A Field Guide to the Classroom Library Ⓐ

REFERENCE

A Field Guide to the Classroom Library A

Lucy Calkins

and

*The Teachers College
Reading and Writing
Project Community*

HEINEMANN
Portsmouth, NH

KH

Heinemann

361 Hanover Street
Portsmouth, NH 03801–3912
www.heinemann.com

Offices and agents throughout the world

© 2002 by Teachers College, Columbia University

Library of Congress Cataloging-in-Publication Data
Calkins, Lucy McCormick.
   A field guide to the classroom library / Lucy Calkins and the Teachers
College Reading and Writing Project community.
      v. cm.
   Includes bibliographical references and index.
   Contents: [v. 1] Library A : kindergarten
   ISBN 0-325-00495-1
   1. Reading (Elementary)—Handbooks, manuals, etc.   2. Children—Books and reading—Handbooks, manuals, etc.   3. Children's literature—Study and teaching (Elementary)—Handbooks, manuals, etc.   4. Classroom libraries—Handbooks, manuals, etc.   I. Teachers College Reading and Writing Project (Columbia University).   II. Title.
LB1573 .C183 2002
372.4—dc21   2002038767

Editor: Kate Montgomery
Production: Abigail M. Heim
Interior design: Catherine Hawkes, Cat & Mouse
Cover design: Jenny Jensen Greenleaf Graphic Design & Illustration
Manufacturing: Louise Richardson

Printed in the United States of America on acid-free paper

12 11 10 09 08   VP   7 8 9 10 11

12/10/10

This field guide is dedicated to

Mary Ann Colbert

The Field Guides to the Classroom Library project is a philanthropic effort. According to the wishes of the scores of contributors, all royalties from the sale of these field guides will be given back entirely to the project in the continued effort to put powerful, beautiful, and thoughtfully chosen literature into the hands of children.

Contents

Acknowledgments

The entire Teachers College Reading and Writing Project community has joined together in the spirit of a barn-raising to contribute to this gigantic effort to put the best of children's literature into the hands of children.

There are hundreds of people to thank. In these pages, I will only be able to give special thanks to a few of the many who made this work possible.

First, we thank Alan and Gail Levenstein who sponsored this effort with a generous personal gift and who helped us remember and hold tight to our mission. We are grateful to Annemarie Powers who worked tirelessly, launching the entire effort in all its many dimensions. Annemarie's passionate love of good literature shines throughout this project.

Kate Montgomery, now an editor at Heinemann and a long-time friend and coauthor, joined me in writing and revising literally hundreds of the field guides. Kate's deep social consciousness, knowledge of reading, and her commitment to children are evident throughout the work. How lucky we were that she became a full-time editor at Heinemann just when this project reached there, and was, therefore, able to guide the project's final stages.

Tasha Kalista coordinated the effort, bringing grace, humor, and an attention to detail to the project. She's been our home base, helping us all stay on track. Tasha has made sure loose ends were tied up, leads pursued, inquiries conducted, and she's woven a graceful tapestry out of all the thousands of books, guides, and people.

Each library is dedicated to a brilliant, passionate educator who took that particular library and the entire effort under her wing. We are thankful to Lynn Holcomb whose deep understanding of early reading informed our work; to Mary Ann Colbert who gave generously of her wisdom of reading recovery and primary texts; to Kathleen Tolan who championed the little chapter books and made us see them with new eyes; to Gaby Layden for her expertise in the area of nonfiction reading; to Isoke Nia for passionate contributions to our upper grade libraries; and to Kathy Doyle who knows books better than anyone we know.

We thank Pam Allyn for her dedication to this effort, Laurie Pessah for working behind the scenes with me, and Beth Neville for keeping the Project on course when this undertaking threatened to swamp us.

Finally, we are grateful to Mayor Guiliani for putting these libraries into every New York City school. To Judith Rizzo, Deputy Chancellor of Instruction, Adele Schroeter, Director of Office of Research, Development and Dissemination, Peter Heaney, Executive Director of the Division of Instructional Support, and William P. Casey, Chief Executive for Instructional Innovation, we also offer our heartfelt thanks for contributing their wisdom, integrity, and precious time to making this miracle happen.

Contributors

Christina Adams
Lisa Ali Chetram
Pam Allyn
Francine Almash
Janet Angelillo
Liz Arfin
Anna Arrigo
Laura Ascenzi-Moreno
Maureen Bilewich
Melissa Biondi
Pat Bleichman
Christine Bluestein
Ellen Braunstein
Dina Bruno
Theresa Burns
Lucy Calkins
Adele Cammarata
Joanne Capozzoli
Laura Cappadona
Justin Charlebois
Linda Chen
Mary Chiarella
Danielle Cione
Erica Cohen
Mary Ann Colbert
Kerri Conlon
Denise Corichi
Danielle Corrao
Sue Dalba
Linda Darro
Mildred De Stefano
Marisa DeChiara
Erica Denman
Claudia Diamond
Renee Dinnerstein
Kathy Doyle
Lizz Errico
Rosemarie Fabbricante
Gabriel Feldberg
Holly Fisher

Sofia Forgione
Judy Friedman
Elizabeth Fuchs
Jerilyn Ganz
Allison Gentile
Linda Gerstman
Jessica Goff
Iris Goldstein-
   Jackman
Ivy Green
Cathy Grimes
David Hackenburg
Amanda Hartman
Grace Heske
Caren Hinckley
Lynn Holcomb
Michelle Hornof
Anne Illardi
Maria Interlandi
Erin Jackman
Debbie Jaffe
Helen Jurios
Kim Kaiser
Tasha Kalista
Beth Kanner
Michele Kaye
Laurie Kemme
Hue Kha
Tara Krebs
Joan Kuntz Verdino
Kathleen Kurtz
Lamson Lam
Gaby Layden
Karen Liebowitz
Adele Long
Cynthia Lopez
Natalie Louis
Eileen Lynch
Theresa Maldarelli
Lucille Malka

Corinne Maracina
Jennifer Marmo
Paula Marron
Marjorie Martinelli
Esther Martinez
Debbie Matz
Teresa Maura
Leah Mermelstein
Melissa Miller
Kate Montgomery
Jessica Moss
Janice Motloenya
Marie Naples
Marcia Nass
Beth Neville
Silvana Ng
Isoke Nia
Jennie Nolan
   Buonocore
Lynn Norton Manna
Beth Nuremberg
Sharon Nurse
Liz O'Connell
Jacqueline O'Connor
Joanne Onolfi
Suzann Pallai
Shefali Parekh
Karen Perepeluk
Laurie Pessah
Jayne Piccola
Laura Polos
Annemarie Powers
Bethany Pray
Carol Puglisi
Alice Ressner
Marcy Rhatigan
Khrishmati Ridgeway
Lisa Ripperger
Barbara Rosenblum
Jennifer Ruggiero

Liz Rusch
Jennifer Ryan
Karen Salzberg
Elizabeth Sandoval
Carmen Santiago
Karen Scher
Adele Schroeter
Shanna Schwartz
India Scott
Marci Seidman
Rosie Silberman
Jessica Silver
Miles Skorpen
Joann Smith
Chandra Smith
Helene Sokol
Gail Wesson Spivey
Barbara Stavetski
Barbara Stavridis
Jean Stehle
Kathleen Stevens
Emma Suarez Baez
Michelle Sufrin
Jane Sullivan
Evelyn Summer
Eileen Tabasko
Patricia Tanzosh
Lyon Terry
Kathleen Tolan
Christine Topf
Joseph Turzo
Cheryl Tyler
Emily Veronese
Anne Marie Vira
Marilyn Walker
Gillan White
Alison Wolensky
Michelle Wolf
Eileen Wolfring

Introduction: What Is This Field Guide?

Lucy Calkins

When I was pregnant with my first-born son, the Teachers College Reading and Writing Project community organized a giant baby shower for me. Each person came with a carefully chosen book, inscribed with a message for baby Miles. Since then, we have commemorated birthdays, engagements, graduations, and good-byes by searching the world for exactly the right poem or picture book, novel or essay, and writing a letter to accompany it. Inside the letter, it says "This is why I chose this piece of literature precisely for you." In this same way, the book lists and the written guides that accompany them in this field guide have become our gift to you, the teachers of our nation's children. We have chosen, from all the books we have ever read, exactly the ones we think could start best in your classroom, and with these books, we have written notes that explain exactly why and how we think these texts will be so powerful in your children's hands.

The book lists and guides in this field guide are the Teachers College Reading and Writing Project's literacy gift to New York City and to the nation. When, two years ago, patrons Alan and Gail Levenstein came to us asking if there was one thing, above all others, which could further our work with teachers and children, we knew our answer in a heartbeat. We couldn't imagine anything more important than giving children the opportunity to trade, collect, talk over, and live by books. We want children to carry poems in their backpacks, to cry with Jess when he finds out that his friend Leslie has drowned, to explore tropical seas from the deck of a ship, to wonder at the life teeming in a drop of water. We want our children's heroes to include the wise and loving spider Charlotte, spinning her web to save the life of Wilbur, and the brave Atticus Finch.

We told the Levensteins that for teachers, as well as for children, there could be no finer gift than the gift of books for their students. We want teachers to be able to read magnificent stories aloud as the prelude to each school day, and to know the joy of putting exactly the right book in the hands of a child and adding, with a wink, "When you finish this book, there are more like it." We want teachers to create libraries with categories of books that peak their students' interests and match their children's passions, with one shelf for Light Sports Books and another shelf for Cousins of the Harry Potter books, one for Books That Make You Cry and another for You'll-Never-Believe-This Books. With this kind of a library, how much easier it becomes to teach children to read, to teach them what they need to become powerful, knowledgeable, literate people!

Even as we embarked on the effort to design magnificent classroom libraries, we knew that the best classroom library would always be the one assembled by a knowledgeable classroom teacher with his or her own students in mind. But, in so many cities, twenty new teachers may arrive in a school in a single year, having had no opportunity to learn about children's books at all. Even though some teachers have studied children's books, they may not be the ones given the opportunity to purchase books. Or, too often, there is no time to make book selections carefully—funds are discovered ten minutes before they must be spent or be taken from the budget. For these situations, we knew it would be enormously helpful to have lists and arrangements of recommended books for classroom libraries. Even without these worries, we all know the value of receiving book recommendations from friends. And so, our commitment to the project grew.

Our plan became this: We'd rally the entire Project community around a gigantic, two-year-long effort to design state-of-the-art classroom libraries and guides, exactly tailored to the classrooms we know so well. Simultaneously, we'd begin working with political, educational, and philanthropic leaders in hopes that individuals or corporations might adopt a school (or a corridor of classrooms) and create in these schools and classrooms the libraries of our dreams. Sharing our enthusiasm, colleagues at the New York City Board of Education proposed that idea to the mayor. Two years later, that dream has come true—In his January 2001 state of the city address, Mayor Giuliani promised $31.5 million of support to put a lending library in every New York City classroom, kindergarten through eighth grade.

Hearing this pronouncement, educational leaders from around the city joined with us in our philanthropic effort. People from the New York City Board of Education reviewed the lists and added suggestions and revisions. The Robin Hood Foundation, which had already been involved in a parallel effort to develop *school* libraries, contributed their knowledge. Readers from the Teachers Union and from the Office of Multicultural Education and of Early Childhood Education and of Literacy Education all joined in, coordinated by Peter Heaney, Executive Director of the Division of Instructional Support, and Adele Schroeter, Director of the Office of Research, Development and Dissemination. The book selections for the classroom libraries became even more carefully honed, and the written guides became richer still.

Over the past few months, boxes upon boxes of books have arrived across New York City, and in every classroom, children are pulling close to watch, big-eyed, as one exquisite, carefully chosen book after another is brought from the box and set on the shelf. Each teacher will receive between three and four hundred books. With most of these books, there will be a carefully crafted guide which says, "We chose this book because . . ." and "On page . . ." and "You'll notice that . . ." and "If you like this book, these are some others like it. . . . " I cannot promise that in every town and city across the nation the effort to put literature in the hands of students and guidance in the hands of their teachers will proceed so smoothly. But I'm hoping these book lists and these ready-made libraries bearing a stamp of approval will catch the eye of funders, of generous patrons, and of foresighted school leaders. And, every penny that comes to the authors from the sale of these field guides will go directly back into this project, directly back into our efforts to get more books into children's hands.

In the meantime, we needn't be idle. We'll comb through the book sales at libraries, and we'll write requests to publishers and companies. In a letter home to our children's parents, we might say, "Instead of sending in cupcakes to honor your child's birthday, I'm hoping you'll send a book. Enclosed is a list of suggestions." We can and will get books into our children's hands, by hook or by crook. And we can and will get the professional support we need for our reading instruction—our vitality and effectiveness as educators depend on it.

About the Books

When hundreds of teachers pool their knowledge of children's books as we have here, the resulting libraries are far richer than anything any one of us could have imagined on our own. We're proud as peacocks of these selections and of the accompanying literary insights and teaching ideas, and can't wait to share them both with teachers and children across the country. Here is a window into some of the crafting that has gone into the book selections:

- We suggest author studies in which the texts that students will study approximately match those they'll write and will inform their own work as authors.

- In upper-grade libraries, we include books that are relatively easy to read, but we have tried to ensure that they contain issues of concern to older children as well.

- We include books that might inform other books in the same library. For example, one library contains three books about dust storms, another contains a variety of books on spiders.

- We know that comprehension and interpretive thinking must be a part of reading from the very beginning, so we include easy to read books that can support thoughtful responses.

- We try to match character ages with student ages, approximately. For example, we have put the book in which Ramona is five in the library we anticipate will be for kindergartners, and put fourth-grade Ramona in the library we anticipate will be for fourth graders.

- We include complementary stories together when possible. For example, Ringgold's *Tar Beach* and Dorros' *Abuela* appear in the same library, anticipating that readers will recognize these as parallel stories in which the narrator has an imagined trip.

- We have never assumed that books in a series are all of the same level. For example, we have determined that some of the *Frog and Toad* books are more challenging, and this is indicated in our libraries.

- We understand that books in a series cannot always be easily read out of sequence. Because we know the *Magic Treehouse* series is best read in a particular sequence, for example, we have been careful with regard to the books we select out of that series.

- We selected our libraries to reflect multicultural values and bring forth characters of many different backgrounds and lives.

- We try to steer clear of books that will not meet with general public approval. We do not believe in censorship, but we do believe that books purchased en masse should not bring storms of criticism upon the unsuspecting teacher.

At the same time that we are proud of the work we've done, we also know that there are countless magnificent books we have omitted and countless helpful and obvious teaching moves we have missed. We are certain that there are authors' names we have inadvertently misspelled, opinions expressed with which we don't all agree, levels assigned that perhaps should be different, and so on. We consider this work to be a letter to a friend and a work in progress, and we are rushing it to you, eager for a response. We are hoping that when you come across areas that need more attention, when you get a bright idea about a guide or booklist, that you will write back to us. We have tried to make this as easy as possible for you to do—just go to our website and contact us!

Choosing the Library for Your Class

We have created seven libraries for kindergarten through sixth grade classrooms. The libraries are each assigned a letter name (A–G) rather than a grade-level in recognition of the fact that the teacher of one class of fourth graders might find that Library D is suited to her students, and another fourth grade teacher might opt for Library E or Library F.

In order to determine which classroom library is most appropriate for a particular class in a particular school, teachers need to determine the approximate reading levels of their students in November, after the teachers have had some time to assess their students as readers. Teachers can compare the book the middle-of-the-class reader tends to be reading with the books we note for each level, and choose the library that corresponds to that average text level. More detail follows this general description. In shorthand, however, the following equivalencies apply:

Library Ⓐ is usually Kindergarten
Library Ⓑ is usually K or 1st grade
Library Ⓒ is usually 1st or 2nd grade
Library Ⓓ is usually 2nd or 3rd grade
Library Ⓔ is usually 3rd or 4th grade
Library Ⓕ is usually 4th or 5th grade
Library Ⓖ is usually 5th or 6th grade

The system of saying, "If in November, your children are reading books like these," usually doesn't work for kindergarten children. Instead, we say Library A is suitable if, in November, the average student cannot yet do a rich, story-like, emergent (or pretend) reading of a familiar storybook, nor can this child write using enough initial and final consonants that an adult can "read" the child's writing.

It is important to note that all of the books in any given library are not at the same level of difficulty. Instead, we have created a mix of levels that tend to represent the mixed levels of ability of readers in the classes we have studied. The composition of the libraries, by level, is described on pages li–lx.

Once you have chosen the library that best corresponds to the average level of your students as readers, you will need to decide which components of the library best suit your curriculum. Each library is divided into components—a core and some modules. The core is the group of books in the library we regard as essential. Each library also contains six modules, each representing a category of books. For example, in each library there is a module of nonfiction books, and in the upper-grade libraries there are modules containing five copies each of ten books we recommend for book clubs. Each module contains approximately fifty titles. The exact quantity from module to module varies slightly because we have tried to keep the cost of each module approximately equal. This means, for example, that the nonfiction module that contains more hardcover books has fewer books overall.

There are a variety of ways to assemble a library. Some teachers will want to purchase the entire library—the core plus the six modules. Sometimes, teachers on the same grade level in a school each purchase the same core but different modules, so a greater variety of books will be available across the hall for their students. In New York City, teachers automatically received the core of their library of choice, 150 books, and then could choose three of the six possible modules.

The Contents of Each Library

Researchers generally agree that a classroom should contain at least twenty books per child. Obviously, the number of books needs to be far greater than this in kindergarten and first grade classrooms, because books for beginning readers often contain fewer than 100 words and can generally only sustain a child's reading for a short while. We would have liked to recommend libraries of 750 titles but decided to select a smaller number of books, trusting that each teacher will have other books of his or her choice to supplement our recommendations.

Because we predict that every teacher will receive or buy the core of a library and only some teachers will receive any particular module, we tried to fill the core of the libraries with great books we couldn't imagine teaching, or living, without. Because we know children will borrow and swap books between classrooms, it is rare for books to be in the core of more than one library, even though some great books could easily belong there.

Usually, these classroom libraries include enough books from a particularly wonderful series to turn that series into a class rage, but the libraries frequently do not contain all the books in a series. Often, more books in the series are included in Modules One and Two, which always contain more books for independent reading, divided into the same levels as those in the core. Our expectation is that once readers have become engrossed in a series, teachers or parents can help them track down sequels in the school or public library.

Within the core of a library, we include about a dozen books of various genres that could be perfect for the teacher to read aloud to the class. These are all tried-and-true read aloud books; each title on the read-aloud list is one that countless teachers have found will create rapt listeners and generate rich conversation.

In every library we have included nonfiction books. They were not chosen to support particular social studies or science units; that would be a different and admirable goal. Instead, our team members have searched for nonfiction texts that captivate readers, and we imagine them being read within the reading workshop. The nonfiction books were chosen either because their topics are generally high-interest ones for children (animals, yo-yo tricks, faraway lands, disgusting animals), or because they represent the best of their genre.

Each library contains about fifteen books that could be splendid mentor texts for young writers. That is, they contain writing that students could emulate and learn from easily since it is somewhat like the writing they are generally able to create themselves.

In each core library, an assortment of other categories is included. These differ somewhat from one library to another. Libraries D and E, for example, contain many early chapter books, but since it is also crucial for children at this level to read the richest picture books imaginable, the core contains a score of carefully chosen picture books. Some cores also contain a set of books perfect for an author study. The categories are indicated on the book lists themselves, and under "Teaching Uses" in the guides.

The vast majority of books in each library are single copies, chosen in hopes that they will be passed eagerly from one reader to another. The challenge was not to find the number of books representing a particular level, but instead to select irresistible books. The chosen books have been field tested in dozens of New York City classrooms, and they've emerged as favorites for teachers and children alike.

The few books that have been selected in duplicate are ones we regard as particularly worthwhile to talk over with a partner. We would have loved to suggest duplicate copies be available for half the books in each library—if libraries had more duplicates, this would allow two readers to move simultaneously through a book, meeting in partnerships to talk and think about the chapters they've read. The duplicate copies would allow readers to have deeper and more text-specific book talks, while growing and researching theories as they read with each other. Duplicates also help books gain social clout in a classroom—allowing the enthusiasm of several readers to urge even more readers to pick the book up. If teachers are looking for ways to supplement these libraries, buying some duplicate copies would be a perfect way to start.

Many of the libraries contain a very small number of multiple (four or five) copies of books intended for use in guided reading and strategy lessons. Once children are reading chapter books, we find teachers are wise to help children into a new series by pulling together a group of four readers, introducing the text, and guiding their early reading. Teachers may also want to offer extra support to children as they read the second book in a series, and so we suggest having a duplicate of this next book as well, so that each child can read it with a partner, meeting to retell and discuss it.

The Levels Within the Libraries

We've leveled many, but purposely not all, of the books in every classroom library. The fact that we have leveled these books doesn't mean that teachers should necessarily convey all of these levels to children. We expect teachers will often make these levels visible on less than half of their books (through the use of colored tabs), giving readers the responsibility of choosing appropriate books for themselves by judging unmarked books against the template of leveled books. "This book looks a lot like the green dot books that have been just-right for me, so I'll give it a try and see if I have a smooth read," a reader might say. It is important that kids learn to navigate different levels of difficulty within a classroom library on their own or with only minimal support from a teacher.

We do not imagine a classroom lending library that is divided into levels as discrete as the levels established by Reading Recovery© or by Gay Su Pinnell and Irene Fountas' book, *Guided Reading: Good First Teaching for All Children* (Heinemann, 1996). These levels were designed for either one-to-one tutorials or intensive, small group guided reading sessions, and in both of these situations a vigilant teacher is present to constantly shepherd children along toward more challenging books. If a classroom lending library is divided into micro-levels and each child's entire independent reading life is slotted into a micro-level, some children might languish at a particular level, and many youngsters might not receive the opportunities to read across a healthy range of somewhat-easier and somewhat-harder books. Most worrisome of all, because we imagine children working often with reading partners who "like to read the same kinds of books as you do," classroom libraries that contain ten micro-levels (instead of say, five more general levels) could inadvertently convey the message that many *children* as well as many *books* were off-limits as partners to particular readers.

There are benefits to micro-levels, however, and therefore within a difficulty level (or a color-dot), some teachers might ascribe a plus sign to certain books, signifying that this book is one of the harder ones at this level. Teachers can then tell a child who is new to a level to steer clear of the books with plus signs, or to be sure that he or she receives a book introduction before tackling a book with this marker.

When assigning books to levels, we have tried to research the difficulty levels that others have given to each text and we have included these levels in our guides. Fairly frequently, however, our close study of a particular text has led us to differ somewhat from the assessments others have made. Of course leveling books is and always will be a subjective and flawed process; and therefore teachers everywhere *should* deviate from assigned levels, ours and others, when confident of their rationale, or when particularly knowledgeable about a reader. You can turn to the tables at the back of this section, on pages xxix–lxiv, to learn more about our leveling system.

Building the Libraries

When we started this project two years ago, we initiated some intensive study groups, each designed to investigate a different terrain in children's literature. Soon, a group led by Lynn Holcomb, one of the first Reading Recovery teachers in Connecticut, was working to select books for a K–1 library. Members of this group also learned from Barbara Peterson, author of *Literary Pathways: Selecting Books to Support New Readers* (Heinemann, 2001), who conducted groundbreaking research at Ohio State University, examining how readers actually experience levels of text complexity. The group also learned from Gay Su Pinnell, well-known scholar of literacy education and coauthor with Irene Fountas of many books including *Guided Reading*. Of course, the group learned especially from intensive work with children in classrooms. The group searched for books that:

- Represent a diverse range of shapes, sizes, authors, and language patterns as possible. The committee went to lengths to be sure that when taken as a whole, primary-level libraries looked more like libraries full of real books than like kits full of "teaching materials."

- Use unstilted language. A book that reads, "Come, Spot. Come, Spot, come," generally would not be selected.

- Contain many high frequency words. If one book contained just one word on a page ("Scissors/paste/paper/etc.") and another book contained the reoccurring refrain of "I see the scissors./ I see the paste." we selected the second option.

- Carry meaning and were written to communicate content with a reader. If the book would probably generate a conversation or spark an insight, it was more apt to be included than one that generally left a reader feeling flat and finished with the book.

- Represent the diversity of people in our world and convey valuable messages about the human spirit.

A second group, under the leadership of Kathleen Tolan, an experienced teacher and staff developer, spent thousands of hours studying early chapter books and the children who read them. This group pored over series, asking questions: Is each book in the series equally difficult? Which series act as good precursors for other series? Do the books in the series make up one continuous story, or can each book stand alone? What are the special demands placed on readers of this series?

Yet another group, led by Gaby Layden, staff developer at the Project, studied nonfiction books to determine which might be included in a balanced, independent reading library. The group studied levels of difficulty in nonfiction books, and found authors and texts that deserved special attention. Carefully, they chose books for teachers to demonstrate and for children to practice working through the special challenges of nonfiction reading.

Meanwhile, renowned teacher-educator Isoke Nia, teacher extraordinaire Kathy Doyle, and their team of educators dove into the search for the very best chapter books available for upper-grade readers. Isoke especially helped us select touchstone texts for writing workshops—books to help us teach children to craft their writing with style, care, and power.

Teacher, staff developer, and researcher Annemarie Powers worked full-time to ensure that our effort was informed by the related work of other groups across the city and nation. We pored over bibliographies and met with librarians and literature professors. We searched for particular kinds of books: books featuring Latino children, anthologies of short stories, Level A and B books which looked and sounded like literature. We researched the class-rooms in our region that are especially famous for their classroom libraries, and took note of the most treasured books we found there. All of this infor-mation fed our work.

Reading Instruction and the Classroom Library: An Introduction to Workshop Structures

These classroom libraries have been developed with the expectation that they will be the centerpiece of reading instruction. When I ask teachers what they are really after in the teaching of reading, many answer, as I do, "I want chil-dren to be lifelong readers. I cannot imagine anything more important than helping children grow up able to read and loving to read. I want students to initiate reading in their own lives, for their own purposes."

There is, of course, no one best way to teach reading so that children become lifelong readers. One of the most straightforward ways to do this is to embrace the age-old, widely shared belief that children benefit from daily opportunities to read books they choose for their own purposes and pleasures (Krashen 1993, Atwell 1987, Cambourne 1993, Smith 1985, Meek 1988).

More and more, however, we've come to realize that students benefit not only from opportunities to read, read, read, but also from instruction that responds to what students do when they are given opportunities to read. I have described the reading workshop in my latest publication, *The Art of Teaching Reading* (Calkins 2001). The reading workshop is an instructional format in which children are given long chunks of time in which to read appropriate texts, and also given explicit and direct instruction. Teachers who come from a writing workshop background may find it helpful to structure the reading workshop in ways that parallel the writing workshop so that chil-dren learn simultaneously to work productively inside each of the two con-gruent structures. Whatever a teacher decides, it is important that the structures of a reading workshop are clear and predictable so that children know how to carry on with some independence, and so that teachers are able to assess and coach individuals as well as partnerships and small groups.

Many teachers begin a reading workshop by pulling students together for a minilesson lasting about eight minutes (unless the read aloud is, for that day, incorporated into the minilesson, which then adds at least twenty min-utes). Children then bring their reading bins, holding the books they are currently reading, to their assigned "reading nooks." As children read inde-pendently, a teacher moves among them, conferring individually with a child or bringing a small group of readers together for a ten- to fifteen-minute guided reading or strategy lesson. After children have read independently for about half an hour, teachers ask them to meet with their partners to talk about their books and their reading. After the partners meet, teachers often call all the readers in a class together for a brief "share session" (Calkins 2001). The following table shows some general guidelines for the length of both inde-pendent reading and the partnership talks based on the approximate level of the texts students are reading in the class.

How Long Might a Class Have Independent Reading and Partnership Talk?		
Class Reading Level	Independent Reading Duration	Partnership Talk Duration
Library A	10 minutes	20 minutes
Library B	15 minutes	20 minutes
Library C	20 minutes	20 minutes
Library D	30 minutes	10 minutes
Library E	40 minutes	10 minutes
Library F	40 minutes	10 minutes
Library G	40 minutes	10 minutes

Periodically, the structure of the minilesson, independent reading, partnership, and then share time is replaced by a structure built around book clubs or "junior" book clubs, our own, reading-intensive version of reading centers.

Minilessons

During a minilesson, the class gathers on the carpet to learn a strategy all readers can use not only during the independent reading workshop but also throughout their reading lives. The content of a minilesson comes, in part, from a teacher deciding that for a period of time, usually a month, he needs to focus his teaching on a particular aspect of reading. For example, many teachers begin the year by devoting a month to reading with stamina and understanding (Calkins 2001). During this unit, teachers might give several minilessons designed to help children choose books they can understand, and they might give others designed to help readers sustain their reading over time. Another minilesson might be designed to help readers make more time for reading in their lives or to help them keep a stack of books-in-waiting to minimize the interval between finishing one book and starting another.

The minilesson, then, often directs the work readers do during independent reading. If the minilessons show students how to make sure their ideas are grounded in the details of the text, teachers may establish an interval between independent reading time and partnership conversations when children can prepare for a talk about their text by marking relevant sections that support their ideas.

Sometimes minilessons are self-standing, separate from the interactive read aloud. Other minilessons include and provide a frame for the day's read aloud. For example, the teacher may read aloud a book and direct that day's talk in a way that demonstrates the importance of thinking about a character's motivations. Then children may be asked to think in similar ways about their independent reading books. Perhaps, when they meet with a partner at the end of reading, the teacher will say, "Please talk about the motivations that drive your central characters and show evidence in the text to support your theories."

Conferences

While children read, a teacher confers. Usually this means that the teacher starts by sitting close to a child as he or she continues reading, watching for external behaviors that can help assess the child. After a moment or two, the teacher usually says, "Can I interrupt?" and conducts a few-minute-long conversation while continuing the assessment. A teacher will often ask, "Can you read to me a bit?" and this, too, informs any hunches about a child and his or her strengths and needs as a reader. Finally, teachers intervene to lift the level of what the child is doing. The following table offers some examples of this.

General Examples of the Conferring That Can Help Readers Grow	
If, in reading, the child is . . .	*Teachers might teach by . . .*
able to demonstrate a basic understanding of the text	nudging the child to grow deeper insights, perhaps by asking: ■ Do any pages (parts) go together in a surprising way? ■ Why do you think the author wrote this book? What is he (she) trying to say? ■ If you were to divide the book into different sections, what would they be? ■ How are you changing as a reader? How are you reading this book differently than you've read others? ■ What's the work you are doing as you read this?
talking mostly about the smallest, most recent details read	generalizing what kind of book it is, giving the child a larger sense of the genre. If it is a story, we can ask questions that will work for any story: ■ How is the main character changing? ■ How much time has gone by? ■ What is the setting for the story? If the text is a non-narrative, we could ask: ■ What are the main chunks (or sections) in the text? ■ How would you divide this up? ■ How do the parts of this text go together? ■ What do you think the author is trying to teach you?
clearly enthralled by the story	asking questions to help the reader tap into the best of this experience to use again later. ■ What do you think it is about this story that draws you in? ■ You seem really engaged, so I'm wondering what can you learn about this reading experience that might inform you as you read other books. ■ When I love a book, as you love this one, I sometimes find myself reading faster and faster, as if I'm trying to gulp it down. But a reading teacher once told me this quote. "Some people think a good book is one you can't put down, but me, I think a good book is one you must put down—to muse over, to question, to think about." Could you set some bookmarks throughout this book and use them to pause in those places to really think and even to write about this book? Make one of those places right now, would you?

Partnerships

When many of us imagine reading, we envision a solitary person curled up with a book. The truth is that reading is always social, always embedded in talk with others. If I think about the texts I am reading now in my life and ask myself, "Is there something *social* about my reading of those texts?" I quickly realize that I read texts because people have recommended them. I read anticipating conversations I will soon have with others, and I read noticing things in this one text that I have discussed with others. My reading, as is true for many readers, is multilayered and sharper because of the talk that surrounds it.

There are a lot of reasons to organize reading time so that children have opportunities to talk with a reading partner. Partner conversations can highlight the social elements of reading, making children enjoy reading more. Talking about books also helps children have more internal conversations (thoughts) as they read. Putting thoughts about texts out into the world by speaking them allows other readers to engage in conversation, in interpretations and ideas, and can push children to ground their ideas in the text, to revise their ideas, to lengthen and deepen their ideas.

For young children, talking with a partner usually doubles the actual unit of time a child spends working with books. In many primary classrooms, the whole class reads and then the teacher asks every child to meet with a partner who can read a similar level of book. Each child brings his bin of books, thus doubling the number of appropriate books available to any one child. The child who has already read a book talks about it with the other child, giving one partner a valuable and authentic reason to retell a book and another child an introduction to the book. Then the two readers discuss how they will read together. After the children read aloud together, the one book held between them as they sit hip to hip, there is always time for the partners to discuss the text. Sometimes, teachers offer students guidance in this conversation.

More proficient readers need a different sort of partnership because once a child can read short chapter books, there are few advantages to the child reading aloud often. Then too, by this time children can sustain reading longer. Typically in third grade, for example, individuals read independently for thirty minutes and then meet with partners for ten minutes to talk over the book. Again, the teacher often guides that conversation, sometimes by modeling—by entertaining with the whole-class read-aloud text—the sort of conversations she expects readers will have in their partnerships.

Book Clubs

Teaching children to read well has a great deal to do with teaching children to talk well about books, because the conversations children have in the air between one another become the conversations they have in their own minds as they read. Children who have talked in small groups about the role of the suitcase in Christopher Paul Curtis's book, *Bud, Not Buddy* will be far more apt to pause as they read another book, asking, "Might *this* object play a significant role in this book, like the suitcase did in *Bud, Not Buddy*?"

When we move children from partnership conversations toward small-group book clubs, we need to provide some scaffolding for them to lean on at first. This is because partnerships are generally easier for children to manage than small group conversations. It is also generally easier for students to read for thirty-minute reading sessions with ten-minute book talks than it is to read for a few days in a row and then sustain extended book talks, as they are expected to do in book clubs.

Children need some support as they begin clubs. One way to do this is to begin with small book club conversations about the read aloud book—the one book we know everyone will be prepared to talk about. Another way to get started with book clubs is for the teacher to suggest that children work in small groups to read multiple copies of, say, a mystery book. The teacher will plan to read a mystery book aloud to the class during the weeks they work in their clubs. Meanwhile, each group of approximately four readers will be reading one mystery that is at an appropriate level for them. The whole class works on and talks about the read-aloud mystery, and this work then guides the small group work. On one day, for example, after reading aloud the whole-class mystery, the teacher could immerse the class in talk about what it's like to read "suspiciously," suspecting everything and everyone. For a few days, the class can try that sort of reading as they listen to the read aloud. Meanwhile, when children disperse to their small groups to read their own mysteries, they can read these books "suspiciously."

Eventually the book clubs can become more independent. One small group of children might be reading several books by an author and talking about what they can learn from the vantage point of having read so many. Another group might read books that deal with a particular theme or subject. Either way, in the classrooms I know best, each book club lasts at least a few weeks. Teachers observe, and coach and teach into these talks, equipping kids with ways to write, talk, and think about texts. However, teachers neither dominate the clubs nor steer readers toward a particular preordained interpretation of a text. Instead, teachers steer readers toward ways of learning and thinking that can help them again and again, in reading after reading, throughout their lives.

Library Ⓐ Contents Description

Library A consists of

I.	Independent Reading & Partner Reading (Levels 1–3)	Level 1	73 Titles	73 Texts
		Level 2	75 Titles	75 Texts
		Level 3	59 Titles	59 Texts
	Emergent Literacy/Shared Reading		41 Titles	177 Texts
	Nonfiction/Concept Books		28 Titles	28 Texts
	Poetry/Song		10 Titles	10 Texts
II.	Guided Reading		30 Titles	120 Texts
III.	Reading Centers/Literature Circles		repeated	59 Texts
IV.	Author Study		10 Titles	10 Texts
V.	Read Alouds		56 Titles	56 Texts
VI.	Books to Support the Writing Process		17 Titles	17 Texts
Total Number of Texts in Library A			**399 Titles**	**684 Texts**

(Because of substitutions made in the ordering process, this number may not be precise.)

Library Ⓐ Book List

Group Description	Level	#	Author	Title	ISBN	Publisher	Quantity	Heinemann Write-Up
CORE								
Independent Reading		1	Harris, Jenny	Amy Goes to School		Rigby	1	
	1	2	Salem, Lynn	Cat Who Loved Red, The	1880612038	Seedling Publications	1	
		1	Aruego, Jose	Look What I Can Do	689712057	Simon & Schuster	1	
		2	Ballinger, Margaret	Making Mountains	439116643	Scholastic Inc.	1	
		3	Browne, Simon	What Can You See?	076356057X	Rigby	1	
		4	Burton, Margie, French, Cathy, and Jones, Tammy	Guess How Many I Have	1583442014	Early Connections	1	
		5	Burton, Margie, French, Cathy, and Jones, Tammy	On the Playground	1583441913	Early Connections	1	
		6	Burton, Margie, French, Cathy, and Jones, Tammy	Things I Like Doing	1583442103	Early Connections	1	
		7	Butler, Andrea	Circus, The	947328068	Rigby	1	
		8	Butler, Andrea	Toy Box, A	947328017	Rigby	1	Y
		9	Butler, Andrea	Zoo, A	947328009	Rigby	1	Y
		10	Canizares, Susan	Monkeys	590769642	Scholastic Inc.	1	Y
		11	Canizares, Susan	Numbers All Around	439045983	Scholastic Inc.	1	
		12	Corrin, Ruth	Paint the Sky	780236971	Early Connections	1	Y
		13	Cousin, Patricia	First Day of School	780281608	Wright Group	1	
		14	Cousin, Patricia	Fruit Trees	780281322	Wright Group	1	
		15	Cowley, Joy	Birthday Cake, A	780274873	Wright Group	1	Y
		16	Cowley, Joy	Bridge, The	780273370	Wright Group	1	
		17	Cowley, Joy	Ghosts	780274083	Wright Group	1	Y
		18	Drew, David	Dear Santa	947328378	Rigby	1	

Group Description	Level	#	Author	Title	ISBN	Publisher	Quantity	Heinemann Write-Up
		19	Eggleton, Jill	My Family		Rigby	1	
		20	Gardner, Marjory	My Cat Muffin	590237861	Scholastic Inc.	1	
	1	21	Giles, Jenny	Out in the Weather	763541567	Rigby	1	Y
		22	Gjording, Nancy	Letter, The	780288696	Wright Group	1	Y
		23	Hughes, Monica	Bobbie and the Parade	763566039	Rigby	1	
		24	Kennedy, Paloma	Wings	763560596	Rigby	1	
		25	Klein, Adria	I Am	439064546	Scholastic Inc.	1	
		26	Levin, Amy	Dogs	439064570	Scholastic Inc.	1	Y
		27	Llewellyn, Claire	Gifts for Everyone	763566012	Rigby	1	
		28	Llewellyn, Claire	I Like To Jump	763566144	Rigby	1	
		29	Maris, Ron	My Book	140505237	Penguin Putnam	1	
		30	McIlwain, J.	Little Seed, A	763541796	Rigby	1	Y
		31	Pandell/dePaola	I Love You Sun, I Love You Moon	399226281	G.P. Putnam's Sons	1	
		32	Ramsey, Joe	My Room	780288645	Wright Group	1	
		33	Randell, Beverly	House, A	763541397	Rigby	1	
		34	Randell, Beverly	Big Things	763541400	Rigby	1	Y
		35	Randell, Beverly	Dad	763541389	Rigby	1	
		36	Randell, Beverly	Go-carts, The	763541494	Rigby	1	Y
		37	Randell, Beverly	Little Things	763541419	Rigby	1	
		38	Randell, Beverly	Playing	763541435	Rigby	1	
		39	Randell, Beverly	We Go Out	763541451	Rigby	1	
		40	Randell, Beverly	Where Are the Babies?	763541583	Rigby	1	
		41	Robinson, Eileen	My Cats	439064635	Scholastic Inc.	1	Y
		42	Roll, Diana	Flower Box, The	780288629	Wright Group	1	
		43	Saunders-Smith, Gail	Autumn Leaves	1560655860	Pebble Books	1	
		44	Saunders-Smith, Gail	Beans	1560654872	Pebble Books	1	

Group Description	Level	#	Author	Title	ISBN	Publisher	Quantity	Heinemann Write-Up
		45	Saunders-Smith, Gail	Eating Apples	156065828	Pebble Books	1	
		46	Schaefer, Lola	Brothers	736802533	Pebble Books	1	
		47	Smith, Annette	Packing My Bag	763541591	Rigby	1	Y
		48	Tafuri, Nancy	Have You Seen My Duckling?	590443852	Scholastic Inc.	1	
		49	Trussell-Cullen, Alan	There's a Mouse in the House	1572555262	Mondo Publishing	1	Y
		50	Wildsmith, Brian	Cat on the Mat	192721232	Oxford University Press	1	Y
		51	Williams, Rebel	Every Morning	780290631	Wright Group	1	
		52	Williams, Rozanne	I Can Write	916119564	Creative Teaching Press	1	
		53	Young, Christine	Seed, The	780206843	Wright Group	1	
	2	1	Berenstain, Stan	Bears on Wheels	039480967X	Random House	1	
		2	Berger, Samantha	Big and Little	439045975	Scholastic Inc.	1	
		3	Butler, Andrea	Teeny Tiny Tina	947328106	Rigby	1	Y
		4	Canizares, Susan	Who's Hiding?	590769634	Scholastic Inc.	1	
		5	Chanko, Pamela	Beak Book, The	590769693	Scholastic Inc.	1	
		6	Chessen, Betsey	Animal Homes	590761668	Scholastic Inc.	1	
		7	Cox, Rhonda	Pigs Peek	1572740302	Richard C. Owen Publishers	1	
		8	Creative Teaching Press	Where's Your Tooth?	916119491	Creative Teaching Press	1	
		9	Cutting, Jillian	After School	780264061	Wright Group	1	
		10	Cutting, Jillian	Day at School, A	780239075	Wright Group	1	
		11	Eriksen, Leonie	Hello Goodbye	763500569	Rigby	1	Y
		12	Fowler, Stephanie	Team Sports	780288726	Wright Group	1	
		13	Frost, Helen	Baby Birds	736802223	Pebble Books	1	
		14	Frost, Miriam	Families	322001730	Wright Group	1	
		15	Giles, Jenny	Can You See the Eggs?	763541753	Rigby	1	
		16	Giles, Jenny	Little Snowman, The	763515043	Rigby	1	Y
		17	Lindgren, Barbro	Sam's Ball	688023592	William Morrow & Co	1	

Group Description	Level	#	Author	Title	ISBN	Publisher	Quantity	Heinemann Write-Up
		18	Lockyer, John	I Like to Eat…	780237331	Wright Group	1	
		19	Melser, June	Look For Me	780275616	Wright Group	1	
		20	Mitchell, Claudette	How to Make a Sandwich	157518074X	Arborlake Publishing	1	
		21	Pomerantz, Charlotte	Where's the Bear?	688109993	Mulberry Books	1	Y
		22	Randell, Beverly	Baby Lamb's First Drink	435049062	Rigby	1	Y
		23	Randell, Beverly	Baby Owls, The	076351506X	Rigby	1	Y
		24	Randell, Beverly	Big Kick, The	435049100	Rigby	1	Y
		25	Randell, Beverly	Home for Little Teddy, A	763515108	Rigby	1	Y
		26	Randell, Beverly	Wake Up, Dad	435067303	Rigby	1	Y
		27	Rigby	My Little Dog	763541699	Rigby	1	
		28	Milios, Rita	Bears, Bears, Everywhere	516420852	Grolier Publishing	1	
		29	Saunders-Smith, Gail	Children	1560654910	Pebble Books	1	
		30	Saunders-Smith, Gail	Trucks	1560654961	Pebble Books	1	
		31	Savage, E.	Making Patterns	780288769	Wright Group	1	Y
		32	Schaefer, Lola	Sisters	736802606	Pebble Books	1	
		33	Williams, Rebel	Call 911	780290712	Wright Group	1	Y
		34	Williams, Rebel	In the Forest	780290739	Wright Group	1	
		35	Williams, Rozanne Lanczak	Bear Went Over the Mountain	916119513	Creative Teaching Press	1	
		36	Williams, Rozanne Lanczak	I Can Read	916119556	Creative Teaching Press	1	Y
		37	Young, Christine	Nests	780206894	Wright Group	1	
	3	1	Bishop, Nic	Green Snake, The	322001463	Wright Group	1	
		2	Canizares, Susan	Treats From a Tree	590161377	Scholastic Inc.	1	
		3	Cox, Rhonda	Chickens	1572740698	Richard C. Owen Publishers	1	
		4	Cox, Rhonda	I Ride the Waves	572743352	Richard C. Owen Publishers	1	
		5	Eggleton, Jill	Clown	763559075	Rigby	1	
		6	Franco, Betsy	Bo & Peter	590273752	Scholastic Inc.	1	

Group Description	Level	#	Author	Title	ISBN	Publisher	Quantity	Heinemann Write-Up
		7	Gardiner, Stewart	Come to My Party	079228660X	National Geographic	1	
		8	Giles, Jenny	Choosing a Puppy	763515140	Rigby	1	
		9	Goss, Janet	It Didn't Frighten Me	157255097X	Mondo Publishing	1	Y
		10	Hall, Kirsten	My Brother the Brat	590485040	Scholastic Inc.	1	
		11	Hancock, Joelie	Saturday Mornings	1572550597	Mondo Publishing	1	
		12	Hill, Eric	Where's Spot?	140566767	Penguin Putnam	1	Y
		13	Ling, Bettina	Kites	590275356	Scholastic Inc.	1	
		14	Mace, Ann	Looking For Bears	1572742682	Richard C. Owen Publishers	1	Y
		15	McPherson, Jan	How Does My Bike Work	792287266	National Geographic	1	
		16	Michaels, Jade	Make My Name	1572559888	Mondo Publishing	1	
		17	Milios, Rita	Bears, Bears, Everywhere	516420852	Grolier Publishing	1	
		18	Neasi, B.	Just Like Me	516020471	Children's Press	1	
		19	Packard, Mary	Where Is Jake?	516453610	Children's Press	1	
		20	Randell, Beverly	Birthday Balloons	76351523X	Rigby	1	Y
		21	Scarffe, Bronwen	Oh No!	1879531585	Mondo Publishing	1	
		22	Seuss, Dr.	Foot Book, The	394809378	Random House	1	Y
		23	Thomas, Rob	Until We Got Princess	157255052X	Mondo Publishing	1	Y
		24	Wall, Julia	All By Myself	780265661	Wright Group	1	
		25	Williams, Rebel	Underground	780290755	Wright Group	1	Y
		26	Windsor, Jo	Max	763558974	Rigby	1	
		27	Yusof, Faridah	In My Family	792286618	National Geographic	1	
Alphabet Books		1	Burningham, John	John Burningham's ABC	517800659	Random House	1	
		2	Ehlert, Lois	Eating the Alphabet	015201036X	Harcourt Brace	1	
		3	Lobel, Anita	Alison's Zinnia	688147372	William Morrow & Co	1	
		4	Lobel, Arnold	On Market Street	688087450	William Morrow & Co	1	
		5	Wildsmith, Brian	Brian Wildsmith's ABC	1887734023	Star Bright	1	

Group Description	Level #	Author	Title	ISBN	Publisher	Quantity	Heinemann Write-Up
Big Books–1 Big Book + 6 Small Copies	1	Cowley, Joy	If You Meet a Dragon	1559111321	Wright Group	1 BB, 6 small copies	
	2	Cowley, Joy	Monster Sandwich, A	780274164	Wright Group	1 BB, 6 small copies	
	3	Eggleton, Jill	Now I Am Six	780255062	Wright Group	1 BB, 6 small copies	
	4	Ehlert, Lois	Feathers for Lunch	590224255	Voyager	1 BB, 6 small copies	Y
	5	Hutchins, Pat	Rosie's Walk	20437501	Simon & Schuster	1 BB, 6 small copies	Y
	6	Keats, Ezra Jack	Peter's Chair	140564411	Penguin Puffin	1 BB, 6 small copies	Y
	7	Melser, June	Sing A Song	780274652	Wright Group	1 BB, 6 small copies	
Counting Books	1	Carle, Eric	1, 2, 3 to the Zoo	698116453	Putnam Publishing	1	
	2	Fleming, Denise	Count!	805042520	Henry Holt & Co	1	
	3	Hoban, Tana	26 Letters and 99 Cents	068814389X	William Morrow & Co	1	
	4	McGrath, Barbara	Cheerios Counting Book, The	590683578	Scholastic Inc.	1	
	5	Wegman, William	37623	786801034	Hyperion Books	1	
Emergent Literacy	1	Brett, Jan	Mitten, The	039921920X	Putnam Publishing	4	Y
	2	Freeman, Don	Corduroy	140501738	Penguin Puffin	4	Y
	3	Galdone, Paul	Three Billy Goats Gruff, The	899190359	Houghton Mifflin	4	Y
	4	Havill, Juanita	Jamaica's Find	590425048	Scholastic Inc.	4	Y
	5	Hyman, Trina Schart	Little Red Riding Hood	823406539	Holiday House	4	
	6	Keats, Ezra Jack	Snowy Day, The	140501827	Penguin Puffin	4	Y
	7	Krauss, Ruth	Carrot Seed, The	64432106	Harper Trophy	4	Y
	8	Slobodkina, Esphyr	Caps for Sale	590410806	Scholastic Inc.	4	Y
	9	Wells, Rosemary	Bunny Cakes	140566678	Penguin Publishing	4	Y
	10	Wood, Don & Audrey	Little Mouse, the Red Ripe Strawberry, and the Big Hungry Bear, The	859530124	Child's Play-International	4	Y
Teaching Writing	1	Baylor, Byrd	I'm in Charge of Celebrations	689806205	Simon & Schuster	1	Y
	2	Collins, Pat Lowery	I Am an Artist	156294729X	Millbrook Press	1	Y

Group Description	Level	#	Author	Title	ISBN	Publisher	Quantity	Heinemann Write-Up
		3	Johnson, Angela	Joshua's Night Whispers	531068471	Scholastic	1	
		4	Zolotow, Charlotte	Snippets: A Gathering of Poems, Pictures, and Possibilities …	006020818X	Harper Collins	1	
Poetry/Song Collections		1	Asch, Frank	Earth and I, The	152004432	Harcourt Brace	1	
		2	Eggleton, Jill	Now I Am Five	078025418X	Wright Group	1	
		3	Hopkins, Lee Bennett	Small Talk	152765778	Harcourt Brace	1	
		4	Kuskin, Karla	Soap Soup and Other Verses	64441741	Harper Collins	1	
		5	Moore, Lilian	I Never Did That Before	689318898	Simon & Schuster	1	
Read-Aloud Texts		1	Brown, Jeff	Flat Stanley Series/Flat Stanley	590675230	Scholastic Inc.	1	
		2	Brown, Margaret Wise	Runaway Bunny, The	64430189	Harper Collins	1	Y
		3	Cleary, Beverly	Ramona the Pest	380709546	William Morrow & Co	1	Y
		4	Cohen, Miriam	Will I Have A Friend?	689713339	Simon & Schuster	1	Y
		5	Crews, Donald	Shortcut	688135765	William Morrow & Co	1	Y
		6	Ehrlich, Amy	Random House Book of Fairy Tales	394856937	Random House	1	
		7	Falconer, Ian	Olivia	689829531	Simon & Schuster	1	Y
		8	Feiffer, Jules	Bark George	62051857	Harper Collins	1	
		9	Fox, Mem	Koala Lou	152005021	Harcourt Brace	1	Y
		10	Freeman, Don	Pocket For Corduroy, A	140503528	Penguin Putnam	1	
		11	Henkes, Kevin	Wemberly Worried	688170277	Greenwillow Books	1	Y
		12	Hoban, Russell	Frances Books Series/Bread and Jam for Frances	64430960	Harper Collins	1	
		13	Kleven, Elisa	Lion and the Little Red Bird, The	140558098	Penguin Publishing	1	Y
		14	Lionni, Leo	Frederick	394826140	Alfred A Knopf	1	
		15	Lionni, Leo	Swimmy	590430491	Scholastic Inc.	1	Y
		16	Steig, William	Pete's A Pizza	62051571	Harper Collins	1	Y
		17	Stewart, Sarah	Library, The	374443947	Farrar Strauss & Giroux	1	Y

Group Description	Level	#	Author	Title	ISBN	Publisher	Quantity	Heinemann Write-Up
		18	Wells, Rosemary	Noisy Nora	140567283	Penguin Publishing	1	

MODULE 1: More Independent and Partnership Reading: Filling in the Lower Portion of the Library

Group Description	Level	#	Author	Title	ISBN	Publisher	Quantity	Heinemann Write-Up
	1	1	Baum, Susan & Harriet Ziefert	City Shapes	61074179	Harper Collins	1	
		2	Blaxland, Wendy	Lunch at the Zoo	590237896	Scholastic Inc.	1	
		3	Burton, Margie, Cathy French & Tammy Jones	Cutting our Food	1583442170	Early Connections	1	
		4	Burton, Margie, Cathy French & Tammy Jones	I Hear!	1583442030	Early Connections	1	
		5	Butler, Andrea	Farm, The	094732805X	Ginn Publishing	1	Y
		6	Canizares, Susan	Nests, Nests, Nests	590761838	Scholastic Inc.	1	Y
		7	Carr, John	Super Hero	780237226	Wright Group	1	Y
		8	Cowley, Joy	Big Hill, The	780274180	Wright Group	1	Y
		9	Cowley, Joy	Feet	078027525X	Wright Group	1	Y
		10	Cowley, Joy	Green Grass	780272633	Wright Group	1	
		11	Cowley, Joy	Huggles Can Juggle…	780248759	Wright Group	1	Y
		12	Cowley, Joy	Little Brother	780274148	Wright Group	1	Y
		13	Depree, Helen	Toys	780232739	Wright Group	1	
		14	Depree, Simon	Making Pictures	780234618	Wright Group	1	
		15	Dufresne, Michele	Fruit Salad	1584530278	Pioneer Valley Educational	1	
		16	Everett, Janie	Faces	67380551	Harper Collins	1	Y
		17	Frost, Miriam	Circus	780290496	Wright Group	1	Y
		18	Herbert, G.	My Pet	1869596463	Rigby	1	
		19	Klein, Adria	I Can See	439064554	Scholastic Inc.	1	
		20	Lee, Millen	We Like Fruit	439064627	Scholastic Inc.	1	Y

Group Description	Level	#	Author	Title	ISBN	Publisher	Quantity	Heinemann Write-Up
		21	Madian, Jon	I Paint	1572555319	Mondo Publishing	1	
		22	Mitchelhill, Barbara	I Like Dogs	076356592X	Rigby	1	
		23	Peters, Catherine	Hats	395882974	Houghton Mifflin	1	
		24	Peters, Catherine	I Am	395883032	Heath	1	
		25	Pinnell, Gay Su	I Like	439064538	Scholastic Inc.	1	Y
		26	Pinnell, Gay Su	Lunch	43906452X	Scholastic Inc.	1	Y
		27	Randell, Beverly	Climbing	76354151	Rigby	1	
		28	Randell, Beverly	Dressing-up	763541427	Rigby	1	
		29	Randell, Beverly	In the Shopping Cart	763541508	Rigby	1	
		30	Randell, Beverly	Way I Go To School, The	763541540	Rigby	1	
		31	Robinson, Fay	What Is It?	763565997	Rigby	1	
		32	Roll, Diana	Bike, The	780288602	Wright Group	1	
		33	Smith, Ben	Ball Games	1586530003	Mondo Publishing	1	
		34	Williams, Rebel	Baby Chimp	780290550	Wright Group	1	Y
		35	Williams, Rebel	Play Ball!	780290542	Wright Group	1	
	2	1		Bus Ride, The		Celebration Press	1	
		2		It's Melting		Creative Teaching Press	1	
		3		On The Go		Creative Teaching Press	1	
		4		See How It Grows		Creative Teaching Press	1	
		5		Where's Your Tooth?		Creative Teaching Press	1	
		6		Who's Hiding		Creative Teaching Press	1	
		7		Whose Forest Is It?		Creative Teaching Press	1	
		8	Bacon, Ron	Sunrise	866878309	Rigby	1	Y
		9	Canizares, Susan	What Do Insects Do?	59039794X	Scholastic Inc.	1	Y
		10	Canizares, Susan	Who Lives in a Tree?	590158562	Scholastic Inc.	1	
		11	Canizares, Susan	Who Lives in the Arctic?	590761501	Scholastic Inc.	1	

Group Description	Level	#	Author	Title	ISBN	Publisher	Quantity	Heinemann Write-Up
		12	Carle, Eric	Do You Want to be My Friend?	64431274	Harper Trophy	1	Y
		13	Chessen, Betsey	Where Do Birds Live?	590769677	Scholastic Inc.	1	
		14	Cutting, Jillian	Child's Day, A	780239121	Wright Group	1	
		15	Cutting, Jillian	Outing, An	78026407X	Wright Group	1	
		16	Eggleton, Jill	What Did Kim Catch?	868677655	Rigby	1	
		17	Gay, Sandy	Raindrops	590273701	Scholastic Inc.	1	Y
		18	Giles, Jenny	My Accident	763541613	Rigby	1	
		19	Gosset, Rachel	Legs	439116627	Scholastic Inc.	1	Y
		20	Kalan, Robert	Rain	688104797	Scholastic Inc.	1	
		21	Lake, Mary Dixon	I Love Bugs		Mondo Publishing	1	
		22	Lindgren, Barbro	Sam's Ball	688023592	William Morrow & Co	1	
		23	Lowe, David	Wheels	868677604	Rigby	1	Y
		24	Petrie, Catherine	Joshua James Likes Trucks	516216392	Children's Press	1	
		25	Randell, Beverly	Birthday Cake for Ben, A	763515051	Rigby	1	Y
		26	Randell, Beverly	Hedgehog is Hungry	435067281	Rigby	1	Y
		27	Randell, Beverly	Lazy Pig, The	43504902X	Rigby	1	Y
		28	Randell, Beverly	Merry-go-round, The	435049046	Rigby	1	Y
		29	Randell, Beverly	Sally's New Shoes	76354163X	Rigby	1	Y
		30	Randell, Beverly	Tiger, Tiger	435049003	Rigby	1	Y
		31	Schreiber, Anne	Boots	59027371X	Scholastic Inc.	1	
		32	Vandine, JoAnn	I Eat Leaves	1572550414	Mondo Publishing	1	Y
		33	Vandine, JoAnn	Run! Run!	1572550422	Mondo Publishing	1	Y

MODULE 2: More Independent and Partnership Reading: Filling in the Middle of the Library

Group Description	Level	#	Author	Title	ISBN	Publisher	Quantity	Heinemann Write-Up
	3	1		Grasshoppers		Pebble Books	1	
		2	Antle, Nancy	Good Bad Cat, The	088743410X	School Zone	1	Y

Group Description	Level	#	Author	Title	ISBN	Publisher	Quantity	Heinemann Write-Up
		3	Bacon, Ron	In My Bed	868677523	Rigby	1	
		4	Bancroft, Gloria	Our School	780288947	Wright Group	1	
		5	Barton, Byron	Boats	694011657	Harper Collins	1	
		6	Benjamin, Cynthia	Footprints in the Snow	590466631	Scholastic Inc.	1	Y
		7	Berenstain, Stan & Jan	Bears in the Night	394822862	Random House	1	
		8	Blanchard, Pat	My Bug Box	1572742739	Richard C. Owen Publishers	1	
		9	Boucher, Carter	Tiger Dave	1572741511	Richard C. Owen Publishers	1	
		10	Christensen, Nancy	Good Night, Little Kitten	051605354X	Children's Press	1	Y
		11	Edwards, Roberta	Five Silly Fisherman	679800921	Random House	1	
		12	Ginsburg, Mirra	Chick and the Duckling, The	06971226X	Aladdin	1	Y
		13	Jensen, Patricia	Funny Man, A	590461931	Scholastic Inc.	1	
		14	King, Susan	Go Back to Sleep	947328467	Rigby	1	
		15	Lawrence, Lucy	Dad's Bike	732718821	Rigby	1	
		16	Lawrence, Lucy	Marvelous Me	947328475	Rigby	1	
		17	Perkins, Al	Ear Book, The	394911997	Random House	1	
		18	Randell, Beverly	Little Bulldozer	435067036	Rigby	1	
		19	Randell, Beverly	Lucky Goes to Dog School	435066919	Rigby	1	
		20	Randell, Beverly	Sally's Beans	435049267	Rigby	1	
		21	Rigby	Roll Over	790101793	Rigby	1	
		22	Robert Kraus	Herman the Helper	671662708	Simon & Schuster	1	
		23	School Zone	Get Lost Becka	887434118	School Zone	1	
		24	Smith, Ben	Centipede's New Shoes	1586530216	Mondo Publishing	1	
		25	Snow, Pegeen	Eat Your Peas, Louise!	516420674	Children's Press / Rookie Readers	1	
		26	Swanson-Natsues, Lyn	Days of Adventure	1572551178	Mondo Publishing	1	Y
		27	Williams, Rebel	Would You Like to Fly?	580290704	Wright Group	1	

Group Description	Level	#	Author	Title	ISBN	Publisher	Quantity	Heinemann Write-Up
		28	Windsor, Jo	Shar	763559040	Rigby	1	
		29	Wiseman, Bernard	Morris the Moose	64441466	Harper Collins	1	
	4	1		Barnyard Math with Farmer Fred		Creative Teaching Press	1	
		2		Cat and Dog Go Shopping		Creative Teaching Press	1	
		3		Celebrating Chinese New Year		Creative Teaching Press	1	
		4		Celebrating Cinco de Mayo		Creative Teaching Press	1	
		5		Monarch Butterflies		Pebble Books	1	
		6		Mr. Noisy Paints His House		Creative Teaching Press	1	
		7		Pack a Picnic		Creative Teaching Press	1	
		8		Ten Little Bears		Celebration Press	1	
		9		The Hungry Farmer		Creative Teaching Press	1	
		10		Time Song, The		Creative Teaching Press	1	
		11	Asch, Frank	Just Like Daddy	671664573	Simon & Schuster	1	Y
		12	Calmenson, Stephanie	My Dog's the Best	590330721	Scholastic Inc.	1	
		13	Capucilli, Alyssa	Happy Birthday Biscuit	60283556	Harper Collins	1	Y
		14	Freeman, Marcia	Giant Pandas	736800980	Pebble Books	1	
		15	Hardin, Suzanne	Dogs at School	1572742569	Richard C. Owen Publishers	1	
		16	Hutchins, Pat	Titch	689716885	Simon & Schuster	1	Y
		17	Maccarone, Grace	Soccer Game	590483692	Hello Reader	1	
		18	Rockwell, Anne	Cars	14154741X	Penguin Puffin	1	
		19	Stadler, John	Hooray for Snail!	64430758	Harper Collins	1	
		20	Ward, Cindy	Cookie's Week	698114353	Penguin Publishing	1	Y
		21	Ziefert, Harriet	New House for a Mole and Mouse, A	14037387X	Viking Penguin	1	

MODULE 3: Filling in the Upper Portion of the Library

Group Description	Level	#	Author	Title	ISBN	Publisher	Quantity	Heinemann Write-Up
	4	1		Celebrating Chanukah		Creative Teaching Press	1	
		2		Celebrating Thanksgiving		Creative Teaching Press	1	
		3		Detective Dog and the Search for Cat		Creative Teaching Press	1	
		4		I Have A New Baby Brother		Creative Teaching Press	1	
		5		It Started as An Egg		Creative Teaching Press	1	
		6		Matthew the Magician		Creative Teaching Press	1	
		7		Tree Is A Home, A		Creative Teaching Press	1	
		8		Where Did It Go?		Creative Teaching Press	1	
		9	Barton, Byron	Planes (Chunky Board Book)	694011665	Harper Collins	1	
		10	Campbell, Ron	Dear Zoo	317621807	Penguin Publishing	1	Y
		11	Capucilli, Alyssa	Happy Halloween, Biscuit!	694012203	Harper Collins	1	
		12	Fehlner, Paul	No Way!	590485148	Scholastic Inc.	1	
		13	Fowler, Allan	Tasting Things	516049119	Childrens Press-Rookie Read-About Science	1	
		14	Latta, Rich	Old Train, The	1572741333	Richard C. Owen Publishers	1	
		15	Maccarone, Grace	Lunch Box Surprise, The	59026267X	Scholastic Inc.	1	
		16	Mayer, Mercer	Critters of the Night Series/Zoom On my Broom	679887105	Random House	1	
		17	Randell, Beverly	Sally's Friends		Rigby	1	
		18	Snowball, Diane	Chickens	1572550465	Mondo Publishing	1	
		19	Strachan, Linda	Ball Called Sam, A	763566306	Rigby	1	
		20	Vaughan, Marcia	Sleepy Bear	790101408	Rigby	1	
		21	West, Colin	"Pardon?" Said the Giraffe	397321732	Harper Collins	1	Y
		22	Wheatley, Nadia	One Is for One	157255133X	Mondo	1	
	5	1		Lion and the Mouse, The	780239318	Wright Group	1	

Group Description	Level	#	Author	Title	ISBN	Publisher	Quantity	Heinemann Write-Up
		2	Bach, Mary	Termites	1572741503	Richard C. Owen Publishers	1	
		3	Cowley, Joy	Ratty-Tatty	780249674	Wright Group	1	
		4	Davidson, Avelyn	Lion Talk	769900429	Shortland Publications	1	
		5	Davidson, Avelyn	Turtle Talk	1572577851	Shortland Publications	1	
		6	Depree, Helen	Three Silly Monkeys Go Fishing	780266072	Wright Group	1	
		7	Dussling, Jennifer	Stars	448411482	Grosset & Dunlap	1	
		8	Fowler, Allan	All the Colors of the Rainbow	51626415X	Childrens Press-Rookie Read-About Science	1	
		9	Fowler, Allan	Feeling Things	516049089 (hc)	Childrens Press-Rookie Read-About Science	1	
		10	Fowler, Allan	So That's How the Moon Changes Shape!	516449176	Children's Press	1	
		11	Fowler, Allan	When You Look Up At the Moon	516460250	Childrens Press-Rookie Read-About Science	1	
		12	Goodrow, Anne	Shapes in the City	322018749	Wright Group	1	
		13	Hawes, Alison	Wind and the Sun, The	763566500	Rigby	1	
		14	Hutchins, Pat	Tidy Titch	688136486	Greenwillow Books	1	
		15	Joyce, William	George Shrinks	64431290	Harper Trophy	1	
		16	Kraus, Robert	Where Are You, Going, Little Mouse?	688087477	William Morrow & Co.	1	
		17	Kuharski, Janice	Raven's Gift	1572741449	Richard C. Owen Publishers	1	
		18	Mitchell, Greg	One Hot Summer Night	157255102X	Mondo Publishing	1	
		19	Moeller, Kathleen Hardcastle	Hoketichee & the Manatee	1572741171	Richard C. Owen Publishers	1	
		20	Preller, James	Wake Me In Spring	510481894	Scholastic Inc.	1	
		21	Rotner, Shelly	Citybook	531071065	Orchard	1	
		22	Sendak, Maurice	Alligators All Around	59045451X	Scholastic Inc.	1	

Group Description	Level	#	Author	Title	ISBN	Publisher	Quantity	Heinemann Write-Up
		23	Wilde, Buck	Squirrels	157257979X	Shortland Publications	1	
		24	Wood, Audrey	Big Hungry Bear	859536599	Child's Play-International	1	
		25	Wright Group	Chicken Licken	780239237	Wright Group	1	
MODULE 4: Genre and Author Studies								
Alphabet Books		1	Carter, David	Alpha Bugs	671866311	Simon & Schuster	1	
		2	Horenstein, Henry	Arf Beg Catch: Dogs from ABC	590033808	Scholastic Inc.	1	
		3	Kaye, Buddy	A You're Adorable, B You're Beautiful	1564025667		1	
		4	Kitchen, Bert	Animal Alphabet	140546014	Viking	1	
		5	Pelham, David	A Is For Animals	671724959	Simon & Schuster	1	
Author Studies		1	Carle, Eric	Have You Seen My Cat?	590044611	Scholastic Inc.	1	Y
		2	Carle, Eric	Tiny Seed, The	590425668	Scholastic Inc.	1	Y
		3	Carle, Eric	Today Is Monday	698115635	Putnam Publishing	1	
		4	Carle, Eric	Very Busy Spider, The	399229191(hc)	Putnam Publishing	1	Y
		5	Carle, Eric	Very Hungry Caterpillar, The	399213015	Philomel Books	1	Y
		6	Ehlert, Lois	Color Farm	694010669	Harper Collins	1	
		7	Ehlert, Lois	Feathers for Lunch	590224255	Voyager	1	Y
		8	Ehlert, Lois	Fish Eyes	152280510	Harcourt Brace	1	
		9	Ehlert, Lois	Planting A Rainbow	152626107	Harcourt Brace	1	
		10	Ehlert, Lois	Red Leaf, Yellow Leaf	152661972	Harcourt Brace	1	Y
Memoir		1	Curtis, Jamie Lee	When I Was Little	64434230	Harper Trophy	1	Y
		2	de Paola, Tomie	Baby Sister, The	698117735	Penguin Putnam	1	
		3	Howard, Arthur	When I Was Five	152020993	Harcourt Brace	1	Y
		4	Rylant, Cynthia	Birthday Presents	531070263	Orchard Books	1	Y
How-To Books		1		How To Make Mud Pie		Creative Teaching Press	1	

Group Description	Level	#	Author	Title	ISBN	Publisher	Quantity	Heinemann Write-Up
		2	Brandenberg, Alexa	Chop, Simmer, Season	152009736	Harcourt Brace	1	
		3	Carlson, Nancy	How to Lose All Your Friends	140558624	Penguin Publishing	1	
		4	Ehlert, Lois	Growing Vegetable Soup	152325808	Harcourt Brace	1	Y
		5	Gibbons, Gail	Tool Book	823406946	Holiday House	1	
Label Books		1		My Little Book of Opposites				
		2	Ahlberg, Janet	Baby's Catalogue, The	316020389	Little Brown & Co	1	
		3	Blos, Joan W.	Seed, A Flower, A Minute, An Hour, A	671886320	Simon & Schuster	1	
		4	Fanelli, Sara	My Map Book	60264551	Harper Collins	1	
		5	Raschka, Chris	Yo! Yes?	531071081	Orchard Books	1	
List Books		1	Cabrera, Jane	Cat's Colors	14056487X	Penguin Putnam	1	
		2	Fox, Mem	Tough Boris	152018913	Harcourt Brace	1	
		3	Ginsburg, Mirra	Where Does the Sun Go At Night?	688070418	William Morrow & Co	1	
		4	Shaw, Charles G.	It Looked Like Spilt Milk	64431592	Harper Trophy	1	Y
		5	Zolotow, Charlotte	Some Things Go Together	64431339	Harper Collins	1	
Nonfiction		1	Gibbons, Gail	Art Box, The	823413861	Holiday House	1	
		2	Onyefulu, Ifeoma	A is for Africa	140562222	Penguin Publishing	1	Y
		3	Rockwell, Anne	Apples and Pumpkins	689718616	Scholastic	1	
		4	Rowe, Jeannette	Whose Nose?	316759333	Little Brown & Co	1	
		5	Woolley, Marilyn	Marks in the Sand	792289269	National Geographic	1	
Wordless Books		1	Banyai, Istvan	Re-Zoom	14055694X	Penguin Putnam	1	
		2	Banyai, Istvan	Zoom	140557741	Viking Penguin	1	
		3	Briggs, Raymond	Snowman, The	679894438	Random House	1	
		4	Day, Alexander	Good Dog Carl	689817711	Simon & Schuster	1	
		5	de Paola, Tomie	Pancakes for Breakfast	156707683	Harcourt Brace	1	Y

Group Description	Level	#	Author	Title	ISBN	Publisher	Quantity	Heinemann Write-Up
MODULE 5: Talking Across Books								
Character–Carl		1	Day, Alexandra	Carl Goes Shopping	374311013	Farrar, Strauss & Giroux	1	
		2	Day, Alexandra	Carl's Afternoon in the Park	374311099	Farrar, Strauss & Giroux	1	
		3	Day, Alexandra	Follow Carl	374343802	Farrar, Strauss & Giroux	1	
Character–Monkeys		1	Martin, David	Monkey Eats Worms		Candlewick Press	1	
		2	Martin, David	Monkey Flies Away		Candlewick Press	1	
		3	Martin, David	Monkey Watch Out		Candlewick Press	1	
		4	Martin, David	Pop Pop Pop		Candlewick Press	1	
Character–Tabby Cat		1	Root, Phyllis	Bump, Thump, Splat		Candlewick Press	1	
		2	Root, Phyllis	Cat Bath		Candlewick Press	1	
		3	Root, Phyllis	Chase, The		Candlewick Press	1	
		4	Root, Phyllis	Hungry Cat		Candlewick Press	1	
Character–Titch		1	Hutchins, Pat	Tidy Titch	688136486	Greenwillow Books	1	
		2	Hutchins, Pat	Titch	689716885	Simon & Schuster	1	Y
		3	Hutchins, Pat	You'll Soon Grow Into Them, Titch	688115071	Mulberry Books	1	Y
Character–Winnie		1		Catch		Candlewick Press	1	
		2		One More Ball		Candlewick Press	1	
		3		Winnie's Birthday		Candlewick Press	1	
		4		Yucky Ball		Candlewick Press	1	
Nonfiction–Animals		1	Canizares, Susan	Nests, Nests, Nests	590761838	Scholastic Inc.	1	Y
		2	Frost, Helen	Baby Birds	736802223	Pebble Books	1	
		3	McMillan, Bruce	Baby Zoo, The	590446355	Scholastic Inc.	1	
		4	Moreton, Daniel	Animal Babies	590761641	Scholastic Inc.	1	
		5	PM Collection	Pets	763541443	Rigby	1	
Nonfiction–Colors		1	Hoban, Tana	Is It Red? Is It Yellow? Is It Blue?	688070345	William Morrow & Co	1	
		2	Lionni, Leo	Little Blue & Little Yellow	688132855	William Morrow & Co	1	

Group Description	Level	#	Author	Title	ISBN	Publisher	Quantity	Heinemann Write-Up
		3	McMillan, Bruce	Growing Colors	688131123	William Morrow & Co	1	Y
		4	Walsh, Ellen	Mouse Paint	152560254	Harcourt Brace	1	
Nonfiction–Community		1		Communities		Capstone	1	
		2	Kalman, Bobbie	What Is a Community from A to Z	865054142	Crabtree Publishing	1	
		3	Keats, Ezra Jack	Apt. 3	689710593	Simon & Schuster	1	
		4	Porter, Gracie	On My Street	780292057	Wright Group	1	
Nonfiction–Family		1	Mayer, Mercer	Just Me and My Dad	307118398	Western Publishing	1	
		2	Mayer, Mercer	Just Me and My Mom	30712584X	Western Publishing	1	
		3	Numeroff, Laura Joffe	What Grandmas Do Best, What Grandpas Do Best	689834918	Simon & Schuster	1	
		4	Numeroff, Laura Joffe	What Mommies Do Best, What Daddies Do Best	689805772	Simon & Schuster	1	
Nonfiction–Transportation		1	Barton, Byron	Airport	64431452	Harper Collins	1	Y
		2	Crews, Donald	Flying	688092357	William Morrow & Co	1	
		3	Crews, Donald	Freight Train	688149006	William Morrow & Co	1	
		4	Rockwell, Anne	Cars	14154741X	Penguin Puffin	1	
		5	Rockwell, Anne	Trucks	140547908	Penguin	1	
Nonfiction–Weather		1	Canizares, Susan	Sun	590107313	Scholastic Inc.	1	
		2	Canizares, Susan	Wind	59007267	Scholastic Inc.	1	
		3	Chanko, Pamela & Daniel Moreton	Weather	590107305	Scholastic Inc.	1	
		4	Kalan, Robert	Rain	688104797	Scholastic Inc.	1	
		5	Neitzel, Shirley	Jacket I Wear In The Snow, The	688045871	William Morrow & Co	1	
Versions of the Gingerbread Man		1	Brett, Jan	Gingerbread Baby	399234446	Penguin Putnam	1	
		2	Galdone, Paul	Gingerbread Boy, The	899191630	Clarion Books	1	

Group Description	Level	#	Author	Title	ISBN	Publisher	Quantity	Heinemann Write-Up
Versions of Three Billy Goats Gruff		3	Ziefert, Harriet	Gingerbread Boy, The	140378189	Penguin Puffin	1	Y
		1	Ferrare, Christine	Three Billy Goats Gruff, The	590411217	Scholastic Inc.	1	
		2	Galdone, Paul	Three Billy Goats Gruff, The	899190359	Houghton Mifflin	1	Y
		3	Stevens, Janet	Three Billy Goats Gruff	152863974	Harcourt Brace	1	
MODULE 6: Shared Reading and Read Aloud								
Big Books + 4 Small Copies		1	Aylesworth, Jim	Old Black Fly	805039244	Henry Holt & Co	1	
		2	Baker, Keith	Big Fat Hen	152019510	Harcourt Brace	1	
		3	Fox, Mem	Time for Bed	152010661	Harcourt Brace	1	
		4	Grover, Max	Accidental Zucchini, The	152015450	Harcourt	1	
		5	Parkes, Brenda	Who's In the Shed?	731200284	Rigby	1	
		6	Shaw, Charles G.	It Looked Like Spilt Milk	64431592	Harper Trophy	1	Y
Chapter Books		1	Cleary, Beverly	Ralph S. Mouse	380709570	Harper Trophy	1	
		2	Gannett, Ruth S.	My Father's Dragon	394890485	Random House	1	Y
		3	Park, Barbara	Junie B. Jones and That Meanie Jim's Birthday	679866957	Random House	1	
		4	Rylant, Cynthia	Gooseberry Park	59094715X	Scholastic Inc.	1	Y
		5	White, E.B.	Charlotte's Web	64400557	Harper Collins	1	
Cumulative Texts		1	Robart, Rose	Cake That Mack Ate, The	316748919	Little Brown & Co	1	
		2	Tafuri, Nancy	This Is the Farmer	688140440	Greenwillow Books	1	
		3	Wood, Audrey	Napping House, The	152567089	Harcourt Brace	1	Y
Emergent Literacy		1	Brown, Margaret Wise	Goodnight Moon	64430170	Harper Collins	4	Y
		2	Clements, Andrew	Big Al	689817223	Simon & Schuster	4	Y
		3	Zion, Gene	Harry the Dirty Dog	006443009X	Harper Collins	4	Y
Repetitive Texts		1	Brown, Ruth	Dark, Dark Tale, A	140546219	Penguin Putnam	1	Y

Group Description	Level	#	Author	Title	ISBN	Publisher	Quantity	Heinemann Write-Up
		2	Carle, Eric	Very Busy Spider, The	399229191	Putnam Publishing	1	Y
		3	Cohen, Caron Lee	Where's The Fly?	688140440	Harper Collins	1	
		4	Cooke, Trish	So Much	763602965	Candlewick Press	1	
		5	Martin, Bill	Brown Bear, Brown Bear, What Do You See?	805047905	Henry Holt & Co	1	Y
		6	Martin, Bill	Chicka Chicka Boom Boom	68983568X	Simon & Schuster	1	
		7	Rosen, Michael	We're Going on a Bear Hunt	673805344	Prentice Hall	1	
		8	Tafuri, Nancy	Spots Feathers and Curly Tails	688075363	William Morrow & Co	1	Y
		9	Williams, Sue	I Went Walking	152380116	Harcourt Brace	1	
Rhyming		1	Grossman, Bill	My Little Sister Ate One Hare	51788576X	Crown Publishing	1	
		2	Hennessey, B.G.	Jake Baked the Cake	140508821	Penguin Putnam	1	
		3	Jorgensen, Gail	Crocodile Beat	689718810	Simon & Schuster	1	
		4	Lotz, Karen	Snowsong Whistling	140558659	Penguin Putnam	1	
		5	Lyon, George Ella	Outside Inn, The	140508821	Orchard Books	1	
		6	Merriam, Eve	Bam Bam Bam	80505796X	Henry Holt & Co	1	
		7	Seuss, Dr.	Cat in the Hat, The	39480001X	Random House	1	
		8	Seuss, Dr.	Fox in Socks	394800389	Random House	1	
Songs		1	Adams, Pam	There Was an Old Lady Who Swallowed a Fly	859530183	Child's Play-International	1	
		2	Carle, Eric	Today Is Monday	698115635	Putnam Publishing	1	
		3	Christelow, Eileen	Five Little Monkeys Jumping On the Bed	395557011	Houghton Mifflin	1	
		4	Hague, Michael	Teddy Bear Teddy Bear	688152511	William Morrow & Co	1	
		5	Moffat, Judith	Who Stole the Cookies?	590065971	Scholastic Inc.	1	
		6	Raffi	Baby Beluga	517709775	Crown Publishing	1	
		7	Raffi	Wheels on the Bus	517576457	Crown Publishing	1	Y
		8	Rosen, Michael	Little Rabbit Foo Foo	671796046	Simon & Schuster	1	

Benchmark Books for Each Text Level

TC Level	Benchmarks: Books that Represent Each Level
1	*A Birthday Cake* (Cowley) *I Can Write* (Williams) *The Cat on the Mat* (Wildsmith)
2	*Rain* (Kaplan) *Fox on the Box* (Gregorich)
3	*It Looked Like Spilt Milk* (Shaw) *I Like Books* (Browne) *Mrs. Wishy-Washy* (Cowley)
4	*Rosie's Walk* (Hutchins) *The Carrot Seed* (Krauss) *Cookie's Week* (Ward)
5	*George Shrinks* (Joyce) *Goodnight Moon* (Brown) *Hattie and the Fox* (Fox)
6	*Danny and the Dinosaur* (Hoff) *Henry and Mudge* (Rylant)
7	*Nate the Great* (Sharmat) *Meet M&M* (Ross)
8	*Horrible Harry* (Kline) *Pinky and Rex* (Howe) Arthur Series (Marc Brown)
9	*Amber Brown* (Danziger) *Ramona Quimby, Age 8* (Cleary)
10	*James and the Giant Peach* (Dahl) *Fudge-A-Mania* (Blume)
11	*Shiloh* (Naylor) *The Great Gilly Hopkins* (Paterson)
12	*Bridge to Terabithia* (Paterson) *Baby* (MacLachlan)
13	*Missing May* (Rylant) *Where the Red Fern Grows* (Rawls)
14	*A Day No Pigs Would Die* (Peck) *Scorpions* (Myers)
15	*The Golden Compass* (Pullman) *The Dark Is Rising* (Cooper) *A Wizard of Earthsea* (Le Guin)

Descriptions of Text Levels One Through Seven

TEXT LEVEL ONE

This level roughly corresponds to the following levels in other systems:

Reading Recovery© (RR) Levels 1–2
Developmental Reading Assessment (DRA) Levels A–2

Text Characteristics for TC Level One

- The font is large, clear, and is usually printed in black on a white background.

- There is exaggerated spacing between words and letters. (In some books, publishers have enlarged the print but have not adjusted the spacing which can create difficulties for readers.)

- There is usually a single word, phrase, or simple sentence on a page, and the text is patterned and predictable. For example, in the book *I Can Read*, once a child knows the title (which is ideally read to a Level One reader) it is not hard for the child to read "I can read the newspaper," "I can read the cereal box." These readers are regarded as "preconventional" because they rely on the illustrations (that support the meaning) and the sounds of language (or syntax) and not on graphophonics or word/letter cues to read a sentence such as, "I can read the newspaper."

- Usually each page contains two or three sight words. A Level One book *may* contain one illustrated word on a page (such as "Mom," "Dad," "sister," "cat") but it's just as easy for a child to read "I see my mom. I see my Dad. I see my sister. I see my cat." because the sight words give the child a way into the text.

- The words are highly supported by illustrations. No one would expect a Level One reader to solve the word "newspaper." We would, however, expect a child at this level to look at the picture and at the text and to read the word "newspaper."

- Words are consistently placed in the same area of each page, preferably top left or bottom left.

Characteristics of the Reader

Readers in this group will demonstrate most of these behaviors.

- Remember the pattern in a predictable text
- Use picture cues

- Use left to right directionality to read one or two lines of print

- Work on matching spoken words with printed words and self-correcting when these don't "come out even"

- Rely on the spaces between words to signify the end of one word and the beginning of another. These readers read the spaces as well as the words, as the words are at first black blobs on white paper

- Locate one or two known words on a page

Benchmarks

The following titles are representative of the kinds of books found in this grouping.

A Birthday Cake, Joy Cowley
Cat on the Mat, Brian Wildsmith
The Farm, Literacy 2000/Stage 1
Growing Colors, Bruce McMillan
I Can Write, Rozanne Williams
Time for Dinner, PM Starters

Assessment

The following titles can be used to determine if a reader is ready to move on to the next grouping of books. This type of assessment is most effective if the text is unfamiliar to the reader. If these titles will be used as assessment texts, they should *not* be part of the classroom library.

My Home, Story Box
The Tree Stump, Little Celebrations
DRA Assessments A–2

We move children from Level One to Level Two books when they are consistently able to match one spoken word with one word written on the page. This means that they can point under words in a Level One book as they read and know when they haven't matched a spoken word to a written word by noticing that, at the end of the line, they still have words left on the page or they've run out of words. When children read multisyllabic words and compound words and point to multiple, instead of one, word on the page, we consider this a successful one-to-one match.

TEXT LEVEL TWO

This level roughly corresponds to the following levels in other systems:

Reading Recovery© (RR) Levels 3–4
Developmental Reading Assessment (DRA) Levels 3–4

Text Characteristics of TC Level Two

- There are usually two lines of print on at least some of the pages in these books, and sometimes there are three. This means readers will become accustomed to making the return sweep to the beginning of a new line.

- The texts are still patterned and predictable, but now the patterns tend to switch at intervals. Almost always, the pattern changes at the end of the book. The repeating unit may be as long as two sentences in length.

- The font continues to be large and clear. The letters might not, however, be black against white although this is generally the case.

- Children still rely on the picture but the pictures tend to give readers more to deal with; children need to search more in the picture to find help in reading the words.

- High frequency words are still helpful and important. The sentences in Level One books tend to begin with 2 to 3 high frequency words, for example, "I like to run. I like to jump." At this level, the pages are more apt to begin with a single high frequency word and then include words that require picture support and attention to first letters, for example, "A mouse has a long tail. A bear has a short tail."

- Sentences are more varied, resulting in texts that include a full range of punctuation.

Characteristics of the Reader

Readers in this group will demonstrate most of these behaviors.

- Get the mouth ready for the initial sound of a word

- Use left to right directionality as well as a return sweep to another line of print

- Locate one or two known words on a page

- Monitor for meaning: check to make sure it makes sense

Benchmarks

The following titles are representative of the kinds of books found in this grouping.

All Fall Down, Brian Wildsmith
I Went Walking, Sue Williams
Rain, Robert Kalan
Shoo, Sunshine

Assessment

The following titles can be used to determine if a reader is ready to move on to the next grouping. This type of assessment is most effective if the text is unfamiliar to a reader. If these titles will be used as assessment texts, they should *not* be part of the classroom library.

The Bus Ride, Little Celebrations, DRA 3
Fox on the Box, School Zone, DRA 4

We generally move children from Level Two to Level Three texts when they know how to use the pictures and the syntax to generate possibilities for the next word, when they attend to the first letters of unknown words. These readers will also read and rely on high frequency words such as *I*, *the*, *a*, *to*, *me*, *mom*, *the child's name*, *like*, *love*, *go*, and *and*.

TEXT LEVEL THREE

This level roughly corresponds to the following levels in other systems:

Reading Recovery© (RR) Levels 5–8
Developmental Reading Assessment (DRA) Levels 6–8

Text Characteristics of TC Level Three

It is important to note that this grouping includes a wide range of levels. This was done deliberately because at this level, readers should be able to select "just right" books for themselves and be able to monitor their own reading.

- Sentences are longer and readers will need to put their words together in order to take in more of the sentence at a time. When they are stuck, it's often helpful to nudge them to reread and try again.

- The pictures are not as supportive as they've been. It's still helpful for children to do picture walks prior to reading an unfamiliar text, but now the goal is less about surmising what words the page contains and more about seeing an overview of the narrative.

- Readers must rely on graphophonics across the whole word. If readers hit a wall at this level, it's often because they're accustomed to predicting words based on a dominant pattern and using the initial letters (only) to confirm their predictions. It takes readers a while to begin checking the print closely enough to adjust their expectations.

- Children will need to use sight words to help with unknown words, using parts of these familiar words as analogies, helping them unlock the unfamiliar words.

- The font size and spacing are less important now.

- Words in the text begin to include contractions. We can help children read these by urging them to look all the way across a word.

Characteristics of the Reader

Readers in this group will demonstrate most of these behaviors.

- Reread and self-correct

- Read with some fluency

- Cross check one cue against another

- Monitor for meaning: check to make sure what has been read makes sense and sounds right

- Recognize common chunks of words

Benchmarks

The following titles are representative of the kinds of books found in this grouping.

Bears in the Night Stan and Jan, Berenstain
The Chick and the Duckling, Ginsburg
It Looked Like Spilt Milk, Charles G. Shaw
Mrs. Wishy-Washy, Joy Cowley

Assessment

The following titles can be used to determine if a reader is ready to move on to the next grouping. This type of assessment is most effective if the text is unfamiliar to a reader. If these titles will be used as assessment texts, they should *not* be part of the classroom library.

Bread, Story Box, DRA 6
Get Lost Becka, School Zone, DRA 8

We move a child to Level Four books if that child can pick up an unfamiliar book like *Bread* or *It Looked Like Spilt Milk* and read it with a little difficulty, but with a lot of independence and with strategies. This reader should know to reread when she is stuck, to use the initial sounds in a word, to chunk word families within a word, and so on.

TEXT LEVEL FOUR

This level roughly corresponds to the following levels in other systems:

Reading Recovery© (RR) Levels 9–12
Developmental Reading Assessment (DRA) Levels 10–12

Text Characteristics of TC Level Four

- In general, the child who is reading Level Four books is able to do more of the same reading work he could do with texts at the previous level. This child reads texts that contain more words, lines, pages, and more challenging vocabulary.

- These texts contain even less picture support than earlier levels.

- Fluency and phrasing are very important for the Level Four reader. If children don't begin to read quickly enough, they won't be able to carry the syntax of the sentence along well enough to comprehend what they are reading.

- These books use brief bits of literary language. That is, in these books the mother may turn to her child and say, "We shall be rich."
- These books are more apt to have a plot (with characters, setting, problem, solution) and they tend to be less patterned than they were at the previous level.

Characteristics of the Reader

Readers in this group will demonstrate most of these behaviors.

- Reread and self-correct
- Read with fluency
- Integrate cues from meaning, structure, and visual sources
- Monitor for meaning: check to make sure what has been read makes sense, sounds right, and looks right
- Make some analogies from known words to figure out unknown words
- Read increasingly difficult chunks within words

Benchmarks

The following titles are representative of the kinds of books found in this grouping.

The Carrot Seed, Ruth Krauss
Cookie's Week, Cindy Ward
Rosie's Walk, Pat Hutchins
Titch, Pat Hutchins

Assessment

The following titles can be used to determine if a reader is ready to move on to the next grouping. This type of assessment is most effective if the text is unfamiliar to a reader. If these titles will be used as assessment texts, they should *not* be part of the classroom library.

Are You There Bear?, Ron Maris, DRA 10
The House in the Tree, Rigby PM Story Books
Nicky Upstairs and Downstairs, Harriet Ziefert
William's Skateboard, Sunshine, DRA 12

We move a child to Level Five books if that reader can independently use a variety of strategies to work through difficult words or parts of a text. The reader must be reading fluently enough to reread quickly, when necessary, so as to keep the flow of the story going. If a reader is reading very slowly, taking too much time to work through the hard parts, then this reader may not be ready to move on to the longer, more challenging texts in Level Five.

TEXT LEVEL FIVE

This level roughly corresponds to the following levels in other systems:

Reading Recovery© (RR) Levels 13–15
Developmental Reading Assessment (DRA) Level 14

Text Characteristics

- Sentences in Level Five books tend to be longer, more varied, and more complex than they were in previous levels.

- Many of the stories are retold folktales or fantasy-like stories that use literary or story language, such as: "Once upon a time, there once lived, a long, long time ago. . . . "

- Many books may be in a cumulative form in which text is added to each page, requiring the reader to read more and more text as the story unfolds, adding a new line with every page turn.

- The illustrations tend to be a representation of just a slice of what is happening in the text. For example, the text may tell of a long journey that a character has taken over time, but the picture may represent just the character reaching his destination.

- There will be more unfamiliar and sometimes complex vocabulary.

Characteristics of the Reader

Readers in this group will demonstrate most of these behaviors.

- Reread and self-correct regularly

- Read with fluency

- Integrate a balance of cues

- Monitor for meaning: check to make sure what has been read makes sense, sounds right, and looks right

- Demonstrate fluent phrasing of longer passages

- Use a repertoire of graphophonic strategies to problem solve through text

Benchmarks

The following titles are representative of the kinds of books found in this grouping.

George Shrinks, William Joyce
Goodnight Moon, Margaret Wise Brown
Hattie and the Fox, Mem Fox
Little Red Hen, Parkes

Assessment

The following titles can be used to determine if a reader is ready to move on to the next grouping. This type of assessment is most effective if the text is unfamiliar to a reader. If these titles will be used as assessment texts, they should *not* be part of the classroom library.

The Old Man's Mitten, Bookshop, Mondo
Who Took the Farmer's Hat?, Joan Nodset, DRA 14

We move children from Level Five to Level Six texts when they are consistently able to use a multitude of strategies to work through challenges quickly and efficiently. These challenges may be brought on by unfamiliar settings, unfamiliar language structures, unfamiliar words, and increased text length. The amount of text on a page and the length of a book should not be a hindrance to the reader who is moving on to Level Six. The reader who is ready to move on is also adept at consistently choosing appropriate books that will make her a stronger reader.

TEXT LEVEL SIX

This level roughly corresponds to the following levels in other systems:

Reading Recovery© (RR) Levels 16–18
Developmental Reading Assessment (DRA) Level 16

Text Characteristics of TC Level Six

- The focus of the book is evident at its start

- Descriptive language is used more frequently than before

- Dialogue often tells a large part of the story

- Texts may include traditional retellings of fairy tales and folktales

- Stories are frequently humorous

- Considerable amount of text is found on each page. A book in this grouping may be a picture book, or a simple chapter book. These books offer extended stretches of text.

- Texts are often simple chapter books, and often have episodic chapters in which each chapter stands as a story on its own

- Texts often center around just two or three main characters who tend to be markedly different from each other (a boy and a girl, a child and a parent)

- There is limited support from the pictures

- Texts includes challenging vocabulary

Characteristics of the Reader

Readers in this group will demonstrate most of these behaviors.

- Reread and self-correct regularly

- Read with fluency

- Integrate a balance of cues

- Demonstrate fluent phrasing of longer passages

- Use a repertoire of graphophonic strategies to problem solve through text

Benchmarks

The following titles are representative of the kinds of books found in this grouping.

Danny and the Dinosaur, Syd Hoff
The Doorbell Rang, Pat Hutchins
Henry and Mudge, Cynthia Rylant
The Very Hungry Caterpillar, Eric Carle

Assessment

The following titles can be used to determine if a reader is ready to move on to the next grouping. This type of assessment is most effective if the text is unfamiliar to a reader. If these titles will be used as assessment texts, they should *not* be part of the classroom library.

Bear Shadow, Frank Asch, DRA 16
Jimmy Lee Did It, Pat Cummings, DRA 18

TEXT LEVEL SEVEN

This level roughly corresponds to the following levels in other systems:

Reading Recovery© (RR) Levels 19–20
Developmental Reading Assessment (DRA) Level 20

Text Characteristics of TC Level Seven

- Dialogue is used frequently to move the story along

- Texts often have 2 to 3 characters. (They tend to have distinctive personalities and usually don't change across a book or series.)

- Texts may include extended description. (The language may set a mood, and may be quite poetic or colorful.)

- Some books have episodic chapters. (In other books, each chapter contributes to the understanding of the entire book and the reader must carry the story line along.)

- There is limited picture support

- Plots are usually linear without large time-gaps

- Texts tend to have larger print and double spacing between lines of print

Characteristics of the Reader

Readers in this group will demonstrate most of these behaviors.

- Reread and self-correct regularly

- Read with fluency, intonation, and phrasing

- Demonstrate the existence of a self-extending (self-improving) system for reading

- Use an increasingly more challenging repertoire of graphophonic strategies to problem solve through text

- Solve unknown words with relative ease

Benchmarks

The following titles are representative of the kinds of books found in this grouping.

A Baby Sister for Frances, Russell Hoban
Meet M&M, Pat Ross
Nate the Great, Marjorie Sharmat
Poppleton, Cynthia Rylant

Asessment

The following titles can be used to determine if a reader is ready to move on to the next grouping. This type of assessment is most effective if the text is unfamiliar to a reader. If these titles will be used as assessment texts, they should *not* be part of the classroom library.

Peter's Pockets, Eve Rice, DRA 20
Uncle Elephant, Arnold Lobel

More Information to Help You Choose the Library That is Best for Your Readers

Library A

Library A is appropriate if your children enter kindergarten in October as very emergent readers with limited experiences hearing books read aloud. Use the following chart to help determine if Library A is about right for your class.

Approximate Distribution of Reading Levels of a Class Matched to Library A		
Benchmark Book	*Reading Level*	*Percentage of the Class Reading at about This Level*
The Cat on the Mat, by Wildsmith	TC Level 1	45%
Fox on the Box, by Gregorich	TC Level 2	30%
Mrs. Wishy-Washy, by Cowley	TC Level 3	25%

Library B

Library B is appropriate for a class of children if, in October, they are reading books like *I Went Walking*. Use the following chart to help determine if Library B is about right for your class. (Note to New York City teachers: Many of your students would score a 3 on the ECLAS correlated with titles such as, *Things I Like to Do* and *My Shadow*.)

Approximate Distribution of Reading Levels of a Class Matched to Library B		
Benchmark Book	*Reading Level*	*Percentage of the Class Reading at about This Level*
The Cat on the Mat, by Wildsmith	TC Level 1	10%
Fox on the Box, by Gregorich	TC Level 2	10%
Mrs. Wishy-Washy, by Cowley	TC Level 3	30%
The Carrot Seed, by Krauss	TC Level 4	25%
Goodnight Moon, by Brown	TC Level 5	15%
Henry and Mudge, by Rylant	TC Level 6	5%
Nate the Great, by Sharmat	TC Level 7	5%

Library C

Library C is appropriate for a class of children if, in October, many of your students are approaching reading books like *Mrs. Wishy-Washy* and *Bears in the Night*. (Note to New York City teachers: Many of your students would be approaching a 4 on the ECLAS that would be correlated with *Baby Bear's Present* and *No Where and Nothing*.)

Approximate Distribution of Reading Levels of a Class Matched to Library C		
Benchmark Book	*Reading Level*	*Percentage of the Class Reading at about This Level*
Fox on the Box, by Gregorich	TC Level 2	8%
Mrs. Wishy-Washy, by Cowley	TC Level 3	8%
The Carrot Seed, by Krauss	TC Level 4	20%
Goodnight Moon, by Brown	TC Level 5	20%
Henry and Mudge, by Carle	TC Level 6	20%
Nate the Great, by Sharmat	TC Level 7	15%
Pinky and Rex, by Howe	TC Level 8	5%
Ramona Quimby, by Cleary	TC Level 9	2%
James and the Giant Peach, by Dahl	TC Level 10	2%

Library D

Use the following chart to help determine if Library D is right for your class.

Approximate Distribution of Reading Levels of a Class Matched to Library D		
Benchmark Book	*Reading Level*	*Percentage of the Class Reading at about This Level*
Good Night Moon, by Brown	Level 5	8%
Henry and Mudge, by Rylant	Level 6	20%
Nate the Great, by Sharmat	Level 7	25%
Pinky and Rex, by Howe	Level 8	30%
Ramona Quimby, by Cleary	Level 9	10%
James and the Giant Peach, by Dahl	Level 10	2%

Library E

Library E is appropriate for a class of children if, in October, a readers list tends to look approximately like the following chart.

Approximate Distribution of Reading Levels of a Class Matched to Library E		
Benchmark Book	*Reading Level*	*Percentage of the Class Reading at about This Level*
Nate the Great, by Sharmat	Level 7	10%
Pinky and Rex, by Howe	Level 8	25%
Ramona Quimby, by Cleary	Level 9	30%
James and the Giant Peach, by Dahl	Level 10	22%
Shiloh, by Naylor	Level 11	5%
Baby, by MacLachlan	Level 12	5%
Missing May, by Rylant	Level 13	2%
Scorpions, by Myers	Level 14	1%

Library F

Library F is appropriate for a class of children if, in October, a readers list tends to look approximately like the following chart.

Approximate Distribution of Reading Levels of a Class Matched to Library F		
Benchmark Book	*Reading Level*	*Percentage of the Class Reading at about This Level*
Pinky and Rex, by Howe	Level 8	2%
Ramona Quimby, by Cleary	Level 9	20%
James and the Giant Peach, by Dahl	Level 10	25%
Shiloh, by Naylor	Level 11	30%
Baby, by MacLachlan	Level 12	20%
Missing May, by Rylant	Level 13	2%
Scorpions, by Myers	Level 14	1%

Library G

Library G is appropriate for a class of children if, in October, a readers list tends to look approximately like the following chart.

Approximate Distribution of Reading Levels of a Class Matched to Library G		
Benchmark Book	*Reading Level*	*Percentage of the Class Reading at about This Level*
James and the Giant Peach, by Dahl	Level 10	10%
Shiloh, by Naylor	Level 11	10%
Baby, by MacLachlan	Level 12	30%
Missing May, by Rylant	Level 13	30%
Scorpions, by Myer	Level 14	20%

About the Guides

Soon we'd begun not only accumulating titles and honing arrangements for dream libraries, but also writing teaching advice to go with the chosen books. Our advice to the contributors was, "Write a letter from you to others who'll use this book with children. Tell folks what you notice in the book, and advise them on teaching opportunities you see. Think about advice you would give a teacher just coming to know the book." The insights, experience, and folk wisdom poured in and onto the pages of the guides.

A written guide accompanies many of the books in the libraries. These guides are not meant to be prescriptions for how a teacher or child should use a book. Instead they are intended to be resources, and we hope thoughtful teachers will tap into particular sections of a guide when it seems fit to do so. For example, a teaching guide might suggest six possible minilessons a teacher could do with a book. Of course, a teacher would never try to do all six of these! Instead we expect one of these minilessons will seem helpful to the teacher, and another minilesson to another teacher. The teaching guides illustrate the following few principles that are important to us.

Teaching One Text Intensely in Order to Learn About Many Texts

When you take a walk in the woods, it can happen that all the trees look the same, that they are just a monotony of foliage and trunks. It is only when you stop to learn about a particular tree, about its special leaf structure and the odd thickness of its bark, about the creatures that inhabit it and the seeds it lets fall, that you begin to see that particular kind of tree among the thickets. It is when you enter a forest knowing something about kinds of trees that you begin to truly see the multiplicity of trees in a forest and the particular attributes and mysteries of each one. Learning about the particulars of one tree leads you to thinking about all of the trees, each in its individuality, each with its unique deep structure, each with its own offerings.

The same is true of texts. The study of one can reveal not just the hidden intricacies of that story, but also the ways in which truths and puzzles can be structured in other writings as well. When one book holds a message in the way a chapter ends, it gives the reader the idea that any book may hold a message in the structure of its chapter's conclusions. When one book is revealed to make a sense that is unintended by the author, we look for unintended sense in other books we read. Within these guides, then, we hope that readers like you will find truths about the particular books they are written about, but more, we hope that you find pathways into all the books you read. By showing some lengthy thinking and meditations on one book, we hope to offer you paths toward thinking about each and every book that crosses your desk and crosses your mind.

Suggesting Classroom Library Arrangements

Many the attributes of a book, detailed in a guide, can become a category in a classroom library. If a group of students in a class seems particularly energized by the Harry Potter books, for example, the guide can be used to help determine which books could be in a bin in the library marked, "If You Like *Harry Potter*—Try These." The similarity between the *Harry Potter* books and the other books in this group may be not only in difficulty gradient, but also in content, story structure, popularity, or genre. That is, a class of children that like *Harry Potter* might benefit from a bin of books on fantasy, or from a collection of best-selling children's books, or from a bin of "Long-Books-You-Can't-Put-Down," or from stories set in imagined places. As you browse through the guides that accompany the books you have chosen, the connections will pop out at you.

Sometimes, the guides will help you determine a new or more interesting placement for a book. Perhaps you have regarded a book as historical fiction, but now you realize it could alternatively be shelved in a collection of books that offer children examples of "Great Leads to Imitate in Your Own Writing." Or, perhaps the guides will suggest entirely new categories that will appeal to your class in ways you and your students haven't yet imagined. Perhaps the guides will help you imagine a "Books That Make You Want to Change the World" category. Or maybe you'll decide to create a shelf in your library titled, "Books with Odd Techniques That Make You Wonder What the Author Is Trying To Do."

Aiding in Conferring

Teachers' knowledge of what to ask and what to teach a reader who says, "this book is boring" comes not only from their knowledge of particular students but also from their knowledge of the text they are talking about. Does "boring" mean that the book is too easy for the reader? Perhaps it means instead that the beginning few chapters of the book are hard to read—confusing because of a series of flashbacks. A guide might explain that the book under discussion has mostly internal, emotional action, and, if the reader is accustomed to avalanche-and-rattlesnake action in books, she may need some time to warm up to this unfamiliar kind of "quiet" action. The guide can point out the kinds of reactions, or troubles, other readers have had with particular books. With the guides at our fingertips, we can more easily determine which questions to ask students, or which pages to turn to, in order to get to the heart of the conference.

Providing a Resource for Curriculum Planning

One Friday, say, we leave the classroom knowing that our students' writing shows that they are thirsting for deeper, more complicated characters to study and imitate. As we plan lessons, we can page through the guides that correspond with some of the books in our library, finding, or remembering, books that students can study that depict fascinating characters.

On the other hand, perhaps we need a book to read aloud to the class, or perhaps we need to recommend a book to a particular struggling reader.

Maybe a reader has finished a book he loves and has turned to you to help him plan his reading for the next weeks. When designing an author study or an inquiry into punctuation and its effects on meaning, it also helps to have the guides with you to point out books that may be helpful in those areas. In each of these cases, and many more, the guides can be a planning aid for you.

Reminding Us, or Teaching Us, About Particular Book Basics

No teacher can read, let alone recall in detail, every book that every child will pick up in the classroom. Of course, we read many of them and learn about many more from our colleagues, but there are far too many books in the world for us to be knowledgeable about them all. Sometimes, the guides will be a reminder of what you have read many years ago. Sometimes, they will provide a framework for you to question or direct your students more effectively than you could if you knew nothing at all about the book. "Probably, you will have to take some time to understand the setting before you can really get a handle on this book, why don't you turn to the picture atlas?" you might say after consulting the guide, or "Sharlene is reading another book that is similar to this one in so many ways! Why don't you go pair up with her to talk." You might learn to ask, "What do you think of Freddy?" in order to learn if the student is catching on to the tone of the narrator, or you might learn you could hint, "Did you get to chapter three yet? Because I bet you won't be bored any more when you get there. . . ." The guides provide a bit of what time constraints deny us: thoughtful insights about the content or unusual features of a given book.

Showcasing Literary Intricacies in Order to Suggest a Reader's Thinking

Sometimes, when we read a book, our idea of the author's message is in our minds before we even finish the story. Because we are experienced readers, much of our inferring and interpreting, our understanding of symbols and contexts, can come to us effortlessly. In the guides, we have tried to slow down some of that thinking so that we can all see it more easily. We have tried to lay out some of the steps young readers may have to go through in order to come to a cohesive idea of what the story is about, or a clear understanding of why a character behaved the way she did. As experienced readers, we may not even realize that our readers are confused by the unorthodox use of italics to show us who is speaking, for example. We may not remember the days when we were confused by changing narrators, the days when it took us a few chapters to figure out a character wasn't to be believed. In these guides, we have tried to go back to those days when we were more naïve readers, and have tried to fill in those thoughts and processes we are now able to skip over so easily.

By bringing forth the noteworthy features of the text, features experienced readers may not even notice, we are reminded of the thinking that our students need to go through in order to make sense of their reading. It gives us an idea of where to offer pointers, of where readers may have gone off in an unhelpful direction, or of where their thinking may need to go instead of where it has gone. By highlighting literary intricacies, we may remember that every bit about the construction of texts is a navigation point for students, and every bit is something we may be able to help students in learning.

Providing a Community of Readers and Teachers

The guides are also intended to help teachers learn from the community of other teachers and readers who have used particular texts already. They make available some of the stories and experiences other teachers have had, in order that we might stand on their shoulders and take our teaching even higher than they could reach. These guides are intended to give you some thinking to go with the books in your classroom library, thinking you can mix with your own ideas.

In the end, we don't all have a community of other teachers with whom we can talk about children's literature. The guides are meant not to stand in for that community, but instead to provide a taste, an appetizer, of the world of supportive professional communities. We hope that by reading these guides and feeling the companionship, guidance and insight they offer, teachers will be nudged to recreate that experience for the other books that have no guides, and that they will ask their colleagues, librarians, and the parents of their students to talk with them about children's literature and young readers. Then, when teachers are creating these guides for themselves, on paper or in their minds' eyes, we will know this project has done the work for which it was created.

Bibliography

Atwell, Nancie. 1987. *In the Middle: Writing, Reading, and Learning with Adolescents.* Portsmouth, NH: Boynton/Cook.

Calkins, Lucy. 2001. *The Art of Teaching Reading.* New York: Addison-Wesley Educational Publishers, Inc.

Cambourne, Brian. 1993. *The Whole Story: Natural Learning and the Acquisition of Literacy in the Classroom.* Auckland, NZ: Ashton Scholastic.

Krashen, Stephen. 1993. *The Power of Reading: Insights from the Research.* Englewood, CO: Libraries Unlimited.

Meek, Margaret. 1988. *How Texts Teach What Readers Learn.* Thimble Press.

Smith, Frank. 1985. *Reading Without Nonsense.* 2nd ed. New York: TC Press.

A Birthday Cake for Ben

Beverley Randell

Book Summary

Ben is in his bed looking at a birthday card from his Dad. The card has a picture of a dinosaur with five balloons around its neck. On the night table is a picture of his Dad in a sailor's uniform. Mom comes into the room when Ben is asleep. She sees the dinosaur card. Mom then goes into the kitchen and reads a book about how to make a dinosaur cake. On the last page, Mom shows her dinosaur cake to Ben.

Basic Book Information

The PM Readers is a series published by Rigby. The PM Readers tend to come in kits where every book looks exactly like every other book. Some teachers think this is less than ideal because at every level, a library should be full of books each with its own individuality. On the other hand, the PM Readers are an important resource for teachers because first, there are many of these at the early reading levels and secondly, the PM Readers recognize and provide the support that early readers need. One notable feature of the PM Readers is their use of complete sentences: I see the cow./I see the pig./. The repetition of high frequency words and the simple sentence syntax provide important reinforcement.

Also, the PM Readers are special because many of even the earliest books are stories. Other early books tend to be label-books, organized in a repetitive list structure, and it's nice to be able to also give beginning readers the opportunity to read stories that have problems and resolutions, as well as characters that appear throughout a series of books. Just as more sophisticated books may feature the Boxcar Children across a series of tales, PM Readers feature Ben or Sally, or other characters, across a series of books.

Noteworthy Features

This book relies upon high frequency words: is, up, on, at, in, look, the, and here. The repetition of these words will give readers a way into the new content on each page. This book, like others at this level, will support early reading behaviors such as directionality, one-to-one correspondence, and monitoring to a known and unknown word. The text is highly supported by colorful illustrations. The print is large and well spaced. Sentences are short, and most pages have only one or two lines of print.

Teaching Ideas

The teacher may confer with a child who is about to read this book, or if multiple copies are available, call a small group of children together to start

Series
Ben books

Illustrator
Genevieve Rees

Publisher
Rigby, 1989

ISBN
0763515051

TC Level
2

them off. She may decide to give a book introduction. There are lots of possible ways to do this. One teacher wanted to set a reader up to do the thinking work called for by this text and by saying, "I like to look over a book before I read it. Should we do that together?" Pointing to the birthday card Ben is holding from his father, she said, "Hmmm. So I'm trying to figure out what Ben is doing." The child speculated that he was looking at a birthday card. "You are probably right!" the teacher confirmed. "Because look..." and she pointed to and began to read the words "Happy..." Soon the child was finishing the phrase, adding the expected "Birthday" and together they read "From Dad." Because a thorough understanding of the book requires some inferring, she then said, "So you're going to have to figure out why his Dad sends a card instead of just saying 'Happy Birthday!' Is he away? I wonder where he could be or what his job could be? And I wonder what other people do for Ben on his birthday. You'll have to find out!"

Whether or not a book introduction is done, the teacher will want to watch as a child reads through the pages of this book to see if the child can match one spoken word to one written one. The reader of this book should be able to point crisply under words, and if the child isn't pointing, the teacher might say, "Point under the words" or "Read with your finger."

Of course, the reader of this text will no doubt point at the wrong words some of the time (and especially if the child exaggerates the separate components of two syllable words such as "birthday"). Sometimes the child won't see the problem until the end of the line when the voicing and pointing don't come out even in the end. Let the child read to this point and let the child say or think, "Oops." If the child goes back to try again, the teacher may want to quietly say, "Good self-correcting," without intervening too much.

Of course, the child may not realize she has encountered difficulty. In which case the teacher can say, "Did that come out even?" or "Did that match?" When the child admits there was trouble the opportunity is there to support this recognition. "Good noticing! It didn't match, did it? So let's go back and try again. That's what good readers do."

The child who is reading books on this level will probably recognize a few sight words and can use those words to "anchor" or pin-down his pointing. If a teacher wants to help a child to do one-to-one matching and also to feel the power of "just knowing" some words, the teacher may, in a conference or a guided reading group, say, "This book has words you know. You know 'the' and 'he' (reviewing these quickly), and you know this word 'comes' don't you?"

If a child encounters difficulty with a word, the teacher will probably want to refrain from jumping in to help right away. It's crucial to give the child time to be an active problem-solver. If the child is not active, the teacher may prompt the child by saying, "Sometimes I check to see if the picture can help," or "Sometimes I reread," or even just saying, "Reread and get your mouth ready for that sound." The latter prompt nudges the child to rely on the syntax of the sentence and then to bring in her knowledge of the first letter sound so as to choose among possible options for what is, at this very early stage of reading, a process of filling in the blank in a sentence.

In a conference, a teacher may want to teach a reader a new word-solving strategy. For example, the text uses the word "book" on page 8. If the child knows the word *look*, a link can be made from look to book, cook, or hook.

A Field Guide to the Classroom Library, Lucy Calkins and the Teachers College Reading and Writing Project, Heinemann, ©2002 Teachers College, Columbia University; http://www.heinemann.com/fieldguides

"Wow! What word power you get from knowing - *ook*" the teacher could say. This, of course, could be the spark behind a mini-lesson another day to the whole class of readers: "Let me tell you about a really cool thing that happened yesterday when (the child's name) and I were reading *A Birthday Cake for Ben...*" the teacher could say. This can be reinforced in word work and shared reading.

This book will support lots of rich thinking and opportunities for discussion. In an independent reading workshop, children know the value of rereading books and they do this expecting to reread with more fluency and phrasing, and also deeper comprehension. Many teachers encourage children to put Post-Its on things they see that help them think more deeply about the book. A child may, for example, notice the picture on Ben's night table of his father in a sailor's uniform and when they talk over the book with a partner, they might speculate that Dad is away on a ship.

Readers can also be encouraged to think about how the different parts of a story fit together. In this story, the father sends a dinosaur card and the mother bakes a dinosaur cake to match the card. It is almost as if the parents work together to give Ben a unified gift, even though the parents are worlds apart. Ben's mother is like the reader of this book. She knows that when you want to learn how to do things, books can really help, and she turns to a book when she wants to learn to bake a special cake.

The reader may want to read about other events in Ben's life in other books about Ben. Soon, the child can be constructing theories about Ben. "What kind of person is he? What are you realizing about Ben?" The child can also theorize about Ben's family and compare the books.

Book Connections

Among the PM Readers, there are a lot of books that go together into a series about Ben: including *Ben's Teddy Bear*, *Ben's Red Car*, *Ben's Treasure Hunt*, *Ben's Dad*, and *Ben's Tooth*.

Genre
Emergent Literacy Book

Teaching Uses
Independent Reading; Small Group Strategy Instruction; Interpretation; Language Conventions

A Field Guide to the Classroom Library, Lucy Calkins and the Teachers College Reading and Writing Project, Heinemann, ©2002 Teachers College, Columbia University; http://www.heinemann.com/fieldguides

A Dark, Dark Tale

Ruth Brown

Book Summary

A Dark, Dark Tale begins "Once upon a time there was a dark, dark moor. On the moor there was a dark, dark wood" and the book continues. In the wood was a house (a dark, dark house, of course) and a door, and a hall . . . leading to a cupboard and in it, a frightened, big-eyed mouse complete with mouse-bed, mouse-slippers, and all the other necessary mouse equipment. The story is complicated by the appearance, midway through, of the black cat that seems to lead the reader deeper into this tale and provides a tragic element. The illustrations and text combine to create an eerie, suspenseful feeling.

Basic Book Information

Puffin publishes this book and it is a real find because it looks and sounds like literature and is published by an outfit that makes trade books for bookstores and town libraries. This is one of the relatively few early books that holds its own in the world of literature. The oversized book doesn't have the appearance of a teaching tool.

Noteworthy Features

This book is supportive of early readers and also has a literary quality to it. The illustrations, together with the language, create an appropriately spooky mood. The book's cover shows a door and in fact, a reader who enters into this book enters the world of story with all its intrigue, suspense, and layered meaning. The book deserves to be read many times and discussed in great detail There is always more for a discerning reader to discover and the book adds up to something that is special and surprising.

Although this book has been leveled as a Level 5 text, it also could be a high-end Level 4 book. The book contains enough of a pattern to lead one to think that every page is basically the same. However, the pattern breaks often and this can sometimes be more challenging than having no pattern at all. The reader expects to read on autopilot, parroting the repeating lines. However, the reader needs to keep an eye on the print in order to notice the variations in pattern. The changes in this pattern mostly involve prepositional phrases. For example, one page begins "Across the passage," while another begins "Behind the curtain. . . . "

The pictures are very detailed with hidden eyes lurking behind trees and shadows that suggest ghosts. Although these pictures might be distracting, they also give the reader helpful information about the text.

Illustrator
Ruth Brown

Publisher
Penguin Books, 1981

ISBN
0140546219

TC Level
5

A Field Guide to the Classroom Library, Lucy Calkins and the Teachers College Reading and Writing Project, Heinemann, ©2002 Teachers College, Columbia University; http://www.heinemann.com/fieldguides

Teaching Ideas

As with other repetitive texts, such as *Brown Bear, Brown Bear*, the book could be introduced as a read aloud. This allows children to delight in the repetitive language and the developing mystery of the text. This is a book that invites children to join in with the story

After children have heard this story read to them, they would enjoy reading it independently and in partnerships. As the teacher observes them, she will want to notice whether their intonation and pacing reflect an understanding of the story. Reading is not just about word solving. It is also about using language to take us to new worlds. If a child is reading it in a staccato fashion, the teacher will want to point out, "This is a beautiful, spooky story. Try to read it aloud so others who listen to you get shivers. Try it again. Put your words together, read it smoothly, and read it to give yourself and others shivers." It may be suggested that when partners get together they try reading it to each other.

When a teacher pulls alongside to confer with a child who is reading the book, she will want to take note of whether the child is attending to the print and is able to self-correct when the pattern changes. The teacher may say, "I like the way you self-corrected" or "You know what? I think you are thinking this will be one of those patterned books you read when you were littler, but you are realizing that this book is trickier. That's a helpful observation. You are going to need to pay really close attention to the words and they will show you what it says."

As children read, they will encounter some long and unfamiliar words, which will provide opportunities for challenging word solving. When children come to "passages" or "curtain" or "cupboard," observe their strategies for dealing with difficulty. Teachers want them to be active, constructive, and resourceful. See if children try to chunk the word, looking at the unknown word for smaller words or chunks of words that they know. Ideally, the child will find "pass" in "passages" and then look at the picture for more helpful information.

Teachers might want to model and encourage a child to mark pages that he is dying to talk about with a partner or with the class.

The cover illustration provides many opportunities for thinking about the text. What is it? A door? A tree? Readers will find hidden animals and may worry that the owl will find them, too. There is a fog or mist in the woods, creating an eerie quality. An observant child might see that although the house-the castle-looks vacant there is an inhabitant . . . a black cat. The cat seems to lead us deeper and deeper into the illustrations. Readers often anticipate that the climax will be a ghost or a witch, and the ending provides an intriguing twist.

Book Connections

In a Dark, Dark Wood published by Wright Group is another book that leads the reader through the wood, into a scary house, and so on, but ends with a ghost yelling "BOO!" instead of the little mouse that is in this tale. *Who's Got My Big Toe* also published by Wright Group is another ghost-like story with a funny ending.

Genre
Emergent Literacy Book

Teaching Uses
Read Aloud; Partnerships; Independent Reading; Interpretation; Language
Conventions

A Home for Little Teddy

Beverley Randell

Book Summary

In this story, Little Teddy decides he cannot sleep on the shelf with the other stuffed animals. He wanders around asking various creatures if he can sleep with them. The bulk of the text is a repeating pattern where Teddy asks animals if he can live with them. The names of the animals are the only things that change on each page. The animals all say no. Finally, the dolls in the dollhouse say "yes" and Little Teddy happily moves in with them.

Basic Book Information

The PM Storybooks, developed in New Zealand and published by Rigby, place a priority on including the traditional story elements. Even texts that at first appear to be lists are, in fact, stories with characters, a problem, and a resolution. The only exceptions are their very earliest books. The PM Readers are known for including a large number of high frequency words, and for controlling vocabulary so that in books of a comparable level of difficulty, the same high frequency words reoccur. The PM Readers use complete sentences: I see a bird./ I see a frog./ to reinforce repetition of high frequency words and simple sentence syntax.

The fact that PM Readers include many high frequency words means that sometimes the resulting sentences seem stilted and unnatural.

Noteworthy Features

About half of this book is dialogue between Little Teddy and the creatures he meets. All dialogue is marked with quotation marks and is referenced with a "speaker tag."

The word "not" in the story is in bold type, to help children catch this crucial word. This helps readers notice the word in particular, and perhaps read it with emphasis, so that they understand that the animals are refusing to offer shelter to the teddy. Without this, some readers would undoubtedly skim over the word and become confused.

The pictures in the story match the text, but will not help readers figure out many particular words, as they are general depictions of scene. They also do not show expressions that would reveal characters' emotions, so they don't offer many clues about the story between the lines either.

Teaching Ideas

Certainly, this book is good for the general teaching uses particular to this

Illustrator
Chantal Stewart

Publisher
Rigby PM Story Book
Collection, 1997

ISBN
0763515108

TC Level
2

level including left to right directionality, one-to-one correspondence, and monitoring to a known and unknown word. Specifically, this book provides practice in reading dialogue, and reading with expression. There aren't any unusual or challenging vocabulary words in the text.

This book is appropriate for readers learning to match one spoken word to one written one. The teacher can cue the reader to find a known sight word, which will serve as an anchor for a one-to-one match. The child who is reading books on this level will probably recognize a few sight words and can use those words to "anchor" or pin-down his pointing. Teachers may refer students to their classroom word wall to check for sight words.

Children who are able to work successfully with a book on this level will benefit not only from the teacher's encouragement to do a one-to-one match, but to "cross-check" as well. Successful reading happens when a reader cross-checks or integrates cues from a variety of sources including sight words, the picture, and the initial letter sound.

In most literature, it is useful for readers to ask themselves why the characters act the way they do in the story. This is particularly true in this book, and this sort of discussion will probably help children gain a deeper understanding of what is going on in the text.

As soon as readers focus on what is really happening, they will undoubtedly have questions for themselves and each other. Why is Little Teddy so adamant about not sleeping with the other stuffed animals? Children sometimes decide from the picture clues that it is too crowded there, or that the cars and trucks on the shelf above make too much noise. Others think Little Teddy just doesn't like the other animals, or that he has been walking along with his suitcase for a long time and this is just another place he won't stop. In any case, when partners are asked to stop and talk after each page, issues generally come up in their book talk right away.

There are also questions about why the other animals turn the teddy away. They say they do it because he is not like them. This can be a great opportunity for children to discuss what they think of reasoning like that. Is that a good reason to turn away someone who needs shelter? And why do the dolls finally let Little Teddy live with them? What is different about them? Is a dollhouse any more suited to a bear than a mouse house? This kind of critical thinking about the book will help children develop their interpretation and critique skills.

Sometimes teachers coach children to read the story looking for the "understory," the emotions under the words-using personal experience to educate their guesses. What is Little Teddy feeling when he is refused shelter? What are the rabbit and the mouse feeling? What are the dolls feeling as they look at the teddy before they tell him he can stay? Why do they feel differently than the other creatures the teddy asked?

Genre
Emergent Literacy Book

A Field Guide to the Classroom Library, Lucy Calkins and the Teachers College Reading and Writing Project, Heinemann, ©2002 Teachers College, Columbia University; http://www.heinemann.com/fieldguides

Teaching Uses
Independent Reading; Language Conventions; Interpretation; Critique; Partnerships; Small Group Strategy Instruction; Whole Group Instruction

A Field Guide to the Classroom Library, Lucy Calkins and the Teachers College Reading and Writing Project, Heinemann, ©2002 Teachers College, Columbia University; http://www.heinemann.com/fieldguides

Book Summary

In *A Is for Africa,* each letter of the alphabet introduces us to a phrase in the Nigerian Igbo culture. The words are chosen to represent all of Africa. They usually refer to artifacts found in everyday life, such as pots, beads, canoes, rivers, feathers and drums.

Basic Book Information

This 25-page, nonfiction picture book, structured alphabetically, focuses on African culture in general and Igbo culture in particular. One or two letters are on each page, followed by a word that begins with that letter and several sentences describing the word's cultural importance. In addition, a colorful photograph that depicts scenes in Nigeria accompanies each word.

The author's note at the book's beginning explains that, although the scenes are Nigerian, they represent all of Africa. Reading this note is not crucial to a basic understanding of *A Is for Africa.* As it follows an alphabet book format, this picture book has no index, table of contents or any other such reference structures often found in nonfiction books.

Noteworthy Features

A Is for Africa's modern photographs of rural Nigeria are inviting and intriguing. The short text chunks separated by the familiar alphabet make the text less intimidating to readers, despite the usually unfamiliar content.

Teaching Ideas

This book can counterbalance some of the skewed images of Africa so prevalent in popular culture. It is important to note, however, that *A Is for Africa* depicts only village life, and only certain aspects of it. Readers should also be aware of Africa's bustling cities, its industries and its diversified economy.

Every situation in *A Is for Africa* is described as a happy one. While the text does not condescend toward village life, there is no mention that many people have no refrigerators or running water, or of the health problems that can be associated with that. The many reasons for these conditions are not mentioned, just as the conditions themselves are passed over lightly.

The author also generalizes about the cultures and peoples of Africa in the opening note and in several places in the text. Teachers may or may not point these instances out to readers, depending on the needs and purposes of the reader. This book's generalizations might lead to interesting work on questioning texts while reading. A teacher might introduce such questioning with a query such as, "Why do you think the author would portray *all*

Illustrator
Ifeoma Onyefulu

Publisher
Puffin Books, 1993

ISBN
0140562222

TC Level
9

A Field Guide to the Classroom Library, Lucy Calkins and the Teachers College Reading and Writing Project, Heinemann, ©2002 Teachers College, Columbia University; http://www.heinemann.com/fieldguides

Africans as welcoming or warm?" Students may go on to develop their own questions, such as "What is the author's point of view?" and "What has the author left out of the book?"

Book Connections

A Is for Africa is very similar both in structure and content to *J is for Jambo*, an alphabet book about the Swahili language and some of the cultures of East Africa. Students might explore other nonfiction books that follow an alphabet structure, such as Jerry Pallotta's *The Desert Alphabet Book* or Joseph Bruchac's *Many Nations: An Alphabet of Native America*.

Genre
Picture Book; Nonfiction

Teaching Uses
Independent Reading; Partnerships; Content Area Study; Critique

A Field Guide to the Classroom Library, Lucy Calkins and the Teachers College Reading and Writing Project, Heinemann, ©2002 Teachers College, Columbia University; http://www.heinemann.com/fieldguides

A Little Seed
John McIlwain

Book Summary

The text of the book uses the form "a little _____" (e.g., water) to describe the tending of a seed. Each page shows a picture of the same little girl going through the process of cultivating a seed. On the last page, the word "big" is substituted for "little" to describe the flower that has grown.

Basic Book Information

Beverly Randell developed the PM series for Rigby and has written many of the books in it. She began to write the books after ten years as a classroom teacher in New Zealand. The PM readers rely upon a traditional story structure, which includes a central character, a problem, a climax or pivotal moment in which readers worry, "Will the problem be solved?" followed by a resolution. Randell, intending to teach early readers to monitor for meaning, writes of these books, ". . . you will find no traces of mad fantasy, certainly no hint of the supernatural, and the very minimum of surprise twists in plots." She believes that books about witches and ghosts or books full of playful nonsense do not teach children the habit of expecting stories to make sense-and of self-correcting when it does not.

Noteworthy Features

The simple text, with its highly supportive illustrations, supports early reading behavior such as one-to-one matching and directionality. Children who are familiar with the process of planting a seed and watching it grow will more easily comprehend this story. The pattern, along with the fact that each page starts with the sight word *a,* helps anchor many readers to the text. The clear division between text and picture also helps early readers to focus on the print.

The repeated word *little* is not supported by the illustrations, so teachers may need to introduce that word to children, or offer it in their introduction to the text.

Teaching Ideas

The teacher may introduce this book by saying: "*A Little Seed* is a book that shows you how to plant and take care of a seed so that it will grow. A girl does this in the book. She begins with a little seed and puts it in a little pot. You can read it to find out what else the seed needs in order to grow." Some teachers also instruct readers about how their reading of commas and ellipses can help their comprehension.

This book is particularly appropriate for readers who are learning to match a spoken word to a written one, predict text from pictures, and

Illustrator
Shirley Tourret

Publisher
Rigby, Smart Series, 1996

ISBN
0763541796

TC Level
1

understand the big idea of a story.

Children might be asked to wonder what would grow from the seed. Students can look at the book as they are reading to see if it offers any clues as to what the seed will become. Readers will find that on the very first page there is an illustration of the seed packet with a flower's picture on it. Another page shows a plant that holds the same flowers that the seed will grow into. This process of looking for clues is the beginning of making educated predictions about how stories will go-a very important skill for beginning readers to acquire.

This text gives children the opportunity to think about the passage of time in a story. How quickly did the seed grow? Children who know that seeds don't grow overnight can ask, or be asked, to look for clues the author gives about how long it takes for a seed to grow. The wordless page with three pictures of the seed growing is one clue, and the ellipses instead of the comma in the pattern is another.

The already-full-grown flowers next to the growing seed may confuse some children. Readers can be pushed to speculate about how such a situation could come about. Children looking closely at details might find it odd when they see that the girl who plants the seed has on the same clothes in every picture-even after the seed has turned into a flower. This might lead some children to think everything happened on the same day. Once they realize this can't be, they will have to supply other reasons for the girl wearing the same clothes and hair bows.

This book is a good addition to a nonfiction study of growing things, or a reading center basket of books on seeds, plants, flowers, or the careful nurturing of anything to make it grow. Children who are watching plants grow in their own classrooms may enjoy labeling the parts of the plant that they can see in the pictures, from roots to stem to petal.

Book Connections

The Carrot Seed by Ruth Krauss is an interesting book to pair with *A Little Seed*. There are many texts at the early levels on related topics by publishers such as Newbridge and Wright Group (Twig and Sunshine series). Others include *The Tiny Seed* by Eric Carle, *From Seed to Plant* by Gail Gibbons, *How a Seed Grows* by Helene J. Jordan and Loretta Krupinski, and *Flower Garden* by Eve Bunting.

Genre
Emergent Literacy Book

Teaching Uses
Independent Reading; Partnerships; Language Conventions; Small Group Strategy Instruction; Content Area Study; Interpretation

A Field Guide to the Classroom Library, Lucy Calkins and the Teachers College Reading and Writing Project, Heinemann, ©2002 Teachers College, Columbia University; http://www.heinemann.com/fieldguides

A Toy Box
Andrea Butler

Book Summary

The text of the book, with one line per page names a list of objects such as "A truck," and "a jack-in-the-box." Each page shows a picture of the object.

Basic Book Information

Andrea Butler, a noted literacy expert and author of *Toward a Reading-Writing Classroom*, a professional book for teachers, wrote this book. *A Toy Box* has eleven words written over eight pages. Most pages have two or three words on a page, except "a jack-in-the-box." There is one line of print on each page. The text is consistently placed at the bottom of the page, with the picture on top. Print is large and well spaced.

Noteworthy Features

This simple text is highly supported by colorful pictures. It will support early reading behaviors such as one-to-one matching and directionality. The repetitive pattern will provide a way into the next page for the reader. The fact that each page starts with the easy sight word "a" will help anchor many readers to the text. The clear division between the text and the picture also helps early readers to focus on the words.

Teaching Ideas

Teachers will be more apt to give book introductions to a child who is reading Level 1 books than to any other readers. A possible book introduction could be, "This is a book about all the things we might find in a toy box. Do you have a toy box at home? What's in it? Let's see what this little boy has in his toy box." This book is particularly appropriate for readers learning to match one spoken word to one written one, readers learning to predict text from pictures, and readers working on directionality.

The teacher can cue the students to find the known sight word, "a" before reading the text. This will serve as an anchor for a one-to-one match. References can be made to the word wall in the classroom if the sight word is on it. It also might be helpful to ask the child to find the word "in" or "the" on page 6. Page 6 reads "a jack-in-the-box"; this will give the teacher an opportunity to see if the readers can hold onto their one-to-one match.

Teachers can use the child's miscues as an opportunity to teach, saying, "Did that match?" Note how the child handles page 5, "a doll." If the child says "a baby," praise him/her for looking at the picture. Then tell the child, "We must use the first letter of the word to help us read. Let's get our mouth ready for the /d/ sound. If a child has a problem with the b/d reversal at this

Illustrator
George Ikonomou

Publisher
Rigby Stage 1, Literacy, 2000

ISBN
0947328017

TC Level
1

 A Field Guide to the Classroom Library, Lucy Calkins and the Teachers College Reading and Writing Project, Heinemann, ©2002 Teachers College, Columbia University; http://www.heinemann.com/fieldguides

stage of reading, that's absolutely normal and is to be expected.

Genre
Emergent Literacy Book

Teaching Uses
Independent Reading; Small Group Strategy Instruction; Partnerships; Language Conventions

A Field Guide to the Classroom Library, Lucy Calkins and the Teachers College Reading and Writing Project, Heinemann, ©2002 Teachers College, Columbia University; http://www.heinemann.com/fieldguides

Airport
Byron Barton

Book Summary

Airport is a book that describes the various happenings of different airplanes at an airport. The reader learns about an airplane that dusts the crops and one that writes a message in the sky. They also learn about a helicopter, a cargo plane and finally follow a jet plane from the beginning of a journey to the end, and then start again at the beginning of the process.

Basic Book Information

More than many other books in this library, this book looks like a picture book. It contains 31 unnumbered pages, with 14 sentences stretched across these pages. The first sentence stretches across four pages, and then successive sentences are stretched across two pages, with illustrations on all pages.

Noteworthy Features

The text placement is fairly consistent on the bottom of each page. After the first page, we read a list of different airplanes and their jobs, spread across the rest of the pages of the book. . However, there is an inconsistent use of words to introduce each sentence shifting between *this*, *here*, *there*, and *these*. Some of the concepts will be unfamiliar to many children. "Dusting the crops" and "writing a message" are examples of what may be tricky parts for many.

At first some children may be confused to find that each sentence crosses over to the next page, but once they become familiar with this structure, they're often able to adapt to it.

Teaching Ideas

Airport is a simple nonfiction book that can be used to introduce a conversation about various types of planes and their purposes. Many teachers will let children study and read the book as best they can with independence because the non-narrative and non-patterned nature of the book makes it good to read in a "dip-in" sort of a way.

After the child has done some work with the text, the teacher may want to introduce the book. One way to do this would be to say, "*Airport* is a book about different types of airplanes and their different jobs." If the reader needed more support, the teacher might incorporate the terms used in the book in her discussions using *here*, *there*, and *this*. A teacher may introduce the tricky pages first. "Let's see what happens when a jet plane starts to journey into the sky," she could say.

Children have loved studying this book as part of an author study of

Illustrator
Byron Barton

Publisher
HarperTrophy, 1982

ISBN
0064431452

TC Level
5

A Field Guide to the Classroom Library, Lucy Calkins and the Teachers College Reading and Writing Project, Heinemann, ©2002 Teachers College, Columbia University; http://www.heinemann.com/fieldguides

Byron Barton. Some children found that this book was similar to many of Barton's other books, such as *Dinosaurs, Dinosaurs*. Students were able to make connections to his list-like writing and bold illustrations, across books. Children who've read other Byron Barton books had more experience negotiating the sentences across two pages.

One teacher used this book as part of a reading center on airplanes. Readers discussed similar books, and with help, thought about how different airplanes have different purposes. This book could be a great addition to a center on airplanes where children can compare various planes and discuss their purposes.

Students might substitute the word *people* for *passengers*, probably because they don't look across the entire word. On a reread of the entire sentence, they are usually able to self-correct.

Genre
Picture Book; Nonfiction

Teaching Uses
Content Area Study; Author Study; Independent Reading

A Field Guide to the Classroom Library, Lucy Calkins and the Teachers College Reading and Writing Project, Heinemann, ©2002 Teachers College, Columbia University; http://www.heinemann.com/fieldguides

Baby Chimp

Rebel Williams

Book Summary

There are two words on each page and the text follows a pattern that combines the word "He" and a series of simple verbs to state the behavior of a chimp. On the first page, for example, the text states, "He eats."

Basic Book Information

This book provides emergent readers with a nonfiction text filled with beautiful photographs of the natural world.

Noteworthy Features

This text follows the "list with a twist" pattern so common in books at this level. In this book, the word that changes on each page is the one that shows action, and that new word is not always well supported by the pictures. For example, on one page the picture shows the chimp in the foliage and it reads, "He hides." The word *hides* may not be totally obvious to the reader from the picture. A reader could think this says, "He peeks" or "He watches." Teachers can coach readers to begin to check the first letter of the word to see if it matches their prediction.

The book contains a sort of epilogue designed to be read by the parent or teacher. The first part of this is a compilation of facts about chimpanzees, which, though written in paragraph form, reads as if it was once a bulleted list that has lost its bullets. There is also a list of "Things to Do" for a teacher who wants to do enrichment activities based on this book. However, rather than making bar graphs comparing the average weight of human and chimp babies or inviting a parent to bring a baby sibling to class as the book suggests, it would probably be more productive for children to be involved in activities that more directly support their emergent reading skills, such as rereading the book and talking about it with a reading partner.

Teaching Ideas

For instructional use in the A library, this book is appropriate for children who are just beginning to focus on print. It is important to be aware that because the book is repetitive, patterned, and the print is supported by pictures, it may appear to teachers that the students understand the text of little books when in fact, the children have committed the text to memory without understanding the links between the text and the words they are

Publisher
Wright Group, 1998

ISBN
0780290550

TC Level
1

A Field Guide to the Classroom Library, Lucy Calkins and the Teachers College Reading and Writing Project, Heinemann, ©2002 Teachers College, Columbia University; http://www.heinemann.com/fieldguides

"reading." In light of this, teachers may want to make sure that children have lots of opportunities to practice emergent reading of familiar story books that have been read aloud to them a number of times. As they do, look for indications that they are ready to make the transition from emergent to conventional reading and, only then, move children toward beginning to read books such as this one. A teacher might determine readiness for this transition by observing a rereading of a familiar emergent storybook such as *Corduroy*. If the teacher *had* been noticing children's rereading sounding more and more like they are actually reading the words-but they now say, for example, "I can't read because I don't know the words," then the teacher would know that they are ready for a book like *Baby Chimp*.

If a child has a sense for how books go and has done enough shared reading, writing workshops, interactive writing, and name study work to know a bit about initial consonants and a few sight words, the child will probably be able to do some productive work with a Level 1 book without a teacher prereading the entire book to the child. A teacher might want to introduce the book title and give the child the added support of an introduction such as, "This book is called *Baby Chimp*. A chimp is a kind of monkey. The book tells about the things he does. Let's look at page 2. I like to look at the picture first. Look, he eats. (She then points to the print and reads.) 'He eats.' Why don't you read and find out what else the chimp does."

As children read, teachers can encourage them to point crisply under each word. If the child's oral text doesn't match the word that she is pointing to, the teacher then has the opportunity to give the child a chance to self-correct. If the child just continues on, the teacher may try to elicit awareness that something is wrong because the one-to-one match isn't coming out evenly. We might say "Did it come out even?" or "Did it match? Try it again and make it match."

If a child miscues, reading the words "He swings" as "He falls" or "He plays," we may want to say, "Check that. Does it say 'plays'? If you were going to write 'plays,' how would you begin?" Since children who are reading these highly-supportive Level 1 texts may not be able to look across entire words and chunk the internal letters just yet, teachers might simply want to help the child by saying, "Could it be 'swings'? Check it and see."

It is helpful for children to reread even very simple books like this one, looking closely at them and thinking about the story. Maybe a child will wonder why the baby chimp is alone for so much of the book. Where is the parent chimp? Maybe the reader will notice how the chimp's feet cling tightly to branches. On one page, the text says, "He jumps" but the accompanying smile makes this page look like the baby chimp is falling, not jumping. Children may talk about these or other observations, and they'll be more apt to do so if the teacher joins them in thinking and talking about the text.

Genre
Emergent Literacy Book; Nonfiction

A Field Guide to the Classroom Library, Lucy Calkins and the Teachers College Reading and Writing Project, Heinemann, ©2002 Teachers College, Columbia University; http://www.heinemann.com/fieldguides

Teaching Uses

Independent Reading; Content Area Study; Small Group Strategy Instruction; Interpretation; Read Aloud

Baby Lamb's First Drink
Beverley Randell

Book Summary

This book tells the story of how a baby lamb is fed by his mother as they enjoy a spring day together.

Basic Book Information

Beverley Randell, the author, lives in New Zealand. The PM Readers tend to come in kits in which every book looks exactly like every other book. Some people think this is less than ideal because at every level a library should include a variety of books, each with its own unique look.

On the other hand, the PM Readers are an important resource for teachers because there are many of these at the early reading levels and they are supportive for readers at this level. Many researchers feel the PM Readers are especially good at providing a lot of easy text, full of high frequency words. That is, instead of saying: "the cow/ the pig/" a PM Reader is apt to say, "I see the cow./ I see the pig./"

Another advantage of the PM Readers is that a great many of even the earliest books are stories. Lots of other early books tend to be label books, organized in a repetitive list structure, and it's nice to be able to give beginning readers the opportunity to read stories that have problems, resolutions, and characters. Just as more sophisticated books may feature the Boxcar Children across a series of tales, PM Readers feature Ben and Sally, or other characters, across a series of books.

Noteworthy Features

This book initially appears to be a "list" book, with one sentence on the left hand page and an illustration on the right hand page. By page 8 the text becomes more complicated and dialogue is introduced. Although the sentences are simple and repetitive, there is a storyline, which opens up many opportunities for discussion (e.g., parent/child relationships, farm animals).

Teaching Ideas

Sometimes a teacher will decide to help a reader (or a group of readers) through a slightly challenging text by giving a book introduction. Then the teacher may watch and listen in as the child or the children read, and use what she sees to decide upon a post-reading teaching point.

On the other hand, teachers do not always need to watch a child's journey through any one book in order to know some strategies that a particular reader will need to read it successfully. The teacher may want to give the child (or a small group of children) a strategy lesson before reading

Illustrator
Ernest Papps

Publisher
Rigby, 1996

ISBN
0435049062

TC Level
2

the text. In a strategy lesson the teacher generally talks about, and often demonstrates, a strategy that effective readers use. He'll then say, "Try using that strategy now with this book while I watch."

Teachers design strategy lessons to remind readers that patterns in books don't always last, and to help them know other ways to find support as they read. In a strategy lesson, one teacher said, "I've noticed you're really good at figuring out the pattern in books, and you've gotten used to books having a change in the pattern on the last page." Then the teacher added, "Sometimes books don't have a pattern to help you, or the pattern only lasts a while, and then switches. This is one of those books. There's a pattern, and then it switches. Then there's another, and you'll see what happens. Read it in partnerships up to the Post-Its I've put in. Pay attention to the patterns you have come to expect and be sure to pay close attention to the surprises you run into."

After talking about the establishment and revision of the first pattern and the presence of a second, looser pattern, children can be encouraged to read one more page together with a partner to see whether or not the pattern continues.

Emergent readers who approach this book should be able to confidently put their finger directly under each word, since they will be asked to read more than just the one or two lines that have been required prior to this level. When a teacher confers with a child who is looking at the cover, it would be important to notice if the child is able to get the title. A child might be tempted to skip over the words *first* and *drink*, if they encounter difficulty, but we would want to give them those words so they would be able to use them to comprehend the story beyond the basic story line.

Many pages contain a word that a reader might find challenging. The teacher can aid the reader in finding a known high frequency word that can serve as an anchor and help keep up the child's reading stamina. On page 2 for example, in the sentence "Spring is here," a young reader is likely to find spring a difficult first word to start the text. "Here" and "is" will be especially strong anchor words in this text. This would be an excellent opportunity to secure other early reading behaviors such as prompting the child to reread, to look at the picture, and to get his mouth ready for the first sound. The child should consistently be asked, "Does that make sense?"

Before beginning a conference, a teacher will want to notice what strategies the child is using for making sense of the text. Is the child searching and checking while reading? For example, did the child match the word "tail," on page 14, with the picture? If not, the teacher can show the child that it helps to look at both the pictures and the letters. If a reader experiences difficulty with the word "hungry," a teacher can encourage the use of different strategies such as: looking at initial and final consonants, looking for parts of the word that they already know (e.g., /un/), seeing if it reminds them of any other word or name that they can read, chunking parts of the word together, and then rereading the sentence to check and see if it makes sense and looks right. The reader can also check the picture and confirm that Baby Lamb looks hungry!

If a teacher wants to gather a group of children with similar needs in a guided reading group, she might begin with the following introduction, "What is Baby Lamb doing?" Children might observe that mother sheep is feeding her baby, and they might add comments such as "Many baby

A Field Guide to the Classroom Library, Lucy Calkins and the Teachers College Reading and Writing Project, Heinemann, ©2002 Teachers College, Columbia University; http://www.heinemann.com/fieldguides

animals on the farm are happy in the spring." The teacher might then say, "Let's turn the pages and see what happens." As the teacher flips through the pages, she'll want to see if the children are able to infer that the baby lamb was just born. In a follow-up lesson at the end, she might teach a word-solving strategy. For example, the word "looking" appears on page 10. She might call attention to the *-ing* ending. Using magnetic letters and a white board, she could make the word "look," and then pull in the *-ing* chunk, explaining how the ending works. Using the magnetic letters to add *-ing* to other commonly used verbs can help children recognize this pattern when it occurs in print.

In a reading partnership, one teacher encouraged each child to practice reading smoothly and with fluency. The partnership decided to take on the roles of the lamb and the sheep. "Baa-baa. Baa-baa" moaned the child who was playing the lamb. In a deep voice, "I am here," said the child who was playing the sheep. The children read and reread as they wrestled with decisions about which part was the sheep and which was the lamb.

Children who have been encouraged to not just read the black marks on a page but also to talk about a book often laugh about the way the baby lamb is getting milk from the mother sheep. Children who have been exposed to parents similarly feeding a newborn sibling might make the connection between the two.

This book might lead to a discussion of other farm animals with babies that have different names, such as cow and calf.

Genre
Emergent Literacy Book

Teaching Uses
Independent Reading; Small Group Strategy Instruction; Partnerships; Interpretation

A Field Guide to the Classroom Library, Lucy Calkins and the Teachers College Reading and Writing Project, Heinemann, ©2002 Teachers College, Columbia University; http://www.heinemann.com/fieldguides

Big Al

Andrew Clements; Andrew Elborn

Book Summary

Big Al, the main character in the story, is a large, lonely, hideous fish who tries to befriend every school of small fish. One day a school of these tiny fish is about to be hauled up in a net when Big Al comes to their rescue. Big Al gets himself trapped in the net and pulled up by the fishermen. Lucky for him, they find him so ugly that he is thrown back in the water and he survives. The small fish that used to scatter when Big Al swam up are now glad to see him back. He becomes their hero and now Big Al has many friends.

Basic Book Information

Every page of this oversized book conveys the expansiveness and the drama of a world that exists beneath the sea. The illustrations, hand-painted on a silken textile, create a three-dimensional quality to the art, which makes Big Al's warts seem puffy, and the ocean blues seem endlessly vast. There are no human characters in this story, unless one counts the fishermen who aren't named or seen. The ocean depths are the setting in this story-nothing else is visible.

Clements, the author of this book, is also the author of the popular chapter book, *Frindle*. Both books rely on his love of stories and his respect for well-hewn plots.

Noteworthy Features

Both the illustrations and the story of Big Al are noteworthy. The illustrations give readers the impression that we have entered the cool vastness of the deep blue sea. The story follows the familiar motif of *The Ugly Duckling* or *Cinderella*. In all of these stories the ugly, or overlooked, character emerges as the star, although while in these stories the character turns out to be lovely after all, Big Al remains warty and brown, looking more like a rotten apple than like the colorful little fish that dart alongside him.

The layout of the text on the page encourages the reader to pay attention to pitch and pacing, creating a sense of drama in the story. Page 1 is typed like any other book. This changes on page 2, where the text is divided in a way that encourages slowing down our voices:

"But Big Al was also very

very

scary."

Next, the author pairs bold print and capital letters to signal when to change the tone of the reader's voice:

"How could he expect **little** fish to trust a great **big** fish with eyes and skin

Illustrator
Yoshi Miyake

Publisher
Simon & Schuster, 1991

ISBN
0689817223

TC Level
8

And **TEETH** like his?"

The narrative follows the classic story structure. In the first page readers learn the setting and the main character's problem-Al has no friends. Then unfolds the attempted but foiled, efforts to solve the problem. Each of these actions is just a page or two long. A longer sequence of events leads to a true resolution and the story ends happily.

Teaching Ideas

This book deserves to be read often and in many different contexts. In the A Library, its primary instructional purpose is an emergent literacy read aloud, along with books like *Caps for Sale*, *Bunny Cakes* and *Mike Mulligan and His Steam Shovel*.

Researchers such as Elizabeth Sulzby and Marie Clay, in their studies of emergent readers, have found that when children are given opportunities to hear stories read often and then "pretend read" (referred to as "reading" or "rereading") they go through a number of predictable stages of reading development. Children begin by simply "labeling" the picture on the page, then telling the story off the pictures, using progressively more dialogue and storybook language, ultimately moving toward a more "conventional" reading where they use the print. To go on this reading journey, it is important for children to hear the story read aloud many times, have lots of opportunities to reread it to a partner, and have a supportive teacher nearby who coaches into the reading. To support this process, teachers can select books with more text than readers could decode, books that can not be easily memorized with elements of drama and suspense and characters that young children can relate to. Multiple copies of several good examples of emergent literacy storybooks are included in the A library and teachers are likely to have other in their own collections.

By reading *Big Al* aloud four or more times over the course of two weeks, teachers support the development of these important emergent reading behaviors as described in the Primary Literacy Standards. After children have been immersed in the story, the teacher gives them opportunities to "read" it as best they can on their own. Over time, children's rereading will tend to go from telling the story off the pictures to a rendition that more closely resembles the actual text. Teachers will want to be aware that in this particular book, though children are exposed to classic story structure and literary language, the pictures don't have many details and therefore do not support the child's use of illustrations to help with "pretend reading" as strongly as most other emergent literacy texts.

Book Connections

After children have heard *Big Al* many times, teachers may read other stories that have a similar theme, and then initiate a discussion around these similarities. *Big Al* is not unlike the little engine that couldn't get over the mountain: "I think I can, I think I can," the train huffed and puffed and eventually succeeded. Usually in these stories the main character shows great resolve. Sometimes, the character has a lucky break and sometimes the character uses magic, trickery, or talent to overcome the problem.

A Field Guide to the Classroom Library, Lucy Calkins and the Teachers College Reading and Writing Project, Heinemann, ©2002 Teachers College, Columbia University; http://www.heinemann.com/fieldguides

Genre
Picture Book

Teaching Uses
Independent Reading; Small Group Strategy Instruction; Language Conventions; Read Aloud

Big Things

Beverley Randell; Jenny Giles; Annette Smith

Book Summary

This book for emergent readers is an organized list of big things-a truck, a bulldozer, a ship, a tractor, a bus, a fire engine, an ambulance, a crane, a plane-each accompanied by a colorful photograph of the object.

Basic Book Information

Many of the PM Storybooks, developed in New Zealand and published by Rigby, are written as stories and structured around traditional story elements. The only exceptions are their very earliest books, including *Big Things*. The PM Readers support very beginning readers by including a large number of high frequency words, and for controlling vocabulary so that in books of a comparable level of difficulty, the same high frequency words reoccur. They also tend to have longer, rather than shorter, sentences. For example, instead of "I see/ a bird/ a frog"/ and so on, the PM Readers are more likely to use complete sentences like I see a bird./I see a frog./.

Noteworthy Features

Throughout this book, text is printed on the left-hand page and is supported by a full color photograph on the right-hand side. Although this is a simple text, it is written in a way that sounds like spoken language-"A truck is big. . . A bulldozer is big." This sentence pattern repeats consistently throughout the book and should enable readers to find their way into each next page. Each page begins with the easy sight word "a" that can help to draw in and anchor readers to the text.

Teaching Ideas

The color photographs could spark a lively conversation about objects that tend to excite young children when they see them in their environment (e.g., an ambulance, a fire engine). The teacher could introduce the book by saying, "This is a story about big things. A truck is big. A ship is big. Let's see what other things are big," as she turns through the pages of the book. Some words in this book could be particularly hard-like "bulldozer" or "crane"-especially if a child isn't familiar with them. If the children make wrong guesses, the teacher can provide the correct word. Also, although the book's pattern is consistent, there are some variations that will be tricky for young readers. On one page "an" is used instead of "a" and this change in vocabulary should be pointed out to readers.

Children reading Level 1 books might first thumb through the book and speculate on what it might say. Some readers will "label" their read, saying, "a truck," or "a ship." Others might make up a story about the big objects.

A Field Guide to the Classroom Library, Lucy Calkins and the Teachers College Reading and Writing Project, Heinemann, ©2002 Teachers College, Columbia University; http://www.heinemann.com/fieldguides

Illustrator
Nelson Price Milburn

Publisher
Rigby PM Starters One, 1996

ISBN
0763541400

TC Level
1

Still others will attempt to read the words. Even at this very early stage, the colorful illustrations and the appealing subject of the book open up opportunities for rich partner conversations.

Assuming that the word "a" has already been taught and is posted on the class word wall or elsewhere in the classroom environment, readers can use that word to find their way into the text on each new page. In a reading conference at this stage, a teacher will want to first observe the child to see if she is pointing under the words on each new page. In order to help keep their reading on track and to emphasize the one-to-one correlation between the written and spoken word, children can be coached to point under each word as they say it. The clear division between the text and the pictures in this book will help early readers to keep their focus on the words.

Again, there are some tricky words in this book (e.g., "bulldozer") and children may read some of them incorrectly. To support the emergent reader, teachers may want to work on the strategy of using the initial consonant to help figure out a new word. For example, readers might say, "A boat is big" rather than "A ship is big." A teacher might respond by saying, "It was really smart of you to use the picture. Let's see if the word 'boat' works. What letter does 'boat' start with?" If the /sh/ sound is too hard for this reader, the teacher could ask, "Could this be the word 'ship'? Yes, it is because ship has the /sh/ sound!" Teachers will want to reinforce this important early strategy in shared reading and word work.

The words "fire engine" on page 8 will often challenge readers but this can provide an opportunity for teaching some self-correction strategies. The text reads, "A fire engine is big." Many readers may think fire engine is one word and find that their pointing does not match the number of words on the page. Sometimes a child will self-correct, saying "Whoops!" and will go back and try it again. If she doesn't catch the mistake, a teacher could ask, "Did that come out even? Let's try it again."

Book Connections

Little Things (PM Collection Starters One) is a book that has the same format, but concentrates on things that are little. These two books might inspire a study of books that focus on big and little or on the theme of opposites. It might also be added to a basket of books about vehicles.

Genre
Emergent Literacy Book; Nonfiction

Teaching Uses
Independent Reading; Partnerships; Small Group Strategy Instruction; Content Area Study; Language Conventions; Interpretation

Birthday Balloons

Beverley Randell

Book Summary

It is Tom's sixth birthday and he is having a party. Tom gets balloons and six cars as presents. His baby sister, Emma, starts to cry. No one can figure out what is troubling baby Emma. Then, Tom notices Emma looking at one of his balloons. He presents her with a red balloon and her crying stops. Dad says, "Emma is lucky to have a big brother like you!" Everyone sings "Happy Birthday" as Emma looks on smiling . . . holding her red balloon.

Basic Book Information

This book contains 174 words over 16 pages. The size and spacing of the print is appropriately matched to a young reader. Throughout the book, the illustrations appear to the left or right of the print, except for page 8 where the illustration is below the text. The illustrations by Ernest Papps are colorful and realistic.

Noteworthy Features

This text presents some challenges for young readers. Pictures, for example, provide only moderate support. One of the most noteworthy features of the book is its use of dialogue. There are four characters in the book that speak: Nana, Poppa, Mom, and Tom. In addition, there are instances of dialogue without a clear reference. For example, on page 4, it reads, " 'Go on Tom,' said Mom. 'Open the box.'" In this case, the speaker is not referenced after the second line of dialogue. The reader must infer that Mom issued the second line, as well as the first.

Another notable feature of the text is its use of bold face print. Throughout the text, there are words in bold (e.g., "'Oh, **thank** you,' said Tom."). The bold font is an indication that the word should be emphasized. For some children, this book may be an introduction to the use of this particular literary device.

Another significant element of this text is its use of italics. On page 16, the entire family sings "Happy Birthday" to Tom. The song lyrics are written in italics to indicate that the song should be sung. Children will most likely be familiar with the "Happy Birthday" song and some may even automatically sing the lyrics. However, equating italics with singing the text may be a new connection for young readers to make.

Readers of this text should probably be well familiar with the return sweep required by sentences that wrap around onto multiple lines. Although there are many such examples in this text, all sentences begin and end on the same page. This makes it easier for readers. They do not have to hold onto the initial idea of a sentence as they turn the page.

Sentences in this text are chunked into paragraph form. These paragraphs

A Field Guide to the Classroom Library, Lucy Calkins and the Teachers College Reading and Writing Project, Heinemann, ©2002 Teachers College, Columbia University; http://www.heinemann.com/fieldguides

Illustrator
Ernest Papps

Publisher
New PM Story Books, 1987

ISBN
076351523X

TC Level
3

are not complex or lengthy. The average length of a paragraph is one to two sentences.

Teaching Ideas

Birthday Balloons contains a substantial number of high frequency words that can serve as anchors for one-to-one matching. Children are likely to recognize a great number of the vocabulary words in the book. When children do encounter unknown words, they will need to rely on multiple cueing systems in order to decode them, as the illustrations are only moderately supportive. Teachers may have to remind students to get their mouths ready for the next sound while they are looking at the word.

Birthday Balloons, like others at this level, presents many possibilities for teaching early reading behaviors to young readers. Children who are matched appropriately to this text will find opportunities to practice such essential skills as one-to-one matching, return sweep, fluency, and phrasing. Depending on the needs of the readers in an individual class, teachers can teach either whole class mini-lessons or individually coach students on these behaviors using books like *Birthday Balloons*.

Since the dialogue in *Birthday Balloons* is somewhat challenging, and a more common feature of books at this level, teachers may choose to introduce this convention to individuals or to the whole class, as appropriate, before children read it independently. In addition, there are many characters and some ambiguously referenced dialogue in *Birthday Balloons*. Because of this, children may benefit from having this book read aloud. Doing so allows students the opportunity to hear distinctions among the characters' voices, helping them to differentiate between them. Teachers may want to reinforce this idea by using this book, or another text that provides similar opportunities, in a shared reading session with children taking on the different character roles. Reading partnerships can be asked to do the same, where appropriate. Teachers can also emphasize a change in voice or tone for different characters in other read aloud books.

Birthday Balloons contains traditional story elements; therefore, it provides lots of opportunities for book talks. Children will probably enjoy the fact that a child is the hero of the story. None of the adults can figure out what is troubling Emma. It is Tom who uses his power of observation and wits to realize that all Emma really wanted was a balloon.

Book Connections

The same cast of characters appears in the book *The Baby-sitter*. Children might want to read both books in sequence. Doing so will help prepare children for reading chapter books in a series as they become more experienced readers. Teachers can build on this in the writing workshop by guiding children to notice that they can create multiple stories with the same characters in their own writing.

Genre
Emergent Literacy Book

A Field Guide to the Classroom Library, Lucy Calkins and the Teachers College Reading and Writing Project, Heinemann, ©2002 Teachers College, Columbia University; http://www.heinemann.com/fieldguides

Teaching Uses
Independent Reading; Small Group Strategy Instruction; Whole Group
Instruction; Partnerships; Interpretation; Language Conventions; Read
Aloud

A Field Guide to the Classroom Library, Lucy Calkins and the Teachers College Reading and Writing Project, Heinemann, ©2002 Teachers
College, Columbia University; http://www.heinemann.com/fieldguides

Birthday Presents

Cynthia Rylant

Book Summary

The narrators of this story are the parents of a child. They remind her of her real birthday, the day she was born and the things she did on that historic day. They also tell her about each of her subsequent birthdays and the things that they did to show her how special she was. Before her sixth birthday, the parents tell the girl how she herself will give the family gifts, make cards and help them to have special days. Then, when her sixth birthday arrives, they tell how the girl talks to them about things in the world, even things they hadn't known, and how they spend time together. The book ends with the words: "Birthday presents."

Basic Book Information

Rylant is a prolific writer of many award-winning children's books. She received the Newbery Honor Award for *A Fine White Dust*, the Caldecott Honor Award for the titles *When I Was Young in the Mountains* and *The Relatives Came. Birthday Presents* and *A Blue-Eyed Daisy* were named Children's Choice books by a joint committee of the International Reading Association and the Children's Book Council.

Noteworthy Features

This is a fairly simple, straightforward book with cute, cartoon-type pictures. Usually, without a teacher's recommending it, boys don't tend to pick it up to read off the shelves, probably because of the girl protagonist pictured on the cover.

The predictable structure of the text in this book lends great support to readers who are not yet confident. Every few pages describes one year's birthday. The descriptions all begin, "On your first [or second or third, etc.] one," and all end "Happy birthday." In the middle, there is always a description of the cake, and of what the little girl and the parents did. Only near the very end of the book does the pattern vary. Instead of a sixth birthday, there is a part beginning "Before your sixth birthday" and containing a description of all the things the little girl did to make other people's birthdays, and lives, special.

Some children find this book hysterically funny. They laugh at the baby's screaming and spitting up, the young child's refusal to share and the chocolate-covered faces of the older child and her friends. These readers seem to enjoy imagining all the shapes a birthday cake can take and the presents and festivities of the party. Because the book is fairly simple, and

Illustrator
Sucie Stevenson

Publisher
Orchard Books, 1987

ISBN
0531070263

TC Level
10

A Field Guide to the Classroom Library, Lucy Calkins and the Teachers College Reading and Writing Project, Heinemann, ©2002 Teachers College, Columbia University; http://www.heinemann.com/fieldguides

very enjoyable, it may be one to keep in mind for the indifferent reader who usually puts everything aside. Of course, a book is always more fun with two readers, so a partnership might also be in order here.

Teaching Ideas

The book lends itself easily to making personal connections. Kids often find themselves comparing what their guardians have told them about their own babyhoods to the little girl's story. Despite this it may not be the easiest book for teachers to use as a starting point to help children make deeper personal connections. There aren't many behaviors in the book that lend themselves to questions about motivations or emotional conflicts that would be fleshed out by personal response. Perhaps this book is best used to get personal response started in an unthreatening way for children who are having trouble vocalizing or writing their reactions.

This story has an unusual narrative voice in that it is told from a second person plural, or "We," point of view. When children are making decisions about which point of view to employ in their own writing, it may be handy to have this book around as a model of this perspective.

The first page may be the hardest of the book. For one thing, the pattern hasn't been established yet, and the reader doesn't know which way the text will go. Next, the writer uses, "little piggies on your hands and feet" to mean fingers and toes. To the literal-minded child or the child not versed in nursery rhymes, this may pose a problem. An early reader might not think that it is normal for a baby to cry, and that reader might startle at the thought that the baby "screamed" upon hearing that her parents loved her. The page ends with the words, "We promised you more...," which can leave the reader wondering, "More what? love? screaming? birthdays?" Of course the answer is birthdays, but the thought process needed to get there might not be a smooth one for the reader. If this book is in the hands of a struggling reader, the teacher or the partner might be better off reading (and perhaps talking through) the first page and then letting the reader get started on the next pages.

Book Connections

Other memoirs structured in this year-by-year fashion are: *When I Was Little* by Jamie Lee Curtis, and *Another Important Book* by Margaret Wise Brown. These books, too, recall one small thing at a time from early childhood, and can all serve as examples for children trying to write memoir.

Of course, Cynthia Rylant has written many, many memoirs and other books for children (see Basic Book Information), a few of which could be paired with this one for an author study.

Genre
Memoir; Picture Book

Teaching Uses
Independent Reading; Read Aloud; Teaching Writing

A Field Guide to the Classroom Library, Lucy Calkins and the Teachers College Reading and Writing Project, Heinemann, ©2002 Teachers College, Columbia University; http://www.heinemann.com/fieldguides

Bunny Cakes

Rosemary Wells

Book Summary

This book tells the story of Rosemary Wells' famous bunny characters, Max and Ruby, making a birthday cake for their grandmother. Ruby, Max's older sister, has decided that the pair should make their grandmother an angel surprise cake instead of the earthworm cake that Max is preparing. Unfortunately, each time Max tries to help he spills some of the ingredients on the floor. Each time he spills, Ruby gets further exasperated and sends Max to the store with a list of replacement ingredients. Max would really like to buy some Red Hot Marshmallow Squirters for the cake, as well, but every time he tries to add this item to the list, the grocer is unable to read his writing. Finally, after his third trip to the store, Max figures out how to write in a way that the grocer will understand: he draws a picture! He gets his Marshmallow Squirters and Grandma is given two cakes: angel food with butter cream roses and sugar hearts AND an earthworm cake with Red Hot Marshmallow Squirters!

Basic Book Information

Bunny Cakes is Rosemary Wells' fourteenth book about the much-loved Max, and one of several that also feature his bossy big sister, Ruby. Wells illustrated the book as well, using colorful, almost cartoon-like pictures that are contained in a box centered on the top of the page. This is a 22-page text.

Noteworthy Features

As is true in many books where the author is also the illustrator, some of the important information in the book is given only in the pictures. For example, the text never tells you that Max spilled the milk. You get this information from the picture, as the text reads simply, "But it was too late."

Most pages have about three to four lines of text. In addition, there is some dialogue in the book, though the characters do not talk back and forth to each other. This book has a very high picture-word correlation, with the pictures telling the story very clearly. Teachers will want readers to notice the repeated use of a colon, and a picture of a grocery list that serves as an important part of the text.

Teaching Ideas

In the A library, *Bunny Cakes* is intended primarily to be used as an emergent literacy read aloud. This instruction is based on the research of Elizabeth Sulzby, whose work with kindergarten children informed her of the importance of recreating parent-child interactions around books in the

Series
Max books

Illustrator
Rosemary Wells

Publisher
Penguin Publishing, 2000

ISBN
0140566678

kindergarten classroom. At home, children often ask parents to "read it again" when they hear a favorite story. In school, the teacher's multiple readings of emergent literacy books helps children become familiar with rich narrative, hear the inflection and pacing of storybook language, and learn to use detailed illustrations to assist them in remembering storyline.

After an emergent literacy storybook has been read to children at least four times, multiple copies of the book should be added to a basket labeled, "Stories We Love," or something similar. Children will have opportunities to return to these books at independent reading time. They will refer to the pictures and use their memory of the teacher's reading to recreate the story in their rereading. Given the opportunity to do this, children pass through different reading stages from simply "labeling" pictures on the page, to telling the story off the pictures, to using progressively more dialogue and storybook language, moving finally toward more "conventional" reading where they use the print. To go on this reading journey, it is important for children to hear the story read aloud many times, have a lot of opportunities to reread it to a partner and have a supportive teacher nearby who thoughtfully coaches into the reading.

Researchers Elizabeth Sulzby and Marie Clay, in their studies of emergent readers, have found that when children are given opportunities to do this type of "pretend" reading (referred to as "reading" or "rereading") they go through these stages of reading development. To support this process, teachers can select books with more text than readers can decode that can not be easily memorized, have elements of drama and suspense, and have characters to which young children can relate.

This book can be an inspiration for early writers because it tells about Max wanting desperately to write for a very important reason. Teachers may seize this as an opportunity to help youngsters understand authentic reasons to write. Max's stages of writing are similar to those that children go through. First he scribbles, then he writes a revised version of his scribbles, and finally he writes with the knowledge that there needs to be a real meaning behind what he writes.

Bunny Cakes is a great book to use as an interactive read aloud. It can be read aloud to the class with pauses at occasional places, inviting children to talk to their partners. Readers will generate things to talk and think about. A teacher may want to go from partner conversations to a whole-group conversation and say, "So, can someone get us started on a conversation?" The teacher can then expect one child to report on what he or she said in the partner talk. Children will not know the importance of talking back to each other until the teacher shows them this. After one child says, "Max keeps messing up," the next child might say something totally unrelated such as, "A worm cake is disgusting." This is an opportunity to emphasize to children the importance of listening to each other and talking back to each other. "So Brian noticed that Max keeps messing up. What do the rest of you think? Can you talk back to Brian?"

In this way, children may grow theories about the book including perhaps, the idea that Ruby wants to show Max how to do more grown-up things, but Max doesn't seem to be able to do them. This may lead to a text-to-text comparison of this story to others about Ruby and Max. It's also an opportunity for children to make text-to-self connections. Do they have bossy older brothers or sisters? The message of this story that writing and

A Field Guide to the Classroom Library, Lucy Calkins and the Teachers College Reading and Writing Project, Heinemann, ©2002 Teachers College, Columbia University; http://www.heinemann.com/fieldguides

pictures can convey important information is one that will allow emergent writers to feel proud of how much they already know about written communication. Just like Max, they can write in ways that others can "read" and understand.

Genre
Picture Book

Teaching Uses
Read Aloud; Language Conventions; Partnerships

A Field Guide to the Classroom Library, Lucy Calkins and the Teachers College Reading and Writing Project, Heinemann, ©2002 Teachers College, Columbia University; http://www.heinemann.com/fieldguides

Call 911
Rebel Williams

Book Summary

This book tells the reader when 911 should be dialed: for fire (firefighters), accidents (paramedics), and kidnapping (police). Each example is displayed on a two-page spread. The final page summarizes it all and has all of the public servants pictured. All of the victims change from one scene to the next.

Basic Book Information

Call 911 has 22 words on 8 pages. The text is consistently located at the bottom of each page, below the picture. Each sentence begins on the left page and is completed on the right. This is a Wright Group book from the nonfiction *Twig* collection.

Noteworthy Features

The pictures and stories in this little book can be quite terrifying. First there is the image of the house burning down, then the woman seriously hurt and grimacing in pain, and then the kidnapper grabbing the child and pulling him into the car. While children certainly need to learn what to do in these instances, the graphic pictures of the situations may disturb some. Teachers will have to use some discretion about using this book in the classroom.

The repetitive text, "Call 911 and _____ will help" appears on each page. The numbers "911" and the word "and" appear on every page. Some of the language is difficult, for example, "paramedics" and "firefighters." The pattern changes at the end of the text.

Teaching Ideas

Children reading this will undoubtedly want to talk about the events in the story with a partner, speculating on what exactly has happened and what is likely to happen next. Picture details can be scrutinized to support the reading of the story. This work in constructing meaning from the words and pictures is critical for a good read of this story.

This book may trigger memories in readers of emergency events in their own lives. Teachers may use this topic in a mini-lesson as an opportunity to help children learn how to use personal responses to support and deepen their reading. How did the events in their lives and those in the book relate to one another? Can one inform the other? This too can be a discussion topic between partners.

Teachers may use this book help children learn how, why, and when to dial 911 for themselves. Do they know how to do it from home? From school? From a pay phone? Considering the tragic events of September 11th,

Illustrator
Cindy Spencer

Publisher
Wright Group, 1998

ISBN
0780290712

TC Level
2

knowing this skill might provide children with a sense of independence and security.

Genre
Nonfiction; Emergent Literacy Book

Teaching Uses
Interpretation; Critique; Content Area Study; Partnerships

Caps for Sale
Esphyr Slobodkina

Book Summary

Each day, a peddler walks carefully up and down the streets, balancing a huge pile of caps on top of his head and saying "Caps! Caps for sale! Fifty cents a cap!" He is very careful not to disturb any of the caps on his head, which are all in a particular color order. One morning, unable to sell a single cap, he walks out into the countryside, sits down under a tree, checks that all of his caps are in place and falls asleep. While the peddler is asleep, a band of mischievous monkeys steals every one of his caps, except for his own checked cap.

When he awakes, he checks for his caps but doesn't find them until he looks up at the tree. On every branch he sees a different monkey wearing one of his caps. Wondering how he is going to get back his caps, he begins talking to the monkeys. They repeat everything he says back to him. The peddler gets so angry that he throws his own cap on the ground and walks away. Not realizing that the monkeys are still copying him, they too throw the caps on the ground. The peddler picks up all of his caps and places them back on his head in the same color order as they were before and begins walking through the town again and saying "Caps! Caps for sale! Fifty cents a cap!"

Basic Book Information

Caps for Sale, subtitled *A Tale of a Peddler, Some Monkeys and Their Monkey Business* is a timeless classic picture book, in print for over fifty years and beloved by generations of readers. The author and illustrator, Esphyr Slobodkina, is a painter, designer, and sculptor as well as a writer and illustrator of children's books. Her paintings are in the permanent collections of the Corcoran Gallery, the Whitney Museum of American Art, the Philadelphia Art Museum, and many others. *Caps for Sale* was featured on the television show Reading Rainbow and it won a Lewis Carroll Shelf Award in 1958. Other works by the author include *The Wonderful Feast* (1955), *The Clock* (1956), *Pinky and the Petunias* (1959) and *The Long Island Ducklings* (1961). Slobodkina has also illustrated *The Little Fireman*, *The Little Cowboy* and *Sleepy ABC's*, all written by Margaret Wise Brown. *Caps for Sale* comes in both hard and soft covers. An audiocassette and a Spanish version of this book are also available.

Noteworthy Features

This book is filled with such warmth, humor, and simplicity that children will ask to hear it over and over again. Although *Caps for Sale* is relatively easy to read, the interest level is high because of its plot, drama, and suspense. The book contains illustrations on one page and text on the next.

Illustrator
Esphyr Slobodkina

Publisher
Scholastic, 1987

ISBN
0590410806

TC Level
6

A Field Guide to the Classroom Library, Lucy Calkins and the Teachers College Reading and Writing Project, Heinemann, ©2002 Teachers College, Columbia University; http://www.heinemann.com/fieldguides

In certain places in the story, the illustrations actually precede the text in their development of the plot, pushing the reader to notice the plot developments before they are described in the text.

The author also uses repetition and wonderful true-to-life dialogue such as when the peddler calls, "You monkeys, you, you give me back my caps." The book also contains onomatopoetic responses as when the monkeys retort, "Tsz, tsz, tsz."

Teaching Ideas

In the A library, the primary instructional purpose of *Caps for Sale* is for use as an emergent literacy read aloud. This instruction is based on the research of Elizabeth Sulzby, whose work with kindergarten children informed her of the importance of recreating parent-child interactions around the reading of books in the kindergarten classroom. At home, children often ask parents to "read it again" when they hear a favorite story. In school, the teacher's multiple reading of emergent literacy books helps children become familiar with rich narrative and to hear the inflection and pacing of storybook language. They also learn to use the detailed illustrations in picture books to assist them in their rereading of the story.

After *Caps for Sale* has been read to the class at least four times, multiple copies of the book could be added to a basket of "Stories We Love" (or some similar label). At independent reading time, children, in partnerships, are invited to read the book to each other "the best way you can." They should be given time to read quietly to themselves and then time to read to their partner. Children will refer to the illustrations, to their memory of the teacher's reading, and to their growing internalization of the story's plot and emotional content as they recreate the story in their rereading.

Given opportunities to hear and read many books that have a strong storyline, characters that they personally relate to, and supportive, detailed illustrations, Sulzby has shown how children move through different reading stages. They go from labeling the pictures on the page, telling the story off the pictures, using progressively more dialogue and storybook language, then moving toward a more conventional, print-based reading. To go on this reading journey it is important for children to hear the story read aloud many times, have many opportunities to reread it to a partner, and to have a supportive teacher nearby to thoughtfully coach into their reading.

Later in the year, *Caps for Sale* can be used as an engaging "accountable talk read aloud." Teachers might consider assigning read aloud partners who will sit together on the rug while the story is read. At significant, pre-selected moments in the reading, the teacher can ask the children to turn to their partner and "say something." This encourages children to remain anchored to the text and to make important personal connections to the characters and the story.

In *The Art of Teaching Reading*, Lucy Calkins writes, "We read aloud to demonstrate to children and to mentor them in the habits, values and strategies of proficient readers and to help them experience the bounties of thoughtful, reflective reading." *Caps for Sale* is the perfect read aloud book, and it can be reread often as we mentor children in different strategies. When teachers stop occasionally to think aloud as they read, sharing thoughts, reactions, or reading strategies, children are given a glimpse into the mind of a skillful reader. Doing so provides children with a powerful model of the kind of active and engaged reading that they can do during their own independent reading.

Book Connections

As of now, this book is not part of a series, but in March 2002 Esphyr Slobodkina will be publishing a new book titled *Circus Caps For Sale*.

Genre
Picture Book

Teaching Uses
Independent Reading; Partnerships; Language Conventions; Read Aloud

Circus

Miriam Frost

Book Summary

This is a counting book about different animals that form part of a circus. The pattern goes like this: one elephant/two lions/three camels, and so on.

Basic Book Information

Developed and published by Wright Group (now, Wright Group/McGraw-Hill), Twig Books were developed as a nonfiction series for emergent readers. Supported by stunning photographs and a variety of illustrative styles, young readers will be inspired by these books about the natural world and everyday life. These titles are most appropriate for small-group instruction and are leveled to support the early reader from the early emergent to upper emergent levels. These simple nonfiction texts are easily integrated across curriculum areas.

Noteworthy Features

This counting book always gives the number of animals and then the name of the animal. For example, page one says, "One elephant," and the pattern continues for six pages with different animals. This counting list book has a twist at the ending because the seventh and last page breaks the pattern with the exclamation: "A circus!"

The illustrations, together with the sentence pattern, will support the early emergent reader. The illustration shows a scene at the circus and contains the bold numeral 1, 2, or 3 and so on that matches the number of animals on the page. The numerals are clearly separated from the text.

Although this is primarily a list book, the illustrations act as a list within a story. We see from the cover that the circus comes to town, enters the tent, and at this point the text begins to list of all the components in the circus. The final page shows all the animals, which have been introduced separately, doing their acts simultaneously, side-by-side.

A reader who studies the pictures closely can notice intriguing incongruities.

Teaching Ideas

If a child has been reading books on this level for a little while and is given this book without an introduction, it's interesting to notice what strategies the child uses when reading the story. It's not likely that the emergent reader will have the skills yet to read this book fluently. It should be informative, however, to take note of what the child does and does not attend to. Does the child focus on the pictures and ignore the print? Does the child zoom in on the letters of the first word and match sounds to accompany letters? It

Illustrator
Joe Veno

Publisher
Wright Group, 1998

ISBN
0780290496

TC Level
1

would not be unusual to observe a child attending to the pictures and creating a narrative, using the pictures and the child's understanding of how books go. A child who is beginning to understand that the print carries the story might begin trying to match the invented story with the text. If the child speculates that the book says, "I see the elephant. / I see the lions." but points to "One elephant" and realizes that the words spoken are not matching up with the printed words, this would signal that this child is ready for more print work.

When the child enters this stage of focusing on print work, we can add support by saying, "I like the way you looked at the picture, then at the print. And you were right-this is an elephant." Teachers could also say, "You are right that this is a pattern book. It could go 'I see the elephant. / I see the lions.' but have you noticed that this is a counting book?" The teacher will probably, at this point, want to simply say, "Let me read you the first page to get you going." It'll be important to model pointing as we read the words.

Teachers will probably want to encourage children to reread this book. This practice will help them develop fluency, to notice more details and to try growing ideas. The observant child might notice that on the final page, the giant elephant seems to shrink in the company of others, a seal makes a trumpet float near to its mouth, the bears are not all the same color, the horse trainer stands directly under the horses' hooves, and the equipment from within the story is replaced by new equipment.

Book Connections

This book would pair up nicely with Eric Carle's *1,2,3 To The Zoo*. Children might want to begin creating a basket of counting books.

Genre
Emergent Literacy Book; Nonfiction

Teaching Uses
Independent Reading; Small Group Strategy Instruction; Content Area Study

Cookie's Week
Cindy Ward

Book Summary

Cookie is a cat that finds trouble to get into every day of the week, thus creating a pattern book for days of the week.

Basic Book Information

This is a 28-page book with full-color illustrations by Caldecott winner Tomie dePaola.

Noteworthy Features

The day of the week pattern is set up on page one as the story begins, "On Monday...Cookie fell in the toilet. There was water everywhere!" Each day of the week follows with a different kind of trouble for Cookie, but whatever the trouble is, it goes *everywhere*. This pattern is consistent until the last two pages where there is a twist.

Teaching Ideas

Some teachers like to use this book for guided reading and feel that a book introduction is particularly helpful to set the reader up for the days-of-the-week pattern. A teacher may choose to introduce this book by saying, "This is a book about a cat named Cookie. Cookie is on every page, and there is a page for every day of the week. It starts with Monday. What do you think will be the next page? Yes! It's Tuesday, and then Wednesday. You can count on this pattern. Find out what kind of trouble Cookie gets into each day. You'll have to look at the picture to help you."

The illustrations are very supportive of the text and should be used for crosschecking. One teacher began her introduction "This is a book about a cat named Cookie who gets into trouble every day. First, it's Monday and Cookie falls in the toilet. What do you think happened? Yuck! Yes, there was water everywhere! Every day Cookie finds more trouble. Remember Cookie is a cat and cats get *into* things. So every time Cookie finds trouble, the stuff that is inside comes out. What do you think comes out of a garbage can? I bet you know! Read and find out what happens with Cookie."

Although much of the vocabulary used won't be in the reader's sight vocabulary, it will be familiar because these are everyday items supported by the illustrations: *garbage, dirt, clothes, curtains.*

Cookie's Week is also a list book and can be used as such for writing and for reading. Having a particular structure, such as the list, can give a book a predictable pattern that young readers can depend on. One teacher introduced *Cookie's Week* to a group of first graders like this: "We've been thinking and talking about list books. What makes a list book, a list book?"

A Field Guide to the Classroom Library, Lucy Calkins and the Teachers College Reading and Writing Project, Heinemann, ©2002 Teachers College, Columbia University; http://www.heinemann.com/fieldguides

One little boy said, "It tells about one kind of thing, like ice cream. My ice cream list has chocolate, vanilla, strawberry and "chunky monkey" on it." The teacher continued, "That's right. Lists are usually about the same kind of thing, or for one particular kind of thing. In *Cookie's Week*, this is a list of what Cookie the cat does every day of the week. On Monday, Cookie falls in the toilet. On every other day of the week, Cookie does something else until we get to Sunday, then on Sunday, it changes a little. What Cookie does on Sunday isn't like what she's done on the other days. Think about that when you get to the last page." The teacher may then give copies of the book to each reader, asking students to make a prediction about what might happen next.

Genre
Picture Book

Teaching Uses
Whole Group Instruction; Independent Reading

A Field Guide to the Classroom Library, Lucy Calkins and the Teachers College Reading and Writing Project, Heinemann, ©2002 Teachers College, Columbia University; http://www.heinemann.com/fieldguides

Corduroy
Don Freeman

Book Summary

Corduroy is a teddy bear that lives in the toy department of a big store. He is waiting for someone to buy him so he can have a real home. One day Lisa and her mom are shopping. Lisa falls in love with Corduroy but her mom says that she does not have enough money to buy Corduroy that day. Lisa's mom also points out that Corduroy is missing a button from his overalls and therefore might not be a good choice. That night Corduroy searches the store for his missing button and ends up in the furniture department. When Corduroy tries to yank what he thinks is his lost button from a mattress, he knocks over a lamp and the security guard comes. He takes Corduroy back to the toy department. Sadly, Corduroy still has no button. The next day Lisa returns to the store with money from her piggy bank. She buys Corduroy and carries him home in her arms. She sews on another button, and hugs him. Corduroy knows that he has at last found a home and a friend.

Basic Book Information

Corduroy is regarded as a classic. Freeman has written many other favorites, including *A Pocket for Corduroy*, *Beady Bear*, *Mop Top* and *A Rainbow of My Own*.

Noteworthy Features

Corduroy is a Level 7 book-and as such, it's way too hard for most kindergartners and early first graders to read. But the story is so irresistible that children ask to hear the book read aloud again and again.

Teaching Ideas

In the A Library, this book is intended primarily for use as an emergent literacy read aloud. This instruction is based on the research of Elizabeth Sulzby, whose work with kindergarten children informed her of the importance of recreating parent-child interactions around books in the kindergarten classroom. At home, children often ask parents to "read it again" when they hear a favorite story. In school, the teacher's multiple readings of emergent literacy books helps children become familiar with rich narrative, hear the inflection and pacing of storybook language, and learn to use detailed illustrations to assist them in remembering storyline.

After the story has been read to them at least four times, multiple copies should be added to a basket of books called, for example, "Stories We Love." Teachers can give children opportunities to return to these books at independent reading time. They will refer to the pictures and use their

Illustrator
Don Freeman

Publisher
Scholastic, 196

ISBN
0140501738

TC Level
7

memory of the teacher's reading to recreate the story in their rereading. Given the opportunity to do this, children pass through different reading stages from simply "labeling" pictures on the page, to telling the story off the pictures using progressively more dialogue and storybook language, and then moving toward a more "conventional" reading which closely resembles the print on the page. To go on this reading journey, it is important for children to hear the story read aloud many times, have a lot of opportunities to reread it to a partner, and to have a supportive teacher nearby who thoughtfully coaches into their reading.

In the B Library, and later in the school year in the A Library, *Corduroy* can be used as an accountable talk read aloud. The first time a teacher reads it, he may want to think aloud in ways that model a response to the book. For example, the teacher might look at the cover of the book, while quietly saying, "I love to read the title of a book and look at the cover, don't you?" then something like, "I'm noticing this cute little bear. I wonder if his name is Corduroy because look, his overalls are made of corduroy? That's a funny name for a bear and for a book. I wonder if the book will be about his overalls? Let's read on. . . . " In a similar way, the teacher might demonstrate one of these reading behaviors during our read aloud sessions: pausing to show children that readers raise questions; speculating about what might happen next; connecting one page of the book with another, and so forth. Of course, teachers will want to be careful that they don't pause too often for these comments. For kindergarten children, especially, it's not advisable to offer weighty lectures about metacognitive processes. Children do, however, benefit from living alongside richly literate adults who sweep children up in their own literacy.

At another reading of *Corduroy*, the teacher might use her inflection to get children wondering, noticing, or anticipating. At passages, which the teacher expects will elicit a response, he might say, "Is your head full of ideas? Turn and talk with a partner." After children have been in school for a while, each child can be assigned a "turn and talk partner." We'll ask them to always sit beside this partner during the read aloud and soon they will have practiced this ritual enough that the logistics become smooth.

The first time a turn and talk is suggested, some children are likely to feel they don't have a lot to say. However, by getting onto the rug and conferring with one or two partnerships, teachers can help children to respond to text and share ideas with each other. It usually isn't advisable to have children report back on their partnership talks to the whole group, because the book is waiting. Creating long intervals for discussion can interrupt the thread of the story.

We might preface another reading of *Corduroy* by telling children that readers reread books often and each time they notice new things about the story. Perhaps the conversation will focus on, "What are you noticing that you didn't notice before?" Over time children's focus can be steered in a particular direction. For example, it could be suggested that readers pay attention to the characters in a story. "Let's really think about Lisa and what she's like," the teacher could say. Alternatively, the teacher might say, "Sometimes I read a book and think, 'Do I agree?' 'Do I disagree?'" This latter prompt could yield some interesting conversation because the teacher (or child) may say, "I disagree with the idea that Corduroy doesn't deserve to be chosen because he is missing a button! That's like saying you can't be

A Field Guide to the Classroom Library, Lucy Calkins and the Teachers College Reading and Writing Project, Heinemann, ©2002 Teachers College, Columbia University; http://www.heinemann.com/fieldguides

adopted if part of you is injured. . . . And how come when Lisa gets Corduroy home, she quickly replaces his missing button and only then hugs him!" The point, of course, won't be to teach this or any other set of ideas about this book, but it is crucial to show children that, as Purves has said, "Books are tools to think with."

Book Connections

In talking and responding to books we can compare books by the same author or about the same characters. The book *A Pocket For Corduroy* would provide a natural opportunity for children to understand that knowing a character in one book may help us to better understand a character in another book.

Genre
Picture Book

Teaching Uses
Partnerships; Read Aloud; Critique; Interpretation; Language Conventions

A Field Guide to the Classroom Library, Lucy Calkins and the Teachers College Reading and Writing Project, Heinemann, ©2002 Teachers College, Columbia University; http://www.heinemann.com/fieldguides

Dear Zoo
Rod Campbell

Book Summary

The child in this story is writing to the zoo for a pet. The zoo sends him a series of zoo animals (elephant, giraffe, lion, camel, snake, monkey, frog). Since each animal is inappropriate as a pet, the child sends each back. This continues as each new pet arrives until the zoo takes time to think. Then the zoo sends the child a puppy. Of course the puppy is perfect, and the child keeps him.

Basic Book Information

This book contains 115 words over 18 unnumbered pages. The size and spacing of the print is appropriate for a reader who understands the left to right directionality of print, the return sweep necessary to read a second line, and one-to-one matching of words spoken with words on the page. The print appears on each left page and under the illustrations on the right page. The reader reads the left page and then lifts the flap on the right page to discover which animal the zoo has sent. The animal's name never appears in print, only in the illustration. So the reader reads "So they sent me a" and lifts the flap on the opposite page. There are many high frequency words.

Noteworthy Features

The colorful illustrations with the interactive flaps will probably keep the reader engaged and motivated. The illustrations do not contain any details of the story. Therefore, the reader is going to have to infer from his knowledge of the animal why this animal may be inappropriate as a pet.

The repetitive pattern is "So they sent me a. . . . He was too_____! I sent him back." The use of the repetitive pattern will enable the reader to use meaning to predict the text and to practice fluent reading. The pattern changes on page 2 and on the last two pages.

Teaching Ideas

Children will have a great time reading this book "as best they can" without needing much support from a teacher or a partner. They'll encounter difficulties, but should be able to use sight word knowledge, phonics, and a focus on meaning to construct a good deal of the text.

If a child has done some independent work and is still needing more support, instead of helping with one hard word, then the next, a teacher might say, "Can we look over the whole book together" and use this as a time to do a belated book introduction. The teacher might say, "The child went to the zoo, didn't he, asking for a pet? But the animals weren't right, were they?" Then turning the pages to the different animals, teachers might

A Field Guide to the Classroom Library, Lucy Calkins and the Teachers College Reading and Writing Project, Heinemann, ©2002 Teachers College, Columbia University; http://www.heinemann.com/fieldguides

want to use-in a conversational way-some of the words they anticipate will be especially tough (*fierce, naughty*). Teachers may want to also teach children a few words they may not know and may not have ready access to, including *thought*. By the time a child can read a book like this one, the child should not read, "He was too big (tall)" on page 5 and not realize that he has made a mistake. The teacher needs to acknowledge that the prediction made sense, but prompt and/or model monitoring and cross-checking a prediction with the letter cues a word offers. The teacher would ask the reader to predict what he would expect to see at the beginning of the word "big" and then check it against the print. In addition the teacher may ask what chunk the reader knows in the word "tall."

The use of a repetitive pattern will offer the teacher an opportunity to model and/or prompt a student for fluent reading.

The change in the repetitive pattern on the last two pages and page 2 will require the reader to do more visual searching than on the patterned pages.

Book Connections

If the reader enjoys the lift-the-flap books some others at this level are *Where is Spot?* and *Here Comes the Bus*.

Genre
Picture Book

Teaching Uses
Independent Reading

Do You Want to Be My Friend?

Eric Carle

Book Summary

A tiny lonely mouse is searching everywhere to find a friend. He follows one animal's tail, but only finds an unfriendly horse. He follows another tail, but only finds an unfriendly crocodile. He continues on this journey, following many animal tails-a giraffe, a kangaroo, a peacock, and so on. Finally he is successful, but not with a different animal, as the reader might expect. Instead he finds another little mouse that gives him the companionship he is craving, and together they spend many happy and loving moments together.

Basic Book Information

This book contains twenty-nine pages all with brilliant illustrations. The one sentence in the book, "Do you want to be my friend?" appears on the first page. At the shift in the story, when the mouse finally finds a friend, we encounter one more word-"Yes!" The pages are beautifully illustrated in Eric Carle's trademark style.

Noteworthy Features

Do You Want to Be My Friend? is a terrific book for emergent readers. Because the book contains only one sentence, children will need to use picture details to help them create the story. The facial expressions of the mouse and the other animals allow the reader to discern feelings of loneliness and then love between the characters in the story. A book introduction would ensure that children have enough prior knowledge of the animals in the illustrations to help them recognize the tails that serve as important clues in the story.

Teaching Ideas

The early emergent reader will use the illustrations and his memory of a teacher's reading, to recreate story. Teachers can help an emergent reader by pre-reading the book or by giving a book introduction. One teacher began by saying to a student, "This is a story about a little mouse who is looking for another animal to be his friend. He keeps following the tails of the animals in front of him, looking for someone, anyone to be his friend. He asks a horse, a crocodile, a lion, a hippopotamus, and other animals. Sometimes, you will see him asking with words and you will see the words, 'Do you want to be my friend?' and other times you can just imagine the words coming out of his mouth."

Teachers may also use this book when working with a reading partnership to show children how to read with two voices. One child can begin reading, "Do you want to be my friend?" and continue that question

Illustrator
Eric Carle

Publisher
Scholastic, 1997

ISBN
0064431274

TC Level
2

on every page where the mouse approaches an animal. The second child may take on the voice of the different animals. The child might insert a common response, such as, "No I don't," until finally, when the mouse meets the other mouse, the young reader should read, enthusiastically, "Yes!"

This book provides an excellent opportunity for a young reader to see the connection between the words on the cover, and finding the same sentence on the first page. In a reading conference, a teacher could begin by supporting the child's reading of the words, "Do you want to be my friend?" If the child is not pointing, the teacher could encourage rereading and pointing to the words to demonstrate one-to-one correspondence. As the student turns the page, they will notice the next page with the exact same words. However, some children will find this to be tricky, since the type font on this page is much larger and not in the configuration of a speech bubble as an emergent reader might expect. By the time they come across the same words on the title page, most children will quickly recognize the words. When the words appear again for the fourth time, which is a copy of the first page of the book, children will have little or no hesitation reading them.

When dialogue is discussed in the writing workshop, this book can demonstrate the use of speech bubbles. A teacher may, in a mini-lesson, share with children that sometimes writers put words in a bubble by the mouth of a character so their readers know who is talking. The teacher might then invite children to "give it a try" when they are writing that day.

Book Connections

Other nearly wordless books that could be studied alongside this one include *Pancakes for Breakfast* by Tomie dePaola, and *Good Dog Carl.*

Genre
Emergent Literacy Book; Picture Book

Teaching Uses
Partnerships; Whole Group Instruction; Interpretation; Teaching Writing

Dogs
Amy Levin

Book Summary

Dogs is a list book in which different children tell us things that each child's dog can do. For example, on the first page, a little girl tells us: "My dog can walk."

Basic Book Information

The simple Scholastic book has 27 words over eight pages, with an average of four words per page.

Noteworthy Features

The single line of large and generously spaced text consistently appears at the bottom of each page, below the picture. The simple text, with highly supportive illustrations, reinforces early reading behaviors such as one-to-one matching and directionality. Most of the meaning in the book is, in fact, conveyed through the illustrations. The familiar words, "My dog can . . . " appear on most pages, helping to anchor children to the text. There is only one simple pattern change at the end and it contains two familiar sight words (i.e., *we, like*). Sentences have natural language structure ("My dog can _____") and end only with periods. The content and language represent experiences that will be familiar to some children.

Children who have not yet mastered strategies and understandings such as one-to-one matching, checking picture against first letter, understanding that print carries the message, or an awareness of first person narrative may substitute "A dog can" or "The dog can. . . . " In this case, the teacher might introduce the book by giving the pattern.

Teaching Ideas

Once children are ready to really focus on print this is a book that will support important early reading behaviors. Children get support from the picture clues and the predictable pattern of the text. They have the opportunity to match spoken words with printed words and to self-correct when these do not "come out even." Children will begin to rely on the spaces between words to signify the end of one word and the start of another. They will begin using a few sight words to anchor them to the text.

This book could be used to support a list book study, either in the reading or writing workshop. It would also be appropriate to use this book in a reading center basket focused, perhaps, on either dogs or pets.

Illustrator
Amy Levin

Publisher
Scholastic, 2000

ISBN
0439064570

TC Level
1

A Field Guide to the Classroom Library, Lucy Calkins and the Teachers College Reading and Writing Project, Heinemann, ©2002 Teachers College, Columbia University; http://www.heinemann.com/fieldguides

Genre
Emergent Literacy Book; Nonfiction

Teaching Uses
Independent Reading; Content Area Study; Teaching Writing

Faces

Janie Everett

Book Summary

This very short book tells about the features that faces have like glasses or spots. It also points out some ways faces can look, like happy, sad, silly, or mad.

Basic Book Information

Faces is one of a collection of *Little Celebrations* books published by Scott Foresman. The book is illustrated with photographs of children's faces performing the actions described in each sentence, giving clues to words like *happy* and *mad* in the sentences. Some of the illustrations may be misleading if students rely too much on the pictures for meaning. This book introduces early readers to the book format, to simple sight vocabulary words in context, and gives them an opportunity to practice their emerging skills. There is no story line, simply a list of things that faces have and show.

Noteworthy Features

There are seven pages in this book, with only sixteen different words overall, making this an easy-read for beginning readers. Each page, with the exception of the last one, has a three-word simple sentence (subject/verb/object). The sentences are consistently placed at the bottom of the page, making reading easier for young students. The word *faces* appears six times. The second and fourth sentences, fifth, and sixth sentences, end in words that rhyme: (*sad*, *mad*, *spots*, and *got*) creating a loosely recognizable poem.

Teaching Ideas

Teachers might introduce this book first by looking at and discussing the pictures with the children, pointing out the actions in the photos and asking "What does this photo show us about faces?" If this book proves to be a favorite, a teacher might duplicate the book, cutting the sentences into strips, separate from the pictures and then ask children to read these sentence strips without picture support and to act them out or to find the matching picture. The teacher might show students the sentences, printed separately in large print on tag board or on the chalkboard and ask one child to act out the sentence. She might then ask "What did . . .show us about faces?"

The rhyming words in the text provide an opportunity for a mini-lesson on rhyming as a strategy for word recognition. The teacher might write a sentence with rhyming words from the book and then underline the rhyming words (perhaps writing the word in a different color and

Illustrator
Alan Shortall

Publisher
HarperCollins, 1993

ISBN
067380551

TC Level
1

A Field Guide to the Classroom Library, Lucy Calkins and the Teachers College Reading and Writing Project, Heinemann, ©2002 Teachers College, Columbia University; http://www.heinemann.com/fieldguides

underlining the rhymed cluster as in *sad* and *mad*). When students listen to the words and look at the underlined part, the teacher may point out the rhyme or ask the students to find the rhyming words. She can then repeat the strategy with the other sentence pair-and ask students to point to the words that rhyme.

Genre
Emergent Literacy Book; Picture Book

Teaching Uses
Independent Reading; Whole Group Instruction; Small Group Strategy Instruction; Interpretation; Language Conventions

A Field Guide to the Classroom Library, Lucy Calkins and the Teachers College Reading and Writing Project, Heinemann, ©2002 Teachers College, Columbia University; http://www.heinemann.com/fieldguides

Feathers for Lunch
Lois Ehlert

Book Summary

The story begins with a cat sneaking outside. The cat looks for lunch because "his food in a can is tame and mild." Although the cat snoops and sneaks up on birds, they hear the jingle of the bells on his collar and the cat ends up eating feathers for lunch.

Basic Book Information

Lois Ehlert is the acclaimed author and illustrator of a number of books for children including *Fish Eyes* and *Eating the Alphabet*. Her books contain bold, dramatic illustrations and those in *Feathers for Lunch* are especially intriguing because of the interplay between the text and the over-sized illustrations.

Ehlert's books seem more like literature than like teaching tools, and this makes them a valuable addition to a classroom library.

Noteworthy Features

This rhyming text will be a good match and provide sufficient support for only some early readers. There are parts of the pictures that are labeled and the students can use details in the picture to help them read these labels. The last page gives additional information about each of the birds featured in the book.

Some books appeal to early readers mainly because they're written and published in ways that suggest attention has been paid to the characteristics of early readers. This book, on the other hand, will appeal to early readers because of its many weird and wonderful features. These features will interest some readers and may confuse others. A teacher might note the very large and very black font and deduce that this book is appropriate for very early readers. This is not the case! In fact, the font seems almost inappropriately large considering the experience and skill levels a child will need in order to work successfully with the text.

There are lots of challenges for early readers in this book and it will be helpful for teachers to be familiar with them. The most obvious are the words scattered among the pictures. On one page, "jingle jingle" is written in red beside the bell on the cat's collar, and "American Robin" is written in black beside the robin's tail feathers. Also, although the main text of the story is written in oversized font, it contains contractions and lots of challenging words that are not at all supported by the picture. One page says, for example, "A spicy treat for today's menu" and shows a blue jay on what is meant to be a pine tree, but this is clear only because the picture is labeled. Then, too, although the font is very large, it seems as if the oversized letters crowd out the white space between words, making this book quite

Illustrator
Lois Ehlert

Publisher
Harcourt Brace, 1990

ISBN
0590224255

TC Level
5

A Field Guide to the Classroom Library, Lucy Calkins and the Teachers College Reading and Writing Project, Heinemann, ©2002 Teachers College, Columbia University; http://www.heinemann.com/fieldguides

challenging for children who aren't yet clear about word boundaries.

The text rhymes, although only readers who read it with some fluency will discover this because the rhymes are not within, but between pages.

The pictures are bold, colorful, and thought provoking. Many show only a particular of the entire scene-the rear half of a cat, the top half of a tulip plant. As mentioned earlier, labels are interspersed among the pictures. The labels in red represent the sounds animals make, and the labels in black give the name of the plants (Rembrandt Tulip, Mourning Dove).

The final four pages contain a chart titled "The Lunch that Got Away" that conveys information about the size, appearance, diet, home, and habitat of the 12 birds that got away from the cat.

Teaching Ideas

Lois Ehlert's books are appealing and accessible to young children. The colorful, detailed illustrations are full of new, scientific information, which children love to learn. The use of bold labels is consistent from one book to another. There is enough information to appeal to readers at varying levels. Teachers can address concepts such as the writer's style, craft, and use of illustrations. Children can use the pictorial details to launch rich conversations. Once children are familiar with at least two of her books, it is easy for them to identify other books that she has written and illustrated. In the A Library, a copy of *Feathers for Lunch* is included in a big book format. This book provides teachers with opportunities to use the text for shared reading.

Teachers might use Lois Ehlert books to introduce the concept of "author study." This could be the first, or an early, reading center cycle. Groups of four children (two sets of partnerships) could be grouped around a basket of books by one particular author (e.g., Donald Crews, Joy Cowley, Gail Gibbons). The entire class could study the books of Lois Ehlert during the mini-lessons and then they could be invited to try using the strategies and ideas practiced together on the rug when they read their own author's books.

Later in the school year, *Feathers for Lunch* could be used as a mentor text in the writing workshop. Teachers may focus children on the use of punctuation (the book contains hyphens, a colon, exclamation points, and so on). There are also examples of good word choice giving added life to the writing. For example, instead of saying "the cat is walking around," she says he is "prowling." The cat is "snooping and sneaking." Children may notice that the title is also the last three words in the story. Teachers can discuss how this is a writing style that takes the reader in a circle. Children can be invited to "give this a try" in their own writing. They may notice the information in the back of the book. Children in their own writing can emulate any or all of these features.

Ehlert has used many techniques that are within the grasp even of children whose spelling may contain little more than beginning and ending consonants. For example, even very inexperienced writers can borrow Ehlert's idea and add sound effects to their stories.

Teachers might invite children to notice the kinds of strategies that Lois Ehlert uses as a writer so that they might try some themselves. Children might notice things such as:

A Field Guide to the Classroom Library, Lucy Calkins and the Teachers College Reading and Writing Project, Heinemann, ©2002 Teachers College, Columbia University; http://www.heinemann.com/fieldguides

Labels (geranium plant)

"Sound" words (jingle jingle)

Use of hyphen (He's snooping and sneaking-those birds sure look good.)

Use of exclamation marks (He could catch that one, he'd eat it, he would!)

Use of the title in the book (but all he catches is feathers for lunch)

A page at the end that gives additional information about the birds featured in the book.

This is a good book to read and discuss with children. They may be eager to talk about how this book is like or unlike their lives. They also might want to talk about whether they think it seems right or wrong for cats to prey on birds.

Genre

Picture Book

Teaching Uses

Author Study; Small Group Strategy Instruction; Whole Group Instruction; Partnerships; Language Conventions; Teaching Writing

Feet

Joy Cowley

Book Summary

This very short book tells about what feet can do: jump, hop, walk, and stop.

Basic Book Information

This is one of the popular Wright Group Story Box books, and is written by the beloved Joy Cowley, author of *Mrs. Wishy-Washy* and countless other books for early readers. As a Story Box book, this book looks like it belongs in a kit of identical little books, but in this library it is interspersed with a lovely variety of shapes and sizes of books. The Wright Company provides professional development as well as books for teachers, and has been a major force in supporting the move towards more literature-based classrooms. The company uses knowledge of readers to publish texts that are supportive of early readers.

Noteworthy Features

There are seven pages in this book, with only thirteen different words overall, making this easy-to-read for beginning readers. The print is in large, bold type and each page, with the exception of the last, has only two-word sentences with a subject/verb. The text is consistently placed at the bottom of each page, making reading easier for young students. There is no story line, simply a list of things that feet do.

The illustrations show children from the waist down performing the actions described in each sentence. Some clearly give clues to the meaning of words like "hop" and "jump;" however, some of the illustrations may be misleading if students over-rely on them for meaning.

The second and fourth sentences, fifth, sixth, and seventh sentences end in words that rhyme: (*hop* and *stop*; *feet*, *meet* and *street*). This creates the feeling of a loosely recognizable poem, but the reader of Level 1 texts probably isn't attending to word endings just yet, or reading in a way that will allow him to notice the rhyme on a first read.

Teaching Ideas

Teachers might introduce this book first by looking at and discussing the pictures with the children, pointing out the action of the feet by asking, "What do the feet do in this picture?" The response should be the text, or close to it. Then the teacher can read a page of the text aloud, pointing to each word as she pronounces it. By this time, students will be able to read the book on their own with some rough degree of accuracy.

This book is written for children who are just beginning to pay attention to the print on the page, pointing under words and making a one-to-one

Illustrator
Sandra Morris

Publisher
Wright Group, 1998

ISBN
078027525X

TC Level
1

match so that one utterance matches one "glob" of letters (a word) on the paper. The reader at this level will know some sound-letter connections but probably isn't yet ready to take words apart, or pay attention to the vowel clusters in them. The child who is reading Level 1 books will just be beginning to match the initial sounds in words with the letters. For this child, it will be an accomplishment indeed if he decides that the person in the picture is galloping and then sees the word *skip* starts with an *S* and says, "Uh-oh."

The rhyming words in the text provide an opportunity for a mini-lesson on rhyming as a strategy for word recognition that is sometimes helpful. Once children are familiar with the text, the teacher might record on chart paper an excerpt from the book that has a few rhyming words and read them aloud, pointing to each word as she does. She can then underline the rhyming words, perhaps writing the rhyming words in different colors. As children listen to the words read aloud and look at the rhyming part they will see that these words rhyme or end with the same sound chunk, and that they also end with the same cluster of letters. She can repeat the strategy with the other sentence pairs-and ask students to read the words that rhyme, and add these to the list as well.

Genre
Emergent Literacy Book; Nonfiction

Teaching Uses
Independent Reading; Small Group Strategy Instruction; Content Area Study; Language Conventions; Read Aloud

A Field Guide to the Classroom Library, Lucy Calkins and the Teachers College Reading and Writing Project, Heinemann, ©2002 Teachers College, Columbia University; http://www.heinemann.com/fieldguides

Footprints in the Snow

Cynthia Benjamin

Book Summary

The book begins by setting the scene. The opening illustration could be from a Christmas card. It shows a white clapboard home in a glen of birch trees. "Winter snow falls./ Winter wind blows." Then the pattern begins, with pairs of pages that show a rabbit and say, "Someone hops/ home." The next show a deer and the text changes appropriately. The animals each return to their own home, and these homes include a den, a dam, a hole in the tree and others. The book ends with an illustration suggesting the child is returning from school, also going home.

Basic Book Information

Footprints in the Snow is a Scholastic *Hello Reader!* book. It has 29 pages with beautiful full-page illustrations. The typeface is large and easy to read. With one exception, the text placement is consistent. Immediately inside the front cover there is a note to parents including some information about reading along with your child, and listening to your child read aloud suggested by Educational Consultant Priscilla Lynch.

Noteworthy Features

This book provides a wise balance of supports and challenges for readers at this level. Looking over the book, a teacher should see that the supports include a large and simple font, fairly large amounts of white space between words, and enough of a pattern to the text that the pictures can help the reader to guess the words that do change.

The challenges include the fact that the title provides no clue as to what the first page will say, so that reading the title to a child won't help much. Also, the first page doesn't have any very early high frequency words to ease the reader into the swing of reading. Throughout the text are a small number of words that will be a bit challenging and the pictures won't provide explicit enough help to encourage children to rely exclusively on the picture for support. The good news is that these words: *someone*, *races*, *stomps* and so forth, are regularly spelled words that provide great opportunities for word work including chunking and using words you know to figure out new words.

Teaching Ideas

A teacher will want to gauge how much support a child needs in order to successfully negotiate this text. If the reader relies on repetitive patterns and supportive pictures to figure out the words, a teacher would need to give a book introduction, perhaps doing some work to help the child with *someone*

A Field Guide to the Classroom Library, Lucy Calkins and the Teachers College Reading and Writing Project, Heinemann, ©2002 Teachers College, Columbia University; http://www.heinemann.com/fieldguides

Illustrator
Jacqueline Rogers

Publisher
Scholastic, 1994

ISBN
0590466631

TC Level
3

(the repeating sight word). The teacher might then choose to walk through most of the pictures and say, for example, "Look, he is running home." The book is ideal for the child who is ready to do just a bit of work on words using what he knows about chunking words and using known words to help with unknown words.

It might be advisable for a teacher to use this book in a strategy lesson. Bringing together a partnership of two readers or a small group of four, the teacher could say, "In our word study time, we've been doing a lot of work with word chunks. You have gotten really good at taking words that seem new to you and finding chunks in them that you know. In this book, you are going to want to use those 'Word Power Muscles' to figure out the words. The pictures will help a bit, but you'll need to also take apart some words." The teacher might say, "Let's get our 'Word Power' going in the title. Let's first look at the picture. . . . What do you see?" Readers will probably say they see a rabbit and they see snow. "Okay, 'rabbit' (pointing to 'footprints') does the title say 'rabbit snow'? No-that doesn't make sense." Then we might say, "Would you work with your partner and see if you can do some word work on this word *footprints*." If partners are able to support each other and they make an effort to rally their energy for some word work, this book should provide some great learning opportunities.

Although the way sentences are stretched out across pages makes the book a poor choice for supporting fluency and phrasing, it will be important to get children rereading parts of the book smoothly. In this book as in others, when children reread it individually, we'll encourage them to use Post-Its on interesting parts and to then meet with partners for conversations. They'll probably notice the different animal homes, and they'll certainly want to name what kind of animal is on each page. With encouragement, they may study and compare the footprints, which after all, are supposed to be a big part of the message.

The book is also special because an observant and thoughtful reader can construct far more meaning from the text than is explicitly conveyed by the words alone. A study of the light suggests that time has passed from page one which may be in the morning and to the final page which is the evening. The animals each live in different homes, which can be named and labeled by the child if she adds own her words to the text.

Footprints in the Snow is organized like countless other early books, and young readers could gather books that follow a similar structure. How are they like and unlike each other? Some may have the opening and closing pages following one pattern and the internal pages, another. Some may have the repeating sentence divided across two pages; many others won't. These books will tend to have a twist at the end of the list, but the ending twists vary in interesting ways.

Book Connections

This book is about footprints in the snow but it is also clearly about how animals move, about animal homes, and about how animals survive in winter. It can be set alongside other books on any one of these topics. For example, there are books about bears in winter (which suggest that bears hibernate rather than stomp through the snow as this book says). Some popular ones include: Denise Fleming's *Time to Sleep*, *DK Readers: A Bed for*

Winter by Karen Wallace, *What Will I do Without You?* by Sally Grindley, *Sleepy Bear* by Lydia Dabovich, and *Animals in Winter* by Henrietta Bancroft. There are also lots of fiction and nonfiction books about animal homes (such as Krauss' famous *A House is a House for Me*).

Genre
Emergent Literacy Book; Picture Book

Teaching Uses
Independent Reading; Small Group Strategy Instruction; Partnerships; Whole Group Instruction

A Field Guide to the Classroom Library, Lucy Calkins and the Teachers College Reading and Writing Project, Heinemann, ©2002 Teachers College, Columbia University; http://www.heinemann.com/fieldguides

Ghost

Joy Cowley

Book Summary

This 26-word book begins with a cover showing a young child wrapped in a bed spread, standing on a stool in order to look in the mirror. A close look shows that nearby there is a paper-bag mask, scissors, and tape. The story starts by listing what the child sees. The text begins "I see the door." When integrated with the pictures, it's clear that the child, dressed in a ghost costume, peers out to see the doorway. Then, as he travels, he sees the table, then the distant armchairs. As he nears the chairs he sees they contain Mom and Dad. Finally he calls out "Boo!" and frightens his parents.

Basic Book Information

This is part of Wright Group's Story Box Collection. Originally published in New Zealand, the Story Box series is well known for its characters and story lines. Joy Cowley, who has written over 400 early reading books, writes most of the titles in the Story Box series. Cowley's Story Box stories contain such memorable characters as *Mrs. Wishy-Washy*, *The Meanies*, and *Hairy Bear*. Wright Group regards this as a level A book.

Noteworthy Features

This book is quite marvelous because its text is extraordinary simple, providing young readers with a great deal of support; and yet, children are required to infer a whole drama, constructing the sequence of events out of phrases, pictures, and their own imaginations.

It's crucial that from the beginning children understand that reading is a process of using every available resource in order to construct meaning. Children who do so with this book will be rewarded with a story complete with a suspenseful build-up toward a climax.

Teaching Ideas

Teachers might have students walk through the story. As students look at each picture, teachers might point out the sentence at the bottom that tells us what "the ghost" sees. For each subsequent page students might respond to the question: What else can the ghost see? Teachers might point to each word in the sentence on that page as the students respond.

If children aren't given a heavy book introduction but are instead left to invent the pattern for themselves, they may find the first page, "I see the door." challenging. The first word *I* should be recognizable and the door is depicted in the illustration, but children will need to do some work to arrive upon the whole sentence of "I see the door."

Teachers will be informed by watching what sources of information

Publisher
Wright Group, 1987

ISBN
0780274083

TC Level
1

children draw upon as they read the first page. Teachers can also watch for how the child reads *the window* (the picture could lead a child to read this as *the moon*).

It'll be interesting to hear a child's retelling of the story and alarm bells should go off for teachers if a child doesn't put the pages and the listed items in the text together in order to create a coherent story.

Book Connections

There are many stories like this in which a character sneaks, slowly, slowly. *The Ghost* can be compared to Ruth Brown's *A Dark, Dark Tale*, *In a Dark, Dark Wood* and *The Big Toe*.

Genre
Emergent Literacy Book

Teaching Uses
Independent Reading; Partnerships; Small Group Strategy Instruction

Good Dog, Carl

Alexandra Day

Book Summary

The mistress of the house goes out and asks Carl, the dog, to watch the baby. While she is away, the dog and the baby get into all kinds of messy, dangerous, and fun mischief. When the mistress returns, she finds everything in perfect order and thanks Carl for his good work.

Basic Book Information

This (nearly) wordless picture book has about 32 pages. The only words are at the beginning where the mistress tells the dog she will be right back and asks him to watch the baby and at the end when she returns and says, "Good dog, Carl." Even if readers can't decode these words, the pictures tell the story beautifully.

Noteworthy Features

The pictures themselves highlight the action of the story, on some pages even leaving out any background that is not relevant to the antics of the dog and the baby. Most of the time, there is one picture per page, but in several cases, there is a sequence of actions told over the course of two pages, with the dog and baby appearing in a montage of illustrations. Readers will have to figure out the sequence of events, since the pictures fall in various places across the two-page spread.

Teaching Ideas

Wordless picture books like this one will always be especially good for helping children focus on the "creating-a-story" part of reading work as opposed to the "decoding the words" part. To create the story with only the pictures, readers have to keep the characters and past events in mind, as well as their knowledge of real world events, and how they relate to what has happened or what will happen in the story. The reader has to feel cumulative effects of the events, and may even create story language to go with the tale, "Once upon a time. . . ."

Without any words to rely on, readers need to really focus on the storyline of the book. They will have to try to make continuous sense out of the events taking place in the pictures. However, there are not entirely new things to figure out with every picture; once readers have figured out that the dog and the baby are going to do fun things that they would normally get into trouble for, then the work is only to figure out precisely what the two are doing each time. The switch to follow in the story comes when the dog looks at the clock and realizes it is time to clean up. Then, the fun changes to work as the dog tidies the baby and the things they've played

A Field Guide to the Classroom Library, Lucy Calkins and the Teachers College Reading and Writing Project, Heinemann, ©2002 Teachers College, Columbia University; http://www.heinemann.com/fieldguides

Illustrator
Alexandra Day

Publisher
Aladdin, Simon & Schuster, 1985

ISBN
0689817711

with. Finally, careful readers can enjoy Carl's exhausted expression as the mistress returns home to find nothing changed.

If children are having a hard time making sense of the book, knowing that first comes the mischief and then comes the clean up may help them pin the smaller events onto the larger framework of the book.

Readers of this book will probably love the trouble that the baby and the dog get into. Many readers may find that the two characters do just the kinds of things that they themselves would love to do alone in the house. Some readers, however, will want to talk to their partners about how strange it is that the lady, presumably the baby's mother, has left the little child alone in the house with only a dog as a babysitter. These concerned readers will rightly point out that the baby could easily have gotten hurt doing some of the life-threatening things that they do together. If there is a reader like that in the group, the discussion will undoubtedly be lively, especially if talk of the message of the book arises.

Book Connections

Teachers may want to explore this technique for developing children's sense of story with other books. If children found this one appealing, there are many other Carl books by Alexandra Day, including *Carl Goes Shopping*, *Carl's Birthday* and *Carl's Afternoon in the Park*. It may be more effective to do some of this same work with different kinds of books and there are a number of good wordless (or almost wordless) ones including: *The Snowman* by Raymond Briggs, *Pancakes for Breakfast* by Tomie dePaola, and *You Can't Take a Balloon into the Metropolitan Museum* by Jacqueline Preiss Weitzman and Robin Preiss Glasser. *Do You Want to Be My Friend?* by Eric Carle can be found in the A Library.

Genre
Picture Book

Teaching Uses
Independent Reading; Critique; Interpretation

Good Night, Little Kitten

Nancy Christensen

Book Summary

It's time for Little Kitten to go to bed, yet that's the last thing that Little Kitten wants to do. Little Kitten would much rather play with the blocks, the fire engine, and the rocking horse. Little Kitten's Mama and Papa keep saying, "Good Night, Little Kitten." Little Kitten replies, " I want to stay up." Finally, Mama and Papa get no response. When they go to look, they find the kitten curled up on the window seat and fast asleep.

Basic Book Information

This is a 29-page book with colorful illustrations by Dennis Hockerman on every page. The pages are numbered. There is a controlled vocabulary consisting of 24 words in this book. The words are listed on the inside cover.

Noteworthy Features

The pictures in this book are very engaging. The whole cat family, Mama, Papa, and Little Kitten all live like humans. Talk about the cat's pajamas! This little kitten is fully decked out in polka dot jammies! Children love to look at the small details in the illustrations, like the hanging picture that Little Kitten drew and the abundance of toys in the bedroom. If young readers turn to the back cover, they'll find yet another scene with Little Kitten. The illustrations, as well as the sentences, are laid out across a two-page spread.

The sentences may seem a bit awkward to adult readers because of the controlled vocabulary. However, in the words of the publisher, "These 24 words are repeated through the story, so that young readers will be able to easily recognize words and understand their meaning."

Good Night, Little Kitten contains a lot of dialogue. All of the dialogue is referenced, which makes it easier for readers who are new to this literary device. Some children may find the dialogue a bit confusing. When Little Kitten's parents say, "Good Night, Little Kitten," they are implying that it is time for him to go to sleep. Children might not make this inference and wonder why Little Kitten's parents keep saying "Good Night, Little Kitten" repetitively, when it is clear that Little Kitten has heard them, has continued playing, and is not interested in going to bed.

Teaching Ideas

Because one sentence is continued over the course of two pages, it may make the phrasing of this book more difficult for early readers to follow. This can be an opportunity to demonstrate the importance of attending to punctuation. This book also presents a chance to introduce quotation marks

Illustrator
Dennis Hockerman

Publisher
Children's Press, 1990

ISBN
051605354X

TC Level
3

A Field Guide to the Classroom Library, Lucy Calkins and the Teachers College Reading and Writing Project, Heinemann, ©2002 Teachers College, Columbia University; http://www.heinemann.com/fieldguides

to students. Teachers may want to read aloud *Good Night, Little Kitten* to demonstrate how punctuation may affect the intonation of your voice as you read. In partnerships, readers will have fun practicing this.

As in all books for the very earliest readers, in *Good Night, Little Kitten* one-to-one matching may not come easily to the child. Teachers can remind students who still need to point under the words, to point crisply under each of the words. Students should also be monitoring to see if there are any words left to point to after they finish reading a line. If there are, students should be aware of this error and be able to self-correct.

There are a number of ellipses throughout *Good Night, Little Kitten.* For children in the upper-elementary grades, this book can be used in a writing workshop. It demonstrates one use of the ellipsis, and therefore, will present a clear message to children who want to begin using this punctuation in their writing. For children in the lower grades, it is important for teachers to explain what this kind of ellipsis means and to model how an ellipsis affects the reading of a text.

Upon inspection of this book, teachers may note the presence of gender stereotypes. Papa cat reads the newspaper while Mama folds the laundry, knits, and dons an apron. This is not a reason to ban the book from the library, but instead can be used by teachers to have discussions with children about other activities and roles moms and dads may take on, in a variety of family configurations. Teachers will want to make sure that their classroom libraries reflect the experiences of their student population.

Genre
Picture Book; Emergent Literacy Book

Teaching Uses
Independent Reading; Language Conventions; Read Aloud; Teaching Writing; Critique; Partnerships

Goodnight Moon
Margaret Wise Brown

Book Summary

This gentle picture book tells about a young rabbit going to sleep. The setting is the rabbit's bedroom, with the rabbit already in bed. The simple text first lists items in the room such as a telephone, a red balloon, and a picture Then the sequence is repeated in a series of lines, each beginning with "Goodnight."

Basic Book Information

Goodnight Moon by Margaret Wise Brown, author of the *Runaway Bunny* and other favorites, is a classic. *Goodnight Moon* uses basic vocabulary and sentence structure in a text of fewer than 150 words. Most pages contain a single line of text. The illustrations alternate, by two-page spread, between color and black and white. The color pages show a view of the entire room, while the black-and-white illustrations portray one item in the room such as the kittens, the mittens, or a mouse, close-up.

Noteworthy Features

Frequent use of rhythm and rhyme add greatly to the charm of this appealing book. Rhyme occurs both at the end of lines and within the text. In addition, the repetitive grammatical patterns establish a satisfying rhythm.

Teaching Ideas

Teachers can introduce this story by telling children that it is a going-to-bed book. After reading the book, teachers might ask children about their own nightly rituals.

Children who choose this book will enjoy studying and talking about it. As they thumb through the book, Clement Hurd's classic illustrations can lead to great discussions. Because the pictures contain many details, much of the conversation may not even center around the written story.

Although the story is virtually plotless, there are subtle changes in the illustrations that a small child will delight in noticing. As the book proceeds, night draws on and the room grows darker. The moon appears outside one window, rising higher in each picture. The mouse appears in a different location on every page. Young children will have fun hunting for him. The final illustration accompanies a line of text that brings closure to the story: "Goodnight noises everywhere." The illustration shows the lamp extinguished, the room in darkness except for the fire and lighted dollhouse windows, the old woman gone, and the little rabbit asleep.

During class partner discussions teachers might also point out that

Illustrator
Clement Hurd

Publisher
Harper & Row, 1947

ISBN
0064430170

TC Level
5

A Field Guide to the Classroom Library, Lucy Calkins and the Teachers College Reading and Writing Project, Heinemann, ©2002 Teachers College, Columbia University; http://www.heinemann.com/fieldguides

Goodnight Moon contains elements drawn from other stories and nursery rhymes children may be familiar with-the cow who jumped over the moon, the three bears, and the kittens who lost their mittens. Partners may reread to find and talk over these elements.

After studying other examples of simpler books in writing workshop, teachers may also want to use this as a model for writing.

Book Connections

Children might enjoy reading other going-to-bed books such as *Goodnight Gorilla*, *The Going To Bed Book*, and *Goodnight, Little Tiger*. *The Napping House* has a similar pattern of slight changes in the lighting in the room throughout the course of the story.

Genre
Picture Book

Teaching Uses
Teaching Writing; Partnerships; Independent Reading; Read Aloud

Gooseberry Park

Cynthia Rylant

Book Summary

Kona, a Labrador retriever, who lives with Professor Albert, and shares his home with Gwendolyn, a wise hermit crab, visits Gooseberry Park often to see his friend Stumpy, the squirrel. Stumpy is preparing to have her children in her nest in the sugar maple at the park. Shortly after the babies are born, an ice storm destroys her home. Her friend Kona, Gwendolyn, and neighbor Murray the bat, all come together with plans to save her children (to bring them to Kona's house) and to find Stumpy, who has wandered away, seeking help. They arrange a sign for Stumpy to find Kona's house. When she is finally reunited with her children, her loyal friends find a new home for the squirrels in a sugar maple in Gooseberry Park, a "split level" with room for Murray, too.

Basic Book Information

Gooseberry Park is written by well-known author, Cynthia Rylant. Other books by Rylant include: *Missing May, When I was young in the mountains, Every Living Thing, The Henry and Mudge Series,* and many more.

   Gooseberry Park has 133 pages, and has 19 titled chapters. The story is told through an omniscient narrator, from the point of view of the animals. Each character has a distinct personality; Kona is the caring friend, who ventures out on the ice to look for Stumpy; Gwendolyn is the gossip lover, who is thoughtful and inventive; Murray is a lover of pop-culture, who protects the babies, although he would rather be eating Mars bars and drinking Pepsi; Stumpy is a collector of objects, she wants to have her cozy nest just right for the day when she will become a mother.

Noteworthy Features

There is some challenging vocabulary that may cause difficulty including: "funereal glow," "senile," "desolation," "exasperation," chapter titles such as: "Rescue and Remorse," and "Yet Another Muckraker." Humorous expressions such as "danced like a Bolshevik," and several others that are uttered by Murray ("He cooks Italian?" " Can't you just call a cab or something?" "Domestic animals-who can figure 'em?") may need explanation. The illustrations by Arthur Howard blend fantasy and reality throughout the story. The beginning chapters slowly introduce the various characters. Chapter 7 "Ice" brings the reader into the ferocious ice storm, with writing that is fast paced.

Teaching Ideas

Teachers may want to introduce this book by telling students about Cynthia

Illustrator
Arthur Howard

Publisher
Scholastic Inc, 1995

ISBN
059094715X

TC Level
10

A Field Guide to the Classroom Library, Lucy Calkins and the Teachers College Reading and Writing Project, Heinemann, ©2002 Teachers College, Columbia University; http://www.heinemann.com/fieldguides

Rylant and some of her other books, with which many will be familiar. The introduction might include a description of the characters, that this is a fantasy fiction story, and the understanding that dangerous events test the strength of friendship

There can be discussion of the omniscient narrator's role in describing the characters through their dialogue and actions, as well as what she/he feels; "Together the two gazed out the window in silence...Each was full of thoughts: thoughts...about mothers and their children, about the profound comfort of shelter and sustenance and the familiarity of home."

Kona and his friends can be compared to characters in *Charlotte's Web* by E.B. White. Students can discuss the ways humor, courage, and persistence enable the friends in both novels to overcome tremendous obstacles. They may notice how the personalities of the characters were clearly developed; Murray and his desire to consume Oreos, marshmallows, or whatever he could find in the professor's kitchen, compared with Templeton the rat who also persisted in his goal of feasting during his nightly forays on the farm.

Readers can discuss the impact some of the other characters have on the plot such as Professor Albert, "...a retired biology professor who loved to grow daylilies and listen to the saxophone"; the wise owl who said to Kona, "She is wandering, my boy, and no one can find a wanderer. The wanderer must first find you"; or the weasel who told Kona, "Yeah, I heard about that squirrel. So What?" Discussions can include Kona and his friends' understanding of the personalities of the other characters and how they use that knowledge to achieve their goal of finding the stolen watch that glows, or to provide a sign for Stumpy to find them.

At the end of the story, spring has turned to summer and Cynthia Rylant leaves the reader with a sense of fulfillment. Students might have a conversation about the changes that have taken place. Readers could explore the significance of the watch that glows in the dark; how it becomes the sign that helps Stumpy find her way back to the children and return to Gooseberry Park, to live near her friend Murray, near the house on Miller Street where Kona and Gwendolyn spend their evenings retelling their adventures.

This book can make a perfect read aloud for very young students. The animals and their antics tend to fascinate and stimulate youngsters.

Genre
Chapter Book

Teaching Uses
Independent Reading; Author Study; Read Aloud

A Field Guide to the Classroom Library, Lucy Calkins and the Teachers College Reading and Writing Project, Heinemann, ©2002 Teachers College, Columbia University; http://www.heinemann.com/fieldguides

Growing Colors
Bruce McMillan

Book Summary

Each right-hand page contains a full color close-up photograph of a fruit or vegetable plant. Each left-hand page has a smaller color photograph of the fruit in its natural habitat, and an extra large word in color, labeling the color of the fruit or vegetable (e.g., GREEN written in the color green). At the end of the book there are two pages full of reduced-size photographs. Each one is placed in between the word for its color and its name.

Basic Book Information

This informative nonfiction book about the colors, names, and parent plants of common fruits and vegetables is published by Mulberry. It's an oversized book that will stand out in many early libraries.

Noteworthy Features

Many Level 1 and Level 2 books are nonfiction books with a list structure, but this one is special because it looks like nonfiction books that more experienced readers will read.

Teaching Ideas

This basic nonfiction text has many features of more advanced nonfiction texts, and so it can be used to introduce children to the genre and to features of nonfiction. The two pages of reduced-size photographs and accompanying labels at the end of the book are like an index. Although this list doesn't have page numbers, readers can still learn that the back of nonfiction books often have listings of what the book contains. They can also learn to move back and forth between the reference page, with all its labels and reduced photographs, and the text of the book itself. This moving back and forth between pages while following one idea is a strategy readers of nonfiction must learn. Readers can learn the name of the fruit or vegetable and then turn back to the page on which it first appeared to get a closer look at it. Because the page numbers are not in this "index," readers must attend closely to the photograph or the color word.

Readers can also use these back pages-if they can maneuver between them and the main text of the book-to confirm or revise their guesses as to what the crops are. Are those round things oranges or apricots? What will the word look like if it is apricots? If children are reading in partnerships, they can check the back pages to verify their predictions.

This book stimulates thinking about its illustrations. In it, the reader has to figure out how the pictures relate to one another. Why is this picture of the tree put together with the word "purple" and the picture of the fruit?

Publisher
Mulberry Books, 1988

ISBN
0688131123

TC Level
1

 A Field Guide to the Classroom Library, Lucy Calkins and the Teachers College Reading and Writing Project, Heinemann, ©2002 Teachers College, Columbia University; http://www.heinemann.com/fieldguides

Why are there these bushy plants near this picture of the yellow vegetable? And what are these tan things? The book shows pictures of the vegetables in various stages of maturity in some pictures, and children will have to figure out for themselves that it is the same plant and same crop. Some children who are familiar with basic fruits and vegetables may be surprised at the varieties of colors these crops come in. Brown peppers? The seemingly odd colors may also provoke questions as to the why's and how's of plants and crops. With a very small amount of text, the book creates fuel for a lot of thinking, wondering, and discussion about the plants it pictures. It may even provoke children to want to try to taste these fruits and vegetables, or grow some themselves if the climate is suitable.

In the A library, this book could be used as part of a reading center that is focused on books about colors. Teachers can introduce this center in a variety of ways. All of the mini-lessons can be centered on this genre. Then, children can choose from a variety of label books. (e.g., Label Books about Food, ABC Label Books, Label Books about Numbers, Label Books about Animals, Label Books about Colors, etc.). Another possibility is to do a nonfiction study as a whole class. Then, centers could have books on a variety of different nonfiction subjects.

Book Connections

In the A Library, this book could be paired in a center with Tana Hoban's *Is it Red? Is It Yellow? Is It Blue?* Ellen Walsh's *Mouse Paint* and Leo Lionni's *Little Blue and Little Yellow*.

Genre
Nonfiction; Picture Book

Teaching Uses
Content Area Study; Reading and Writing Nonfiction; Partnerships; Whole Group Instruction; Small Group Strategy Instruction

A Field Guide to the Classroom Library, Lucy Calkins and the Teachers College Reading and Writing Project, Heinemann, ©2002 Teachers College, Columbia University; http://www.heinemann.com/fieldguides

Hairy Bear

Joy Cowley

Book Summary

Hairy Bear is an emergent level book about a mother and father bear that hear noises in the night. Mother bear tries to get Hairy Bear to do something about the "robbers" that she hears. Hairy Bear threatens to "fim-fam-fight 'em," and "bim-bam bash 'em," but doesn't seem to want to go downstairs to find them.

Basic Book Information

This 16-page book has 109 words.

Noteworthy Features

The author uses rhyme, rhythm, and repetition to make her stories fun and familiar. The large font, generous spacing, and repetitive patterned text help make this book accessible to early readers, but the pictures are much less supportive of the text than many readers at this level have been accustomed to.

   The appearance of nonsense words can offer challenges to readers who are expecting real words. The fact that what is happening in the picture seems to contradict what the text is saying will also challenge some readers if they don't put the two together and infer that Hairy Bear's words are a lot braver than his actions.

Teaching Ideas

If a teacher wanted to support readers' first experience of this text, one way to do this would be with a book introduction. One teacher did this by saying, "In this book, Hairy Bear and Mother Bear think they hear robbers downstairs. Mother Bear thinks Hairy Bear is a scaredy bear because he won't go get them. Let's look on page 3. The picture on this page doesn't help us much to figure out what the words say, so we have to look all the way across our words to help us. Let's look at the last line on page 3, 'I'll fim-fam-fight 'em.' Can anyone try the first part of that? F-I-M. Now try taking the *f* off of the next part of the word F-am . . . let's put it together: 'Fim-Fam...fight 'em.' Let's practice reading that all together, saying it the way Hairy Bear might say it. . . . "

   Once the readers understand that the last line on many of the pages consists of nonsense-type words, they will have a better feel for the way the book is supposed to sound as well as how it should be read. Readers attempting this book should have an understanding of how to use words they know to get to words they don't know (i.e., using word analogies so that *light* can help the reader get to *right, night, might*) and how to blend

Publisher
Wright Group, 1998

ISBN
0780274636

TC Level
4

A Field Guide to the Classroom Library, Lucy Calkins and the Teachers College Reading and Writing Project, Heinemann, ©2002 Teachers College, Columbia University; http://www.heinemann.com/fieldguides

sounds of unknown words together (crim-cram-crash). To fully enjoy the story, the reader needs to read it fluently and with expression so multiple rereadings will be important.

Along with the Big Book version, teachers are provided with several small copies of the same text. Teachers may want to have children practice what has been modeled right there on the rug with a partner before going off to try it in their independent reading. While listening in, teachers will want to hold back a bit, allowing readers to work through the nonsense words. This will give them an opportunity to observe what graphophonic knowledge the reader is using in order to make his way through these difficult syllables. Once the reader has tried a few ways to get at the words, the teacher could then try one of several prompts. Teachers can prompt the reader to use words he knows to work out unknown words by asking, "Do you know any words that look like this word?" If he can't come up with a word, a teacher might supply a word that he knows, "Would the word *him* help you here?" (*crim, fim, bim*). We might also prompt him to look all the way across the words and chunk them into parts (*f-im, f-am, f-ight*).

In addition, the reader must study the pictures carefully to understand that there is much more going on in the story than the words are saying. For example, Hairy Bear may be threatening to get the robbers, but in the picture, Mother Bear is attempting to drag Hairy Bear out of the bedroom while he is still holding on to the bed. Only together do we get the whole story.

This book is a perfect text for teaching readers that the illustrator can show us a different story in the pictures than what might be in the text. The words tell us that father bear wants to get those robbers and fight them, but the pictures show us a completely different story in which mama bear has to drag father bear out of the bedroom in order to find out who the robbers are.

Hairy Bear is part of a set of books meant for shared reading, but also works well as a guided reading book or a book for independent reading.

Genre
Emergent Literacy Book

Teaching Uses
Independent Reading; Critique; Interpretation; Whole Group Instruction; Read Aloud; Language Conventions; Partnerships

A Field Guide to the Classroom Library, Lucy Calkins and the Teachers College Reading and Writing Project, Heinemann, ©2002 Teachers College, Columbia University; http://www.heinemann.com/fieldguides

Happy Birthday, Danny and the Dinosaur!

Syd Hoff

Book Summary

Danny finds his friend the dinosaur at the museum and invites him to his sixth birthday party. He discovers that it is the dinosaur's birthday, too. The dinosaur is "a hundred million years and one day old!" They decide to celebrate together. They hang balloons, wear party hats, sing songs, play pin-the-tail-on-the-donkey, and blow out the candles on the birthday cake. At the end of the day, they make their birthday wish, which is to be together again the following year.

Basic Book Information

Happy Birthday, Danny and the Dinosaur! is part of the An I Can Read Book series. There are 32 pages and no chapter breaks. There are between one and four lines of text per page and most pages contain a single sentence. Each page is brightly illustrated with pictures that match at least one sentence on the page, but the picture alone won't tell readers what the text says.

Begun in 1958, Syd Hoff's *Danny and the Dinosaur* series, like Else Holmelund Minarik's *Little Bear* series, have been an important step into longer books. The dinosaur is huge, but in no way intimidating. He is instead friendly to Danny and the rest of the neighborhood kids.

Noteworthy Features

Children will love this simple funny tale of Danny and his dinosaur in the familiar world of birthday parties. For a text that is this simple, Syd Hoff does a good job of creating humor. He does this by placing the dinosaur in activities that are familiar for children, yet silly for a dinosaur. The story is simple, but because many children fantasize about having a dinosaur as a loyal pet, the story will hold the interest of most readers at this level. The *Danny and the Dinosaur* books offer the challenge of a single, continuous plot. The story in all the *Danny and The Dinosaur* books is made up of a series of linked and chronological episodes.

The majority of the text is written with high frequency words, such as *was, friend, said, would, rode, today, your, children, helped, asked,* and *everybody*. There is a sprinkling of more difficult words that may challenge the reader, such as *delighted, museum, million, balloons,* and *furniture*. Quotation marks and exclamation points are used simply throughout. Some

Illustrator
Syd Hoff

Publisher
Harper Collins, 1996

ISBN
0064442373

TC Level
5

A Field Guide to the Classroom Library, Lucy Calkins and the Teachers College Reading and Writing Project, Heinemann, ©2002 Teachers College, Columbia University; http://www.heinemann.com/fieldguides

of the sentences are compound. There is referenced dialogue (readers are explicitly told who the speaker is), with references always coming at the beginning or end of the sentence.

Teaching Ideas

Happy Birthday, Danny and the Dinosaur can be used as a read aloud, in a guided reading group, as an independent reading book for early readers, or as part of an author study of Syd Hoff. Readers can discuss the ways in which most Syd Hoff books are alike. For example, most Syd Hoff books have a child with an unlikely, talking animal friend. Readers can also discuss recurring characters such as Danny and the dinosaur.

The most obvious and strongest characteristic of books written by Syd Hoff is the humor. When introducing *Happy Birthday, Danny and the Dinosaur*, a teacher may say, "This is the story of a boy who has a dinosaur as a friend. They decide to have a birthday party together and do all sorts of birthday things, like wearing party hats, playing pin-the-tail-on-the-donkey, and making a wish on a birthday cake. Can you imagine having a dinosaur at your party? What funny things might happen? Could a dinosaur really come to your house?" Readers will enjoy discussing their fantasies of what it would be like to be visited by a dinosaur.

Primary grade readers who have mastered early reading skills, such as one-to-one matching, directionality, checking the picture against the text, or "getting their mouth ready" for an unfamiliar word can use this book to support those behaviors. At the same time, the book also enables children to attempt new skills, including reading text that does not have pictures that match each sentence, reading longer and often compound sentences, reading with quotation marks and punctuation, tackling harder words, and reading with increasing fluency, for longer and longer periods of time.

Teachers may work with readers on developing self-checking skills; strategies for figuring out unfamiliar words such as using context, rereading and looking for the unfamiliar word in other parts of the text; retelling; and how to talk about funny, interesting or confusing parts with other readers.

As it is written in the past tense, *Happy Birthday, Danny and the Dinosaur!* is a good book to use to help children pay special attention to words with -ed endings.

Book Connections

Happy Birthday, Danny and the Dinosaur! is one of three books about the same characters. The others are *Danny and the Dinosaur* and *Danny and the Dinosaur Go to Camp.* Other titles by Syd Hoff at a similar level include *Sammy the Seal, The Firehouse Cat, Captain Cat,* and *Oliver.* Before reading *Danny and the Dinosaur* books, children may want to read *Rex and Lilly,* a somewhat easier book that also has a dinosaur as a character.

Genre
Picture Book

A Field Guide to the Classroom Library, Lucy Calkins and the Teachers College Reading and Writing Project, Heinemann, ©2002 Teachers College, Columbia University; http://www.heinemann.com/fieldguides

Teaching Uses
Read Aloud; Character Study; Independent Reading; Small Group Strategy
Instruction; Author Study

A Field Guide to the Classroom Library, Lucy Calkins and the Teachers College Reading and Writing Project, Heinemann, ©2002 Teachers
College, Columbia University; http://www.heinemann.com/fieldguides

Hats, Hats, Hats

Ann Morris

Book Summary

Hats, Hats, Hats is a "round-the-world" tour of different kinds of hats: how hats are worn for worship, protection, as part of a tradition, custom or uniform, and during work and play. Hats are shown as part of an expression and representation of who we are and where we come from.

Basic Book Information

Hats, Hats, Hats is a picture book. There are 28 pages and the text begins on page 5. The amount and placement of text varies. There are pages with no text, pages with one sentence, and pages with a few words from a long sentence that spans two to three pages. There are brightly colored photographs on each page. Some pages contain full-page photographs, some have photographs with the text at the bottom or top, some have photographs with the text on the side, and some have three to four photographs with the text under each photograph. Each photograph supports the text in some way, usually in direct correspondence with some part of the text. But, the photographs have a lot of information that can be "read" besides the information that matches the text

The font is large and well spaced. There is an "index " at the back of the book, which describes the type of hat, culture and/or nationality of the people in the photograph, the country where the photograph has been taken, and the way in which the hat is being shown that corresponds to each page in the book. The photographs represent: Israel, the United States, Peru, England, Egypt, France, El Salvador, India, Indonesia, Nigeria, Japan, and Denmark. The index is written in language that is more complex and the font is quite small. Early readers are likely to need help with this section of the book.

Noteworthy Features

This book is beautifully photographed and fascinating to read. The variety of hats, and uses for hats across cultures is well represented, yet simply and succinctly explained. The inclusion of people from around the world, many of them wearing the clothing, using the tools, and shown as part of, their obviously differing environments is lovely and remarkable. Each page lends itself to long discussions about various aspects of what is represented in the individual photograph. The index, also, is well stocked with even more detailed and equally interesting information about culture, tradition, and types of hats.

Although the book has a number of supportive features (e.g., the format is large in size, the font is large, there are a lot of high frequency words, and there is very little text overall) it could still be challenging for early readers.

Illustrator
Ken Heyman

Publisher
Lothrop, Lee & Shepard, 1989

ISBN
0688122744

TC Level
3

Some challenges include the use of ellipses, sentences that stretch over two to three pages, and some vocabulary that is not easily decoded or gleaned from the context.

Teaching Ideas

Hats, Hats, Hats makes a good addition to an author study of Ann Morris books (particularly those photographed by Ken Heyman). Many of her books have a similar format, a simple premise, and photographs from around the world that support the premise. Readers may find similarities and differences in all the Ann Morris books.

This book may be used as part of a study of the genre of nonfiction. Teachers may model for children how we sometimes read nonfiction differently than fiction. Readers can practice reading smaller chunks, as they often do withnonfiction, rather than straight through from start to finish. Teachers may model for children the many opportunities for, and the necessity of, frequent and interesting discussions that nonfiction text presents to the reader.

A teacher might also give a strategy lesson on the nonfiction elements of this book. A teacher may say, "You'll be seeing many indexes as we read nonfiction books. If you turn to the index, you'll see a variety of hats and a description of the culture or nationality of the people who wear the hats and the country where the photograph was taken. When I read nonfiction texts, I always like to look over the index because I know it gives me even more information." Many of the details included in the index lend themselves to opportunities for teachers to have rich discussions with the class.

Hats, Hats, Hats may be used as part of a reading center that is organized around several different principles. This book may be used in a center about: community workers, books about uniforms and costumes, or books about things that cultures share. In fact, one great exercise for young readers is to build their own centers with a handful of books and to define the organizing principle of those centers by themselves. Young readers will often need help choosing reading center books that belong together. At first, their topics may be too broad, too vague or too esoteric to do good reading center work.

Hats, Hats, Hats is also available as a Big Book, and it may be used with a small group or with the whole class to support early reading behaviors. This book lends itself to doing word work because there are a lot of high frequency words, as well as words that are unfamiliar and will be challenging for the early reader. Teachers may use this book to support lessons on one-to-one matching, "getting your mouth ready" for an upcoming word, and predicting or figuring out text from looking at the picture and asking yourself: "What would make sense here?" Young readers may memorize the text through repeated readings, and then may work with the big book or a smaller version in small groups or reading partnerships, practicing all of the above early reading strategies.

As readers become more familiar with the text, they may use *Hats, Hats, Hats* as a "touchstone text" to help them write their own simple nonfiction books. Readers may choose a small topic and write their own nonfiction books in a similar format to this one. They may use *Hats, Hats, Hats* to guide them with their own writing.

A Field Guide to the Classroom Library, Lucy Calkins and the Teachers College Reading and Writing Project, Heinemann, ©2002 Teachers College, Columbia University; http://www.heinemann.com/fieldguides

Hats, Hats, Hats may be used to support other areas of the curriculum, particularly Social Studies. Many teachers in early grades do whole class studies of community and cultures. These often include such topics as uniforms of community workers and/or or the similarities and differences of cultures around the world-in which the subject of traditional dress, including hats, is often included. This book would be a rich and valuable source of information about any of these topics. Teachers may show readers how to use this book as a "reference" for their studies. Teachers may pose questions to readers that help them think critically about people, their work, play, and customs as they read. Teachers may lead readers to discover how many hats are designed with their uses or the demands of the environment in mind. For example, on page 10, construction workers are wearing hard hats. Teachers might ask children, "Why are these called 'hard hats'? Why do these workers need hats that are hard?"

This book can be used as a springboard to an art lesson or choice time activity where children make their own hats. The hats they make can either represent some part of their personality or culture, or help them in their "work" or play!

Book Connections

There are several other books written by Ann Morris and photographed by Ken Heyman that follow a similar format, including *Bread, Bread, Bread*, which can also be found in the A library. There are also many other books at this level about clothing, costumes, and uniforms.

Genre
Nonfiction; Picture Book

Teaching Uses
Author Study; Content Area Study; Critique; Interpretation; Partnerships; Small Group Strategy Instruction; Reading and Writing Nonfiction

Have You Seen My Cat?

Eric Carle

Book Summary

In this story, a boy travels the world asking people in a variety of cultural settings, "Have you seen my cat?" Each time, the individual points to a cat but when the boy sees it, he says, "This is not *my* cat." The book ends with people who look like they could be the boy's parents pointing and the boy finding a mother cat with six babies. "This is my cat!" the boy says.

Basic Book Information

This 22-page picture book is richly illustrated by Eric Carle, who has written and illustrated over 70 books for children, many of which have become bestsellers.

The question "Have you seen my cat?" and answer "This is not *my* cat!" is repeated on each double-page spread until the last page, "This is my cat!"

The black font is small and handwritten in appearance on a white background. The same double-page spread of cats including a lion, bobcat, and cheetah to name a few, is included before and after the text of the story, with a label naming each beneath the illustrations.

Noteworthy Features

Carle's trademark collage illustrations give this book its distinctive style. It's also interesting to note the way that pictures, like words, can be combined in a list-like way with each item on the list containing parallel elements. Each picture showing the boy asking each individual, "Have you seen my cat?" is similar to every other page in its basic component parts. Always the boy is shown interacting with a person, or people, in a setting unlike our own. The vignette with the boy inquiring after his lost cat is always small, and on each subsequent page there is an oversized cat that is not the boy's cat.

Teaching Ideas

One way to enter this book is to predict what it may be about. The teacher might say, "This book is called *Have You Seen My Cat?* by Eric Carle. The cover can help us know about the book. What do you see on the cover?" The teacher may then open up the book and show the picture of a cat with kittens that continues across the back cover as well. There is also a blurb on the back cover. A teacher might say "The words here tell us about the book. Listen while I read them to you."

Because the book has a repetitive pattern, a child will be able to read the text, working on pointing to words while he progresses along, matching spoken words with printed words and self-correcting when these don't

Illustrator
Eric Carle

Publisher
Scholastic, 1997

ISBN
0590444611

TC Level
1

"come out even."

Children who choose this book will enjoy talking about it. As they thumb through the book, a close look at the detailed illustrations can lead to many discussions and much speculation about who and where are the people who point to the exotic cats. Readers in partnerships may also attempt to problem-solve for the names of the cats (illustrated on the front and end pages of the book) using the picture and the first letter of the word as cues.

Young writers can learn to think and plan out their own books before actually writing them as Carle has clearly planned out his book. Instead of simply drawing whatever comes to mind on each page, a child might decide to make a book using *Have You Seen My Cat?* as a model text, exploring, for example, the use of both drawings and text to tell a story, or a question and answer format.

Genre
Emergent Literacy Book; Picture Book

Teaching Uses
Independent Reading; Teaching Writing; Language Conventions; Interpretation; Partnerships; Small Group Strategy Instruction

Hedgehog is Hungry

Beverley Randell

Book Summary

First it is winter and Hedgehog sleeps. Then it is spring and hedgehog awakens with a hearty appetite. He eats a variety of bugs and small creatures one by one. The book ends by saying "Hedgehog is hungry in the spring."

Basic Book Information

The New PM Story Books are part of the Rigby PM Collection. The books tend to come in kits in where every book looks exactly like every other book. Some teachers think this is less than ideal because at every level a library should include a variety of books, each with its own individuality. On the other hand, these Story Books are an important resource for teachers for two important reasons. First, there are many of these at the early reading levels and secondly, they recognize the supports beginning readers need and offer them. Teachers feel that the PM Story Books are especially good at providing a lot of easy text, full of high frequency words. The PM Story Books use complete sentences: I see the cow./ I see the pig./ to reinforce the repetition of high frequency words and simple syntax.

The PM Readers are also somewhat unique in that a great many of even the earliest books, are stories. Many other early books tend to be label books, organized in a repetitive list structure, and it's nice to be able to also give beginning readers the opportunity to read stories that have not only problems and resolutions, but also characters children can follow through a series of books. The PM Readers contain many books about Ben and Sally.

Noteworthy Features

This book has sixteen numbered pages, with one or two lines per page, with only the last page wrapping a sentence over onto two lines. Each sentence is three to four words long. New words are highly supported by the illustrations. The print is large and well spaced. For each creature that the hedgehog comes across, there is a picture both in the illustration, and on the page with the text, right next to the word. In some cases though, readers may not know exactly what the creature in the picture is supposed to be, especially if they aren't familiar with slugs, snails, or other garden critters.

Teaching Ideas

Teachers may want to give a book introduction to introduce what may be an unfamiliar animal to the readers, the hedgehog. As students check the cover the teacher may read the title, *Hedgehog is Hungry,* and ask what kind of food a hedgehog might eat. Readers will then go off to find out for themselves, as the teacher moves among them.

Illustrator
Drew Aitken

Publisher
Rigby PM Story Book Collection, 1987

ISBN
0435067281

TC Level
2

This book is appropriate for readers learning to match one spoken word to one written one. The teacher can cue the reader to find a known sight word, which will serve as an anchor for a one-to-one match. The child who is reading books on this level will probably recognize a few sight words and can use these words to "anchor" or pin down his pointing.

Independent readers will also benefit from the teacher's encouragement to "cross-check" as well. Successful readers cross-check, or integrate cues from a variety of sources including sight words, the picture, and the initial letter sound to make meaning.

It is not as easy as it may at first seem to comprehend what is happening in this story, despite the few repetitive words. If a reader reads this book with a partner and the two of them stop to talk often (perhaps putting Post-Its every few pages) this will help them comprehend the tale. In a conference with the partners, a teacher might suggest that sometimes when reading a book it helps to talk about how much time is going by in the story. It is winter when the story opens, and spring on the next page. Some readers may assume spring came rather abruptly, and some may assume a great deal of time has passed from one page to the next.

Also the words on the last page, that say, "Hedgehog is hungry in the spring," seem to imply that he hasn't eaten yet. Or is it that he hasn't yet eaten his fill? In partner discussions, readers will debate these points, and use their inferring skills and personal experience to support their inferences.

Book Connections

The Very Hungry Caterpillar by Eric Carle, although written at a much more difficult reading level, is about a similar topic and has a similar structure to this book. Both are about creatures that eat everything that comes across their paths. Children might find that having *The Very Hungry Caterpillar* read aloud to them serves as an excellent introduction to *Hedgehog is Hungry*.

Genre
Emergent Literacy Book

Teaching Uses
Independent Reading; Language Conventions; Partnerships; Interpretation; Whole Group Instruction

A Field Guide to the Classroom Library, Lucy Calkins and the Teachers College Reading and Writing Project, Heinemann, ©2002 Teachers College, Columbia University; http://www.heinemann.com/fieldguides

Hello, Goodbye

Leonie Eriksen

Book Summary

This is a simple story with a plot that develops through the pictures. In the text each animal says "hello" to another one and the other one says "goodbye." The pairing of the animals that are traditional "enemies"-cat with dog, bird with the fly, and so on, along with the expressions on the faces of the animals, explains why the "goodbye" animal departs. The surprise ending, with the spider licking its lips and only one wing of the fly left, lends a bit of humor to the story.

Basic Book Information

The story is told in seven pages of text. There is one sentence per page. Each sentence repeats either the pattern "'Hello,' said the ___." or "'Goodbye,' said the ___." There is an exception on the last page. The spider says both "hello" and "goodbye" as it swallows the fly.

The text consistently appears at the top of each page, making reading easier for the beginning reader. The illustrations are clever, cartoon-like drawings that tell the story. The story is intended to be humorous and the illustrations reflect this. While there is a hint of a problem/resolution plot, it is only a hint.

Noteworthy Features

This is a third-person narration told in dialogue. The sentence construction consists of a greeting within quotation marks followed by a "speaker-tag." Readers must infer the story from the pictures. Eight different words are used in the text. The repeated sentence pattern makes the introduction and practice in context of such high frequency words as *said*, *hello*, and *goodbye* easier for the beginning reader.

Teaching Ideas

Teachers might want to introduce this book by discussing the title, asking the questions, "What do we usually say when we see a friend?" and "When we are leaving, what might we say?" They might prompt students to look at the letters in the words for clues to the word. Once the students have identified the title, teachers might want to continue the discussion by asking: Do cats and dogs *usually* get along? Students will no doubt share examples of exceptions-comments that teachers can use to emphasize the meaning of "usually." Teachers might follow such a discussion by asking students to predict what the cat and dog might be saying. Since each of the sentences in the story involves quotation marks, teachers might want to give an example of that sentence structure, perhaps using the suggestions

Illustrator
Ian McNee

Publisher
Rigby, 1988

ISBN
0763500569

TC Level
2

A Field Guide to the Classroom Library, Lucy Calkins and the Teachers College Reading and Writing Project, Heinemann, ©2002 Teachers College, Columbia University; http://www.heinemann.com/fieldguides

students give about what the dog or cat is saying.

The story is told through the illustrations. Teachers might do a picture walk or "walkthrough" with students, guiding them to interpret the action in each of the pictures. They might prompt an inference by asking a question such as "Why is the cat running away, do you think?" Teachers might also ask students to find the title words "hello" or "goodbye" in the sentence, the name of each animal, and notice the quotation marks, indicating "talk" or "conversation."

Teachers might follow such a walk through with a shared reading, reading each sentence aloud and inviting students to join in. This is also an opportunity for teachers to emphasize the importance of reading with expression. Students should reread the story silently.

Teachers might want to have students draw one of the animals, placing the "Hello" and "Goodbye" in a "balloon" above the head of the animal. They might follow this by holding a "Readers Theater" performance, where each student "reads" the part of the animal in the drawing. Teachers might encourage students to improvise, perhaps making the sound the animal makes, as well as saying "hello" or "goodbye."

To check comprehension, teachers might invite students to retell the story to their reading partners, explaining why each animal said "Goodbye" and drawing conclusions about what happened to the fly. This may lead to a lively discussion or debate.

Book Connections

Students would probably enjoy listening to the book *There Was an Old Woman Who Swallowed a Fly* as a follow-up to this book, since there are similar events in that story.

Genre
Emergent Literacy Book; Picture Book

Teaching Uses
Independent Reading; Whole Group Instruction; Interpretation; Partnerships

Huggles Can Juggle . . .

Joy Cowley

Book Summary

Huggles Can Juggle . . . is an amusing story of a whimsical, indigo-colored creature who loves to juggle. The book is a list of the things Huggles juggles. The picture shows that he juggles first with one hand, then two hands. He balances on one foot, then on one hand, and then on the other foot. He even balances an egg on his nose. On each page one more object is added to the items being juggled. The story comes to a much-anticipated conclusion when everything, including Huggles, comes tumbling down. The last two words of the book state simply, "an accident."

Basic Book Information

Written by Joy Cowley, the famous New Zealand author of *Mrs. Wishy-Washy*, this fictional book is part of the Sunshine Collection of books published by Wright Group/McGraw-Hill. The book is tiny, and it looks like it belongs on a rack full of identical books, but it has been specifically written and designed to support very early readers. This book is part of a series about Huggles.

The Sunshine Reading Program was first developed by Wendy Pye, Inc. of New Zealand, and continued by Wright Group/McGraw-Hill in the United States. The books incorporate predictable sentence patterns, rhyme, rhythm, repetition, and illustrations that match the text. Together, these features support the earliest readers. Each story has a surprise ending.

Noteworthy Features

Although this is about as simple a book as one could find, it does contain ellipsis after the title and before the conclusion, indicating something is about to happen. The high frequency word "an" occurs on every page. The sans-serif typeface is clear and the words are well spaced, allowing for one-to-one matching. Interest is sustained by Huggles' ever-changing positions portrayed on each page in lighthearted, watercolor illustrations. Each successive page adds one more recognizable item to the picture and the accompanying text names it. The humorous character makes children laugh and they love anticipating the ultimate outcome.

Teaching Ideas

The teacher will need to read this title aloud, while pointing out the words to the child. Though some titles can be deduced based on the picture and knowledge of a few sight words, this title is way out of range for children who are reading Level 1 books. Readers will not be able to decode the title on their own. Some teachers might decide to do a more full-blown book

Illustrator
Elizabeth Fuller

Publisher
Wright Group, 1986

ISBN
0780248759

TC Level
1

A Field Guide to the Classroom Library, Lucy Calkins and the Teachers College Reading and Writing Project, Heinemann, ©2002 Teachers College, Columbia University; http://www.heinemann.com/fieldguides

introduction, asking the reader if he knows what juggling is and saying, "In this book, you'll see Huggles can juggle more and more things, but something happens at the end. . . . " However, teachers shouldn't push for this sort of full introduction because a reader can figure the story out and it is best to leave this thinking work in the child's hands.

A teacher who knows early readers well might wish that this book had more words on each page. If each page had read, "Huggles can juggle an orange. / Huggles can juggle an.../" rather than just "an orange, / an apple..." readers would have easier access into each new page (they'd expect it to repeat) and would get more practice pointing under the words. Nonetheless, this book encourages students to develop the early reading behaviors of using left to right directionality, one-to-one matching to anchor pointing, and self-correction.

A teacher may want to resist teaching this reader that Huggles rhymes with juggles. A reader comfortable with Level 3 books could profitably reread books such as this one looking for rhymes and discover this, but readers reading Level 1 books are well off if they notice first consonants. Vowel clusters-and especially one as long and complex as - *uggles*-aren't next on their horizon!

The reader of this book may miscue by reading "an" as "the" (i.e., reading "the orange" for "an orange"). This child will profit from a bit of work on these sight words and also from work on pointing under the words, making sure each spoken word is represented by a written word. Teachers should let the child mispoint and self-correct and avoid rushing in to prevent the problem in the first place.

A reader of Level 1 books shouldn't be expected to "sound out" or "chunk" words such as *elephant* or *umbrella*. These are easily recognizable objects from the picture, and children who stall over reading these words simply need to be reminded to check the picture. There will be lots of chances, when children are reading books with less picture support and easier-to-chunk words, for teachers to coach children to do some word work. Now may not be the best time for this.

Comprehension needs to be a huge and vital part of reading from Day One. Children can be encouraged to place Post-Its on pages that help them to think about the text or later to reread the book with a partner and then talk about the sections marked. One can imagine the great conversations and questions partners might have: What if the umbrella opened? (And, why doesn't it?) Wouldn't the ice cream cone fall apart? Why does his belly button change colors?

Book Connections

Huggles Can Juggle . . . is part of a series of books from Sunshine Level One Books. Other titles include *Huggles' Breakfast*, *Huggles Goes Away*, *What Is a Huggles?*, and *A Hug Is Warm*, all by Joy Cowley.

Genre
Emergent Literacy Book

A Field Guide to the Classroom Library, Lucy Calkins and the Teachers College Reading and Writing Project, Heinemann, ©2002 Teachers College, Columbia University; http://www.heinemann.com/fieldguides

Teaching Uses
Independent Reading; Language Conventions; Interpretation; Read Aloud;
Partnerships; Small Group Strategy Instruction

I Can See

Adria Klein

Book Summary

I Can See is a list book of animals and their colors. It's written in a consistent pattern, "I can see a . . . " with a different colored animal on each page.

Basic Book Information

This eight page book is written in a consistent pattern, "I can see a . . . " until the last page, which breaks the pattern by asking the question, "What can you see?" Color photographs illustrate the one new word, an animal, on each page.

Noteworthy Features

I Can See has many supports for beginning readers. The text is large, well spaced, and in an easy to read font. The text is consistently placed at the bottom of the page on a white background. Spacing between words is enlarged to support one-to-one matching. Each page begins with the same four high frequency words: *I, can, see, a.* The word that corresponds to the color of the animal on each page is the color of the animal. For example, on the page "I can see a yellow snake." the word "yellow" is actually in yellow type. Like many pattern books, the last page breaks the pattern.

Although color words are familiar to many beginning readers, it may be challenging for some to determine the word "gray" and that the whale is "black" and not "blue."

Teaching Ideas

Some teachers may want to preview the animals and colors depicted in the text. If a teacher does decide to pre-teach the animals, a quick picture walk is enough. "Oh, look, there's a _____," can be said without making the tone of this introduction that of "drill-and-kill" on vocabulary words. If a teacher wants to do less pre-teaching she may choose to leave more words in the child's hands, and to allow some misnaming of animals, at least in the child's initial journey through the text.

A child who is ready to do some good reading work with this book will have already spent time writing her own stories and will have joined with the class in shared readings of books like this one. From all these opportunities, the child may already have learned to recognize the word "I," to expect books to make sense, and that words go with the pictures. On her own, such a child might construct a version of this book, perhaps thinking that it says, "I see a _____." This child will have done a lot of things right, recognizing "I," looking between the picture and the print, expecting this

A Field Guide to the Classroom Library, Lucy Calkins and the Teachers College Reading and Writing Project, Heinemann, ©2002 Teachers College, Columbia University; http://www.heinemann.com/fieldguides

book to be like others she has read, anticipating a pattern, and so on. But, the child may not be pointing at the print at all, or may be doing this loosely without self-correcting when it doesn't come out evenly.

When a teacher pulls alongside this child or a partnership of two children who are having a go at this text independently, the teacher may want to stay quiet for a bit. If the child or children pause when the teacher approaches expecting him to take charge, the teacher needs to say, "Keep going. I'm just watching." After a bit, teachers can coach children to point under the words, to "read with their fingers." A teacher might say, "Can I read the title and the first page to you? That might help." Pointing under the words while reading the first page can show them how the color of the word matches what the word says.

The high frequency words at the start of each page make this book a good one for readers who are getting better at pointing to words while they say them. The fact that the print is colored to match what the word says is a nice twist because the colored font draws readers to the font as a source of information, reinforcing that it isn't only the picture that tells them what the word says-the letters do as well. Of course, the last page with its pattern change will present some challenges.

A teacher might want to say, "The last page of this book has a twist, doesn't it?" so that readers come to expect a change on the last page and therefore are ready to attend more closely to the text when they reach that page.

Book Connections

A Birthday Cake by Joy Cowley also includes text written in different colors.

Genre
Emergent Literacy Book

Teaching Uses
Independent Reading; Language Conventions; Partnerships; Small Group Strategy Instruction; Whole Group Instruction

I Eat Leaves

JoAnn Vandine

Book Summary

I Eat Leaves is a beginning nonfiction book that introduces young readers to creatures who eat leaves. Each animal (and one invertebrate) introduces itself and then states what it eats. For example, "I am a koala. I eat leaves." The other herbivores in the book include a panda, a rabbit, and a giraffe, as well as a caterpillar. The book ends with a child asking the question, "Do I eat leaves?" The answer, of course, is "Yes!"

Basic Book Information

I Eat Leaves has 47 words, not including the one-word labels found in the illustrations specifically naming the type of leaf, from eucalyptus to lettuce. The book has eight pages. Each page of text includes two short sentences placed below the illustration. The second sentence, "I eat leaves," is repeated on each page, with the exception of the last two pages. Most sentences end with a period, one ends with a question mark, and an exclamation mark follows the word "Yes!" on the last page. The clearly spaced words encourage one-to-one correspondence and directionality. High frequency words used are: *I, am, a,* and *eat.*

Noteworthy Features

The text provides the supports beginning readers need through its use of repetition and predictable language patterns. Each large, colorful illustration shows both animal and fauna in naturalistic detail and closely matches the text below. Labels identify the name of each plant being eaten, like eucalyptus and acacia, which adds to the book's authenticity. The overall attractiveness of the book will entice readers to return to it over and over again.

The book presents a change-up at the end when the pattern shifts from repetitive statements to a question being asked instead. This invites the young reader to learn and apply new skills and strategies, while using what is known to figure out the unknown. A closer attention to the print is also required.

Teaching Ideas

I Eat Leaves introduces informational text to emergent readers. The familiar theme of animals has meaning and appeal to most young children. There may be some unknown creatures in the book depending on a child's experience, so a book introduction might include a discussion of the animals in the pictures. Animals may be named and where the students might have seen them may be discussed.

A Field Guide to the Classroom Library, Lucy Calkins and the Teachers College Reading and Writing Project, Heinemann, ©2002 Teachers College, Columbia University; http://www.heinemann.com/fieldguides

Illustrator
Cynthia A. Belcher

Publisher
Mondo Publishing, 1995

ISBN
1572550414

TC Level
2

This book can also offer an introduction to the features of nonfiction text, the purpose for reading such texts, and how such texts can be read. Nonfiction features that can be pointed out are the graphic use of labels to identify things and how information can be gained through the pictures, as well as the text. This book may also be in a nonfiction genre study.

This book may also be used in a reading center about animals and their habitats. Readers can ask what is the same and what is different about these creatures. For example, they all eat leaves, but they eat different kinds of leaves.

Book Connections

Other titles in this series from Book Shop from Mondo Publishing include: *Fun With Hats, Honk!, My Circus Family*, *Run! Run!*, and *Will You Play With Us?*

Newbridge also publishes many rich resources that would enhance a study of nonfiction and that are appropriate for the K-1 emergent reader. Some titles that could be used along with *I Eat Leaves*, include *Everyone Eats, Animals Hide*, and *Who Lives in a Tree?*

Genre
Nonfiction; Emergent Literacy Book

Teaching Uses
Independent Reading; Content Area Study; Reading and Writing Nonfiction

I Went Walking

Sue Williams

Book Summary

I Went Walking tells the story of a young boy who is on a walk. Along the way he meets many farm animals. There is a refrain throughout the book as the boy encounters each animal. The little boy says, "I went walking." An unidentified voice asks, "What do you see?" The little boy then responds, "I saw a _____ (e.g., brown cow) looking at me." At the end of the book the little boy turns around and finds that all the animals are following him. On the last page, the parade of animals and the young boy dance merrily.

Basic Book Information

This is a 30-page book with vibrant illustrations by Julie Vivas. The fantastical illustrations resemble watercolor paintings. The text is clearly printed in a black font against a white background. Text placement varies from page to page. There are a number of high frequency vocabulary words throughout the story.

Noteworthy Features

One of the most distinguishing features of this book is its three-phrase refrain, repeated throughout the book. The only two words that change each time the refrain appears, are the color and name of the animal (i.e., pink pig).

This book is representative of many other books in Library A. The book focuses on animals and colors, which are popular themes in this library. Like many other books, there is also a twist at the end. The last page of the book, reads, "I saw a lot of animals following me!"

Another way in which this book is like many others in Library A, is its cumulative structure. Throughout the book, as the boy meets the animals, they add onto a parade following the young boy on his walk.

There is one feature of *I Went Walking* that is somewhat puzzling. There are wrap-around sentences throughout the book. But the part of the sentence that appears on the second line, has initial capitalization (i.e., first line: "I saw a green duck" second line: "Looking at me."). Children who have learned that only the start of a new sentence or proper names should appear in caps may be confused. Teachers can perhaps present a disclaimer and explain to children that it is incorrect to use capital letters in the middle of a sentence.

Another slightly confusing element of the story is its colors. The "red" cow could easily be identified as "brown." Children who are using the pictures to figure out the colors of the animals might easily misidentify the color. Checking the initial consonant will help them self-correct.

Another noteworthy feature of this book is its unidentified narrator. The

Illustrator
Julie Vivas

Publisher
Voyager Books, Harcourt Brace, 1989

ISBN
0152380116

TC Level
2

boy says, "I went walking." A voice responds, "What did you see?" There is no reference as to who this speaker may be throughout the book.

Teaching Ideas

I Went Walking provides a lot of support for young readers. It is highly repetitive. There are only 4-lines throughout the entire book. The only words that change in the refrain are the color and name of the animal. These words can be decoded by using the corresponding pictures that depict the animal.

When the teacher pulls alongside readers who are reading this book she may want to coach one child by prompting him to reread when he encounters difficulty and encourage another to look at the picture and get her mouth ready to look at the sound. All students should be encouraged to check for meaning.

I Went Walking is a wonderful book to use in reading partnerships. The question and answer format lends itself to readers taking on the different roles of the speakers. One student might say, "I went walking." Then the other student would reply, "What did you see?" Children have a lot of fun with this playful back and forth. This type of reading should sound more conversational and will help to develop students' fluency with reading text, an important factor in building comprehension.

The illustrations in *I Went Walking* are really spectacular. They help to create a sense of suspense that young children can enjoy. On the pages that say, "What did you see?" there is a small part of the animal peeking out (e.g., the tail of a black cat sticking out from a basket). Children will probably be yelling out, "It's a black cat!" but until they turn the page, they won't find out if they guessed right.

Teachers who want to use this book as a basis for a related phonics lesson might want to work on the *-ing* ending: *looking*, *walking* and *following* are all words in this book that use this ending. If teachers wanted to add *-ing* words on a word wall, they should make sure that every student in the class is able to read these words. Every student should feel that the words on the word wall are ones they are confident reading and using in their writing.

Genre
Picture Book

Teaching Uses
Independent Reading; Partnerships; Small Group Strategy Instruction

A Field Guide to the Classroom Library, Lucy Calkins and the Teachers College Reading and Writing Project, Heinemann, ©2002 Teachers College, Columbia University; http://www.heinemann.com/fieldguides

I'm in Charge of Celebrations

Byrd Baylor

Book Summary

The narrator tells us about some of the 108 celebrations she has created for herself in the desert of the southwestern United States. After she takes part in an extraordinary natural event, such as observing a green cloud shaped like a parrot or walking along a trail close to a coyote, she records the occasion in her notebook and decides on a fitting way to celebrate the anniversary in the future. She laughs when people ask her if she is lonely in the desert, because she has become so familiar with the desert and the creatures that inhabit it.

Basic Book Information

Two-page spreads of text and illustrations comprise this 26-page picture book. Each double-page spread contains two or three columns of text, with columns holding from one to five words. Streaks of color from the sparse illustrations angle around the text. Byrd Baylor is the author of four Caldecott Honor books, including three illustrated by Peter Parnall.

Noteworthy Features

Short lines and stanzas give *I'm in Charge of Celebrations* the feel of a poem. With words such as "you" and "Friend," the narrator addresses readers directly. Though her voice is simple and colloquial, her language occasionally becomes lyrical. For example, when describing the gyrations of whirlwinds she has seen, the narrator uses a series of line breaks and the repeated word *and* to convey a sense of a twisting that picks up speed like a whirlwind itself: ". . . moving / up from the flats, / swirling / and swaying / and falling / and turning, / picking up sticks / and sand / and feathers / and dry tumbleweeds."

The book is arranged so that each celebration begins on a different page, much like the books that contain a compilation of poems about the holidays in a calendar year.

Many readers will not be familiar with the desert landscape in this book. Some will imagine that a desert is nothing but sand, and be surprised that the text names so many plants and animals that thrive in this habitat. Many will not know what a yucca is, and some might not know what a cactus is. In general, the least familiar words in the book are not likely to interfere with basic comprehension, though teachers can remind children of strategies to get the gist of unknown words.

Teaching Ideas

I'm in Charge of Celebrations serves the writing workshop not only as a

Illustrator
Peter Parnall

Publisher
Simon and Schuster, 1986

ISBN
0689806205

TC Level
7

model of good writing, but also as a model of writers' habits. In the story, the narrator keeps a notebook. She tells what she writes down and why. Students can look at how the narrator uses her notebook and get ideas for working with their own writers' notebook. Teachers might encourage children to notice the natural world-even the ants crawling through cracks in the playground blacktop-to see if they can find something to write about and celebrate.

Before reading *I'm in Charge of Celebrations*, teachers may begin by reading a different book about the everyday events that children experience (e.g., Sandra Cisneros' *Hairs /Pelitos*). Teachers might ask, "How do you suppose this author got the idea to write a whole book about this? I bet that because she's a writer, she really notices the littlest things. I could write a book about my hands. I've got this green magic marker on my thumb from this morning when we were working on our science studies, and I've got a scar on my finger from when I fell off my bike when I was six. I'm noticing that there are a lot of stories, right in my hand." Soon the class might imagine stories from daily life they could put down on paper.

The illustrations of the book, with their broad swaths of unusual colors, often do not immediately attract children's attention, though they do invite questions. Why is the rabbit portrayed in the middle of a circle? Why is the tail of the falling star touching the narrator and going all around her?

Book Connections

Byrd Baylor and Peter Parnall's Caldecott Honor books are *The Desert Is Theirs*; *Hawk, I'm Your Brother*; and *The Way to Start a Day*. Eve Merriam's *The Wise Woman and Her Secret* and Norma Farber's books of poems are good companion texts.

Genre
Picture Book

Teaching Uses
Teaching Writing; Read Aloud; Independent Reading

A Field Guide to the Classroom Library, Lucy Calkins and the Teachers College Reading and Writing Project, Heinemann, ©2002 Teachers College, Columbia University; http://www.heinemann.com/fieldguides

It Didn't Frighten Me

Janet Gross; Jerome Harste

Book Summary

This book begins with a picture of a child sitting up in bed after his dad had turned out the light for the night. The child sees an orange alligator in the tree outside his window. Then the next page shows the view outside the child's window and says, "But . . . that orange alligator didn't frighten me!" The text continues like this with the child seeing a purple witch, a pink dinosaur, and a lot of other scary and funny things. On the last page, the child sees a big brown owl saying, "Whooo me?" and the refrain changes to "And did it ever frighten me!"

Basic Book Information

This book was written by Janet Gross and by the renowned language arts researcher Jerry Harste who is known for coauthoring *Creating Classrooms for Authors and Inquirers*, with his colleague, Kathy Short.

This is a 23-page book with vivid, humorous illustrations. Each double-page spread has consistent text placement with the poem/refrain repeated on the left hand side of the page, and text supporting the picture of each new "creature" on the right hand side of the page.

Noteworthy Features

The book is a pitch black book with letters in white print, making a striking effect and matching the content and theme of the story.

The book reads like a song. Each verse in that song begins with a phrase that many of us know from scary stories, "One pitch black, very dark night. . . ." Like many early books the text is repetitive, but the unit that repeats is larger in this book than in many other books for beginning readers. In this book, the entire four-line "poem" repeats, with each stanza containing two words that vary-those words identify the new creature that is in the window frame.

Teaching Ideas

Because of its rhyme, song-like, and literary qualities, this would make a good choice for a shared reading text. If readers who are reading books at lots of different levels all hear this book read aloud to them and all join in chorus-like shared readings of the text, then this book need not be reserved only for Level 3 readers. If it's been a shared reading text, all children should feel they have it "under their belts." Even readers who cannot yet unlock the puzzle of unknown words using graphophonics may choose to read this book relying on the memorized refrain and the strong picture support just as they have done with easier but somewhat similar books such as *Brown*

Illustrator
Steve Romney

Publisher
Mondo Publishing, 1986

ISBN
157255097X

TC Level
3

Bear, Brown Bear What Do You See? or *Five Little Monkeys Jumping on the Bed*.

The teacher may decide to do a book introduction to offer an independent reader some support. If a teacher has access to additional copies, a book introduction could also be given to a small group of readers. In her introduction, one teacher said, "This book is arranged a little differently than many. It is kind of a song or poem. Once you've read the first page through one time, go back and read it again so you can pull it all together and make it sound like a song."

The sheer quantity of print on page 2 may intimidate a reader. A teacher therefore, may decide to scaffold the child through the first page. If, on the other hand, she's done an introduction with a group, she might say, "Why don't the four of you work on this first page together? Read it through and help each other. Then, when you have got it, go back and reread it to make it smooth." When giving an introduction to a single reader or a partner pair the teacher might say, "I'll stay here while you read this first page. I don't think you are going to need my help, but I'll be here." She wouldn't say, "I will be here just waiting to help" because she always want to be teaching toward independence.

A reader who is ready for this text will be able to use phonics knowledge to work out an unknown word, looking not just at the initial and final letters, but looking all the way across the word. The reader should also be cross-checking one cue against another, as well as self-correcting and monitoring for meaning.

It is very important to resist the urge to pre-teach a word like "pitch" to a Level 3 reader. Some teachers might be tempted to do this simply because the word "pitch" is sure to challenge a reader-but the word should be within the grasp of these readers and especially so if we encourage them to word-solve together. Human beings learn words best by using them in meaningful contexts and once the child reads this page with intonation, the child will probably recall the phrase "pitch black night."

Whether or not the teacher does an introduction, she will listen to children read and encourage them to "put the words together to make it smooth." This is a great book for teaching fluency and phrasing and readers, when they get to books with more text like this, often get bogged down and begin to read word by word. This is especially common for children reading at this difficulty level because when readers get to Level 3 and 4 books, the texts require them to slow down and chunk across words.

The book is full of literary language. A perfect example is the phrase, "I looked out my window only to see a . . ." a seven- or eight-year-old is unlikely to actually say "I looked out my window only to see," or even to say, "One pitch black, very dark night. . . ." The book is as challenging as it is because of this literary language, and readers of Level 3 and Level 4 books benefit when we tell them that the words in books sound like a story, and that writers often use literary or storybook language. This is a new feature of books at this level and beyond, and children benefit from being encouraged to feel and delight in and enjoy the sounds of a story. Because there are few challenges in this text other than the use of literary language, the book is a great one for this purpose.

A Field Guide to the Classroom Library, Lucy Calkins and the Teachers College Reading and Writing Project, Heinemann, ©2002 Teachers College, Columbia University; http://www.heinemann.com/fieldguides

Genre
Emergent Literacy Book; Poetry

Teaching Uses
Independent Reading; Partnerships; Small Group Strategy Instruction; Read Aloud

A Field Guide to the Classroom Library, Lucy Calkins and the Teachers College Reading and Writing Project, Heinemann, ©2002 Teachers College, Columbia University; http://www.heinemann.com/fieldguides

Jamaica's Find
Juanita Havill

FIELD GUIDE

Ⓐ Ⓑ Ⓒ Ⓓ

Book Summary

Jamaica, while playing alone in the park, comes across a red sock hat and a cuddly, stuffed gray dog. Instead of placing both items in the lost and found at the park house, Jamaica returns only the hat and takes the stuffed animal home. At home, Jamaica shows off her dog to her family, which is not thrilled about having a dirty stuffed dog sitting at the dinner table. Once Jamaica is asked to take it out of the kitchen area, she begins to think about whether she did the right thing by keeping the dog. She overhears her mother mention, "It probably belongs to a girl just like Jamaica." While sitting in her room and talking to her mother, Jamaica feels empathy for the owner and decides that she wants to return the dog to the park house. After bringing back the stuffed dog, Jamaica meets a girl named Kristin, the original owner of the stuffed animal. As Jamaica happily reunites Kristin with her missing dog, the girls exchange smiles and become friends.

Basic Book Information

This picture book is a winner of the 1987 Ezra Jack Keats New Writer Award and a Reading Rainbow Selection. This 32-page picture book has at least one illustration for each pair of facing pages. The text in the book can be found on both sides of the page and superimposed over some pictures. The watercolor illustrations in the book closely represent the written text.

Noteworthy Features

The text itself has been placed to fit around the illustrations. As such, words are not in any consistent place on the page. The illustrations, however, support the text carefully. The characters' expressive faces and postures can help children understand the emotions the text on each page describes.

Teaching Ideas

This book is about honesty, compassion, and making good decisions. Jamaica's moral dilemma of dealing with right and wrong is a thread woven from the beginning to the end of the book. In and outside the classroom, there are many ways in which children can learn from this book.

The book can be a mentor text for children who are trying to write their own personal narratives. Many children retell incidents in their own lives without consciously shaping them as stories. They would benefit from a reminder of the features of narrative, and from examples of successful, cohesive stories.

This book also lends itself to teaching the strategy of prediction. Readers could use prior knowledge and looking at the cover to predict what the story

Series
Jamaica series

Publisher
Houghton Mifflin Company, 1986

ISBN
0590425048

TC Level
5

will be about. Throughout the text, they can predict what will happen next and explain the textual basis for their predictions.

Book Connections

Juanita Havill has written two other books with the same main character, *Jamaica and Brianna* and *Jamaica Tag-Along*. In this text, as well as Rod Clement's *Grandpa's Teeth*, the main characters deal with issues of honesty, making choices and attending to their consciences. *Believing Sophie*, by Hazel Hutchins, and *Fanny's Dream*, by Caralyn Buehner, both address the major themes presented in *Jamaica's Find* and show how characters resolve similar problems.

Genre
Picture Book

Teaching Uses
Independent Reading; Teaching Writing; Character Study; Critique

A Field Guide to the Classroom Library, Lucy Calkins and the Teachers College Reading and Writing Project, Heinemann, ©2002 Teachers College, Columbia University; http://www.heinemann.com/fieldguides

Just Like Daddy

Frank Asch

Book Summary

This story is written in first person by a young bear who retells his day from waking up until he catches a big fish. After every episode, he says "...Just like Daddy." The story begins, "When I got up this morning, I yawned a big yawn...Just like Daddy." There is a surprise ending when the bear catches the fish "...Just like Mommy!" On the final page the illustration alone tells the ending of the story: the family frying fish over a campfire.

Basic Book Information

Some texts are narratives that contain a central character and move through time. Other books are lists, stringing equal episodes together. This book is a combination of the two structures. The young bear is retelling the chronological sequence of the day he went fishing, but because he adds the chorus of "Just like Daddy" after every event, the text also reads as if it were a list of what the young bear does in a day that is just like what Daddy does.

Noteworthy Features

The structure and repetitive refrains in this book, which are described above, provide support that readers need as they tackle the linguistic complexity of this book. For most readers, the challenge of this text lies not in accumulating the text into a cohesive whole (the patterns and steady progression through time make that easier), nor do they lie in the words themselves (although there are tough words here). Instead, the challenge lies especially in the syntax of those long, rich and varied sentences. Many of the sentences include clauses. The episodes do not occur in a simple next, next, next fashion. Instead there are passages such as "On the way, I picked a flower" and "When we got to the lake...."

   Even in books that move chronologically through time or through a catalog of different topics, there are often repeating elements that tie the text together and provide unity to it. These repeated elements might be a metaphor or color. In this relatively simple book, there are several repeating elements; the repeating text is one. Another is the little red bird who visits every page.

Teaching Ideas

As children read this book, they can become more accustomed to reading long, complex sentences that contain adverbial clauses. The children will receive support in this from the very simple chronological structure of the book and its repeating refrains, because both of these elements will help readers have the confidence to tackle the challenges the book poses.

Illustrator
Frank Asch

Publisher
Simon & Schuster, 1981

ISBN
0671664573

TC Level
4

 A Field Guide to the Classroom Library, Lucy Calkins and the Teachers College Reading and Writing Project, Heinemann, ©2002 Teachers College, Columbia University; http://www.heinemann.com/fieldguides

Teachers may want to use the text as a model for writing by asking: "What do you like to do that is 'just like Mommy or Daddy'or somebody else in your family?"

Book Connections

Frank Asch has written many books about Little Bear. Teachers may want to collect them in a reading center so that students may follow the character (and Little Bird) through several adventures.

Genre
Emergent Literacy Book; Picture Book

Teaching Uses
Independent Reading; Language Conventions; Small Group Strategy Instruction; Character Study; Interpretation

Koala Lou

Mem Fox

Book Summary

A young koala bear, longing to hear her mother speak lovingly to her as she did before all the other children came along, plans to win her distracted parent's attention. Little Koala Lou enters the Bush Olympics gum tree climbing event, but only comes in second. Her mother finds and comforts her with the words she had been waiting for, and reassurance that Koala Lou is as loved as ever.

Basic Book Information

This is an extremely popular book among both adults and children. The realistic and adorable illustrations, poignant story and the easy-to-identify-with feelings in the story, seem to appeal to everyone.

Mem Fox has written more than twenty-five picture books for children, including *Zoo-Looking*, *Feathers and Fools*, andHattie *and the Fox*. More information about Mem Fox can be found on her website at www.memfox.net.

Noteworthy Features

The story is straightforward, and the pictures in the text provide support to children trying to figure out the general storyline. However, in most cases the pictures won't help children with particular words, and the vocabulary is both lyrical and occasionally sophisticated. All of the animal characters are species native to Australia, and some may be unknown to the American reader. Occasionally in the story, there are some words written as they sound phonetically, in order to communicate the animals' Australian way of speaking English. Readers can usually figure these out on their own by reading them aloud a time or two like *platypus*, *emu*, and *kookaburra*.

The story revolves around the "Bush Olympics" with the "gum tree climbing event," but neither one is explained. Readers who hold on to the story can formulate guesses as to what the Bush Olympics will involve and what the gum tree climbing event will entail. As they read on the story will support these guesses.

The story is filled with literary language and is written for the ear. "At last the day of the Olympics arrived." Hearing books like this one read aloud many times will help readers develop a sense of literary story language.

Teaching Ideas

This is an all-time favorite read aloud book for many teachers. The book's lyrical language, drama and pace all combine to make it the sort of book that children long to hear over and over. No one should hesitate to give in

Illustrator
Pamela Lofts

Publisher
Harcourt, Brace & Company, 1988

ISBN
0152005021

TC Level
8

A Field Guide to the Classroom Library, Lucy Calkins and the Teachers College Reading and Writing Project, Heinemann, ©2002 Teachers College, Columbia University; http://www.heinemann.com/fieldguides

to everyone's fondest hopes and do just that, for children benefit from hearing books such as this one read aloud so often that the structure and music of stories is internalized. It is from hearing stories like this read aloud that children come to sense that there's a time, in a story, for something to happen, that they learn to feel tension mounting, to catch their breath in suspense, to turn the page just a little bit faster because soon they'll know how it all turns out. When children grow up with a sense for how good stories flow, they'll instinctively write and tell their own stories that work for readers, and they'll read books expecting to find those elements that good authors always include.

A teacher won't want to read this aloud without reading it herself first several times, learning to hurry the pacing in some places and to slow it down in others. By reading a book such as this one well, teachers can help children fall in love with all books.

The first time a teacher reads *Koala Lou* to a group, she may want to read it straight through. Then the teacher may read it again to give children opportunities to talk to partners, or to listen for what Mem Fox has done as a writer so they can emulate her, etc.

Some teachers encourage listeners to talk early and often about the connections between a text and their own lives. One of the big life themes for many children is the arrival of siblings who compete for attention. It may be wise, however, to postpone this discussion and to first help children linger over and attend to the story at hand and perhaps the characters. What kind of characters are these? How do you know this? In this story, the main character is Koala Lou and she's a koala, but children can begin to think, "If she were a person, what kind of a person would she be?" A reader might say, "We don't know," because her characteristics are not spelled out in the text. But the reader can get to know a character by her actions, and surely Koala Lou's actions show determination, resolve, energy and a longing to be loved. The reader also gets to know a character by seeing what others think of them, and this book says that she was so soft and round that all who saw her loved her.

More sophisticated readers can notice not only the traits of characters, but the ways authors help readers know and care about the characters they create. Koala Lou is a richly developed character because she isn't just one thing. She isn't just lovely, brave and good. She's also brooding and able to sulk and be competitive. It's not important for children to produce these adjectives to describe her, but it is important for them to see they care about her all the more because she's complex and life-like; she's what some might call "human."

A teacher may want to point out that one of the most memorable lines in the story is the line Koala Lou's mother says (and then, as Koala Lou got older, doesn't say) "Koala Lou, I do love you!" Mem Fox could have written this differently. She could have had the mother say, "Koala Lou, I love you." But Mem knows how to write for the ear, to write so this and countless other passages of the text have an irresistible rhythm.

In their own writing, children may want to find an important section and to rewrite it so that it sounds good to the ear. Mem Fox rewrote her opening more than 50 times before she had it right! The passage is also memorable because these are the actual words a character says. Throughout the text, there aren't a lot of quotes, but the quoted passages are very important, each

A Field Guide to the Classroom Library, Lucy Calkins and the Teachers College Reading and Writing Project, Heinemann, ©2002 Teachers College, Columbia University; http://www.heinemann.com/fieldguides

one helping to explain much about the character speaking. The way characters talk (as well as the content of the talk) reveals them. Again, children may want to reread their own writing and consider, "Do I have any characters talking from time to time? Does the way they talk reveal their characters?"

This book clearly conveys messages. With younger readers a teacher might simply ask, "What is the whole story trying to tell us?" With older, more experienced readers, the book can provide an opportunity for teachers to help them interpret texts.

Many readers feel that the book's message is that a child will get sad when another child is born and the parent has less time to spend, but that the parent really loves the first child as much as ever. Or, readers might decide the message is that even if someone has no time to tell you she loves you, she does love you, and you needn't try to win a big prize to gain her love.

If teachers want to push their student's thinking about the book, and give them reason to find textual support for their ideas, they may want to offer alternate conclusions about the message of the story. When they do this, students have to turn to the text to decide which interpretation fits best, and why. Perhaps the message of the story is that you need to at least try for the big prize to get the attention, or perhaps it is that only when you feel really low down will you finally get the affection you need. Perhaps the message, intended or not, is about what happens when you strive for attention for yourself, instead of simply asking for more or sharing in whatever is keeping the attention-giver so busy! In any case, students can discuss and find evidence to support their interpretations and decide what they think about the truth or justness of the messages they find.

Book Connections

Mem Fox has written more than twenty-five picture books for children, including
Zoo-Looking, Feathers and Fools, and *Hattie and the Fox.* More information about Mem Fox can be found on her website at www.memfox.net.

Genre
Picture Book

Teaching Uses
Author Study; Read Aloud; Interpretation; Critique

A Field Guide to the Classroom Library, Lucy Calkins and the Teachers College Reading and Writing Project, Heinemann, ©2002 Teachers College, Columbia University; http://www.heinemann.com/fieldguides

Legs

Rachel Gosset; Margaret Ballinger

Book Summary

This book depicts creatures grouped according to how many legs they have: 0, 2, 4, 6, or 8. It ends with a picture of some real and some made-up creatures with large or questionable numbers of legs.

Basic Book Information

This book has seven pages. On each page there are several creatures in the cut-paper illustration, and the text below the picture reads simply, "No legs." or, "Two legs." and so on. The last page, with the illustration of children together in a dragon costume and a centipede, asks readers "How many legs?"

Noteworthy Features

The two-word captions under the pictures are followed by a period, although they are not full sentences.

Teaching Ideas

Some teachers teach the word "legs" to children as they introduce the book and tell them the title. Once children can identify this key word, they can read most of the book independently. If they then realize that the number corresponds to the number of legs found on the animals on the page, they can count legs to discover what the second word on each page says. Teachers may also remind readers that when encountering an unknown word, the picture can help but it's also important to look at the first letter.

Readers who are practicing emergent skills such as one-to-one matching, directionality, "getting their month ready" for an unfamiliar word, or locating a known word to help problem-solve for an unknown word can use this book to support those behaviors.

Some children end up using this book as the starting point for a scientific exploration of legs. The open-ended last page of the book invites readers to ask questions like, "Why did the book stop there? Aren't there creatures with ten legs? Twelve? And for that matter, why do the numbers of legs go up by twos? Do centipedes and millipedes really need an even number of legs for balance? Are there any creatures that have an odd number of legs? Why or why not?" Teachers may want to discreetly add creatures and objects like starfish, sea anemones, and tables or stools into the mix to give children more fuel for discussions of exactly what legs are and are not.

Illustrator
Celina Mosbauer

Publisher
Scholastic, Reading Discovery, 1996

ISBN
0439116627

TC Level
2

Genre
Emergent Literacy Book

Teaching Uses
Partnerships; Small Group Strategy Instruction; Independent Reading; Content Area Study

Little Brother

Joy Cowley

Book Summary

Little Brother describes how a family gets ready for a new baby. Each member of the family makes a gift for the baby. They all bring their gifts to Mother in the hospital.

Basic Book Information

This is one of the Story Box books, and is written by Joy Cowley, the beloved author of *Mrs. Wishy-Washy* and countless other books for early readers. As a Story Box book, this book looks like it belongs in a kit of identical little books but in this library it is interspersed with a lovely variety of shapes and sizes of books. The Wright Company provides professional development as well as books for teachers, and has been a major force in supporting the move toward literature-based classrooms. The company uses its knowledge of early reading development to publish texts that are supportive of early readers.

Noteworthy Features

There are fifteen different words used over the seven pages of text in this storybook. Six of these words are repeated at least once. The sentence structure follows a simple subject/predicate pattern. The first four pages use the sentence pattern: _____ made a _____. The fifth sentence adds the words, "to give to mother" to the sentence. The next sentence breaks the pattern: "Mother had a baby." And the last sentence continues that thought: "my baby brother."

The illustrations on each page support the accompanying text and will help children figure out some words. The illustrations are realistic and sensitively wrought. The male figures break gender stereotypes: Father bakes a cake, Uncle knits a blanket. The illustrations fill the page, leaving just enough room at the bottom for the sentence they illustrate. The story is a simple list of gifts that members of the family make for the new arrival.

There is no dialogue. The narrator is the sister of the new baby. Although the text does not reveal this, the pictures do. Since the story is really told through the pictures, readers must make inferences by matching details in the picture with the words in the sentence.

While this book is slightly more challenging for the beginning reader than some others at this level, it provides enough assistance by way of picture clues and the repeated sentence pattern to make it manageable.

Teaching Ideas

If readers have been taught to look through the book before reading the

A Field Guide to the Classroom Library, Lucy Calkins and the Teachers College Reading and Writing Project, Heinemann, ©2002 Teachers College, Columbia University; http://www.heinemann.com/fieldguides

Illustrator
Jo Davies

Publisher
Wright Group, 1998

ISBN
0780274148

TC Level
1

print, they'll probably notice that each of the people is working on something. If the teacher is present to do a book introduction, he could support the child's experience of the book by asking, on a few of the pages, "What did this person make?" If the teacher thought readers needed an even more supportive introduction, he could ask, "Who could all these presents be for?"

This book allows students to discuss some of the cultural features the story depicts. For example, teachers might want students to react to the gifts each of the characters has prepared and if their family members might make similar gifts.

Students might also discuss what having a new baby brother might be like. Teachers might have students draw and label pictures of their own family, using words like *mother*, *father*, *sister*, *brother*, *aunt*, and *uncle*.

Book Connections

Peter's Chair by Ezra Jack Keats talks about a new addition to the family and the changes Peter goes through in accepting this new addition.

Genre
Emergent Literacy Book

Teaching Uses
Critique; Language Conventions; Interpretation; Independent Reading; Partnerships; Small Group Strategy Instruction

A Field Guide to the Classroom Library, Lucy Calkins and the Teachers College Reading and Writing Project, Heinemann, ©2002 Teachers College, Columbia University; http://www.heinemann.com/fieldguides

Looking for Bears
Ann Mace

Book Summary

School closes for the summer and a carefully equipped teacher drives off into the mountains of the local national park in search of live bears. She looks in the most likely places: by the lake, along the river, on the mountainside, and in the blackberry patch. The teacher concludes her search at the bottom of the mountain where she finds lots and lots of bears in the gift shop.

Basic Book Information

On most of the 12 pages in this text there are bears clearly shown in the illustrations. The bears not only help to reinforce the theme of the book but their placement within the colorful illustrations is useful in supporting the reader's decoding of unfamiliar words.

Noteworthy Features

The text is consistently placed on the bottom of each page. The repetition of the phrases "went looking for bears" and "she looked" helps to support early readers.

The discrepancy between the illustrations and the text on the opening page might pose a bit of a problem for some readers.

Teaching Ideas

This book is appropriate for young readers who have a solid but limited sight vocabulary and need texts with simple, predictable patterns.

The play between the illustrations and the text make it a good book to read with a partner. After the first reading, readers can spend time viewing the back cover to trace the route of the teacher. In a second read, partners can turn back to the cover to place themselves along the route. Partners can have the opportunity to practice retelling and to engage in good book talk. Teachers might model how readers might first read to themselves and use Post-Its to mark specific places in the text where they want to "stop and talk" with a partner.

If teachers are using reading centers as part of their independent reading work, this is a good book to use in a fact book center on animals. It answers the questions: Where do bears live? What do bears like to eat? What do bears do in the wild?

Book Connections

Where's the Bear? by Charlotte Pomerantz offers a different point of view

Illustrator
Ann Mace

Publisher
Richard C. Owens, 2000

ISBN
1572742682

TC Level
3

toward bears.

Genre
Emergent Literacy Book; Picture Book

Teaching Uses
Independent Reading; Partnerships; Small Group Strategy Instruction; Language Conventions; Content Area Study

Making a Memory
Margaret Ballinger

Book Summary

A little girl reflects on special memories that are represented through artifacts that are displayed on a shelf. Each object elicits a memory, beginning when she was five years old, and, in descending order, ending with a memory from when she was one year old. On each page, the little the girl discusses things she bought, drank, and so on at a given age. The book culminates with the little girl "making a memory"-a drawing for her father, so he too, will be able to have artifacts.

Basic Book Information

There are seven pages in the book, each with one line of text. A "memory bubble" illustration appears on each page, providing the reader with more information about the details of the memory.

Noteworthy Features

On each of the seven pages, there is one line of text that is consistently placed under the illustrations. Sentences switch between past and present tense. Pictures provide moderate support with the exception of the first and last pages. Each page begins with "I" followed by an action verb, and then followed by the word "this" (i.e., I bought this, I found this, I made this, etc.). The text contains many high frequency words including: *I, on, my, this, was, when, got, from, made, am, for*, and *dad*.

Teaching Ideas

A child who is reading this book will need to be able to read and make sense of the word "memory" in order to comprehend the text. A teacher might give a book introduction by saying, "*Making a Memory* is a story about a girl who thinks about her memories from the time she was little. She remembers special times when she was five, and four, and three, and so on. And then at the end, she makes a gift of memory for someone special."

This is an excellent book to use in a writing workshop, to support children in understanding that authors often write about childhood memories. Some primary teachers use this book as a touchstone text in a study of family stories. In a kindergarten or first grade class, children quickly notice the memory bubbles and relate them to speech bubbles. Sometimes, children borrow the memory bubbles and use them in their own writing. One child made a memory bubble about when he was three. In the center of his memory bubble was a little figure, which he said was his baby sister, and around the figure was what he said was his crib, his toys and all his clothes. In approximated spelling, he wrote that when his sister was

A Field Guide to the Classroom Library, Lucy Calkins and the Teachers College Reading and Writing Project, Heinemann, ©2002 Teachers College, Columbia University; http://www.heinemann.com/fieldguides

Publisher
Scholastic, 1996

ISBN
0590237926

TC Level
3

born, because he was a big boy, he gave her a lot of his things. Some teachers even use paper with "memory bubbles" as a paper choice during a memoir genre study.

Children who have studied list books will quickly recognize this as fitting into that genre though it's more sophisticated than most early list books. Children will recognize this as a list of memories and see this text as an example of a sophisticated list book.

If the class is using reading centers, this book might be included in a basket of books about personal memories. In these centers children read and talk across books, finding similarities and differences among them, and making text to life connections. A group of young readers took turns pretending that they were the little girl. Each child "told" her story by reading the words and the memory bubble.

Book Connections

Other Library A books in a center with this one might include *Birthday Presents* by Cynthia Rylant, and *When I Was Five* by Arthur Howard. *Wilfrid Gordon McDonald Partridge* by Mem Fox would be another good addition to such a center, and in the writing workshop both can serve as a model of the way in which objects can trigger memories.

Genre
Emergent Literacy Book

Teaching Uses
Partnerships; Small Group Strategy Instruction; Independent Reading; Language Conventions; Teaching Writing

A Field Guide to the Classroom Library, Lucy Calkins and the Teachers College Reading and Writing Project, Heinemann, ©2002 Teachers College, Columbia University; http://www.heinemann.com/fieldguides

Making Patterns

Elizabeth Savage

Book Summary

This book is a list of ways children make patterns. The title page shows a busy scene at a beach. Then the text follows the simple pattern "Making patterns in the _____" moving from sand to snow to dirt to dough and so forth. There is a rhyme scheme linking together alternate pages: snow/dough/oh no!

Basic Book Information

Like most of Wright Group's Twig books, *Making Patterns* shows an awareness of the ways a text can support beginning readers as they consolidate their knowledge of such important print concepts as one-to-one correspondence, picture-to-text match, language patterns, and so on.

In this book, as in other books in this collection, the back cover contains information about activities that teachers might want to do with children. These are sometimes of questionable use and in this case it's particularly confusing. It's unclear why a teacher or child reading a book at this level would want to know about the Fibonacci sequence, a fairly sophisticated mathematical concept. Instead, after reading this book, rather than making calendars or taking pattern walks to nearby parks, children can reread it or talk about it or read another like it.

Noteworthy Features

Making Patterns offers a few special challenges for readers. The first word on each page is not an easy word. The words in the title, "Making patterns," become the first two words on each page and this should help anchor young readers to the text. For some children, teachers might need to introduce new vocabulary. For example, some children won't have had opportunities to bake cookies and may not know the word "dough."

The children in the pictures change from one page to the next, and there is no constant character. The illustrations show young children of various ethnicities.

There are more patterns incorporated within each illustration than first meets the eye. For example, the children's clothing has geometric patterns, symmetry, and color alternation.

Teaching Ideas

Children can read this book independently or in partnerships. If they begin to search for patterns in the pictures, the book will support a lot of thinking and study. Teachers may support children's reading by beginning with a book introduction such as, "We've been making patterns in math and the

Illustrator
Diana Magnuson

Publisher
Wright Group, 1998

ISBN
0780288769

TC Level
2

children in this book are making patterns, too. We can see what the children are doing to make patterns." Teachers probably will want to make children aware of the repetitive pattern to the text to would help them to read more smoothly.

Genre
Emergent Literacy Book

Teaching Uses
Language Conventions; Independent Reading; Partnerships; Small Group Strategy Instruction

A Field Guide to the Classroom Library, Lucy Calkins and the Teachers College Reading and Writing Project, Heinemann, ©2002 Teachers College, Columbia University; http://www.heinemann.com/fieldguides

Monkeys

Susan Canizares; Pamela Chanko

Book Summary

This engaging book has color photographs and captions that show eleven things monkeys do. The photographs show different species of monkeys engaging in the actions cited in the text. The text begins with the question "What do monkeys do?" and the rest of the text follows with eleven declarative statements answering the question, for example "Monkeys climb."

Basic Book Information

This is part of the Scholastic Science Series for emergent readers. The book is large and colorful, with pictures that are sure to elicit responses from readers.

The book ends with two pages that have been written for the teacher, with more information about monkeys. This information is linked to six of the twelve photographs in the book. The link is made subtly with a black-and white-thumbnail sketch of the photographed page set alongside the paragraph. Also included is an index naming the type of monkey depicted on each page. From the end pages, we learn that monkeys' tails can wrap around branches, holding on as tight as if the tail was a hand. Knowing this, a teacher could pause at the suggested particular page to chat with the reader about some of the pages in this book, bringing out a lot of information that isn't contained in the print or the photographs.

Noteworthy Features

This is a repetitive patterned book, written to support a child who is just beginning to attend to the print. The photographs are impressive, the subjects are "cute and cuddly," and children will find these books more interesting than many of similar difficulty. The open book holds two photographs that fit one to a page, though occasionally the pictures are especially wide, spanning across the double-page spread.

The book is made a bit easier because the title, *Monkeys* is also the first word on each page. The verb that tells just what this monkey is doing (and *all* monkeys can do) however, will often not be discernible from the picture alone.

Teaching Ideas

Teachers may use this text to support the early reading behaviors of

Publisher
Scholastic Science
Emergent Readers, 1998

ISBN
0590769642

TC Level
1

directionality, "getting your mouth ready" for an unfamiliar word, and for cross-checking the picture against the text.

Some teachers may also use this book to help demonstrate how readers use a variety of strategies to figure out unknown words. Since there are two words per page the first of which is *monkey*, a teacher may want to help children read the second words on each page, as needed. Students' attention can be brought to picture supports as well as graphophonic cues.

Monkeys contains four words that begin with consonant blends: *climb, swing, screech,* and *store*. A teacher might use this book to launch a word study of these and other consonant blends. A chart might be created (and added to) throughout the word study.

As teachers confer, or listen in on partner conversations about this book, they should hear some talk about the pictures and kids' strategies for confirming what they think the monkeys are doing in each. In addition, teachers may want to nudge readers to reread the text and to put Post-Its on places they find interesting. Teachers might even be more specific or tell readers that it is smart to look between pages and notice things that are similar or that go together. Do they see any patterns? A reader might also find pages that raise questions that would generate more discussion: Are the kissing monkeys in love? Do monkeys have feelings?

Many teachers find that it's exciting to bring children into the world of nonfiction reading by organizing inquiry centers (or reading centers) that promote reading, talking, thinking, and learning about a subject. It might be, for example, that the teacher decides to pull together one group of children to learn more about monkeys, another to learn about insects, another to learn about mammals, and so on.

In a mini-lesson, teachers might show students that nonfiction readers, who are really trying to learn about a subject, reread their books and study even the tiniest details in the pictures. The class could spend a few minutes trying that work together on the rug with their own independent reading books. Then the teacher could disperse readers to their various "animal groups," reminding them, "Today and often when you read, try to really notice the tiniest details in pictures. Let these get you thinking."

After rereading their texts over the course of a few sessions, a teacher might encourage readers to look between the pages in any one book, or across books, so as to "grow ideas" on particular topics. For example, although this book is about what monkeys do, a reader could reread the book looking for information about where monkeys live, and the reader might find a number of pages which link together around that topic.

In writing workshop this book could be a mentor text for children who are writing books about topics on which they are experts. They would notice that some nonfiction books begin with a question that is then answered in a number of ways throughout the text, or that some of these books might be structured like a list.

Genre
Emergent Literacy Book; Nonfiction

A Field Guide to the Classroom Library, Lucy Calkins and the Teachers College Reading and Writing Project, Heinemann, ©2002 Teachers College, Columbia University; http://www.heinemann.com/fieldguides

Teaching Uses
Independent Reading; Content Area Study; Partnerships; Small Group
Strategy Instruction; Language Conventions; Teaching Writing

A Field Guide to the Classroom Library, Lucy Calkins and the Teachers College Reading and Writing Project, Heinemann, ©2002 Teachers
College, Columbia University; http://www.heinemann.com/fieldguides

Mrs. Wishy-Washy

Joy Cowley

Book Summary

This book is an extended version of the simpler text, *Mrs. Wishy-Washy's Tub*, also by Joy Cowley. The cow, the pig, and the duck all play in the mud. Mrs. Wishy-Washy finds them, puts each in the tub and scrubs them down. Satisfied that they are now clean, she leads them into the yard and heads inside. No sooner is she gone then the three animals head back for the puddle and the lovely mud.

Basic Book Information

This is one of the Story Box books, and is written by Joy Cowley, the beloved author of countless books for early readers. As a Story Box book, this book looks like it belongs in a kit of identical little books but in this library it is interspersed with a lovely variety of shapes and sizes of books. The Wright Company provides professional development as well as books for teachers, and has been a major force in supporting the move toward literature-based classrooms. The company uses its knowledge of reading development to publish texts that are supportive of early readers.

There are fifteen pages of text in this story. The sentences are short-most contain only four or five words. The repeating patterns of some of the sentences make reading easier. The syntax is varied, with a number of the sentences in reverse order, that is, predicate/subject. Elizabeth Fuller's cartoon-like illustrations portray the action well, making word recognition easier for the young reader.

The layout has features that put this text at a higher difficulty level than the introductory books from Wright Group. The text is located inside the lines that frame the picture, and placement varies. Sometimes it appears at the top of the page, other times at the bottom. On one page, the sentence begins at the top and continues underneath the illustration. On a couple of other pages, the sentence begins on the left-hand page and continues onto the right-hand one. In these cases, the sentence is a compound one, the division coming before the conjunction "and."

There are thirty-six different words in this story, a fact that also increases the difficulty level of the book. The plot sequence is a simple problem/resolution with a circular structure-at the end, the animals wind up where they began, making a humorous ending that is enjoyable for beginning readers.

Noteworthy Features

The third person narration, with sentence patterns that provide practice in less common sentence structure, introduces students to more varied text. Clues in the pictures encourage inferring-the expressions on the faces of the

A Field Guide to the Classroom Library, Lucy Calkins and the Teachers College Reading and Writing Project, Heinemann, ©2002 Teachers College, Columbia University; http://www.heinemann.com/fieldguides

characters, as well as their movements, add to the humor of the story. There is some dialogue in the form of comments made by Mrs. Wishy-Washy, rather than conversation. The vocabulary Cowley uses is made up of common words that will be familiar to some young readers.

Teaching Ideas

If students have read the simpler version of this story, *Mrs. Wishy-Washy's Tub*, teachers might introduce this book by comparing the two, and asking for someone to recall the simpler version. If this book is their first encounter with Mrs. Wishy-Washy, teachers might introduce the book by giving the title and asking them why they think she might have a name like that, and to predict from the cover and title page what Mrs. Wishy-Washy may be getting ready to do.

Teachers might do a very brief walk-through of the book, discussing a few of the illustrations with students. Because the story has a humorous, unexpected ending, teachers may want to save the last page for children to discover in their independent reading. Students can discuss the illustrations, particularly the expressions on the characters' faces and their gestures, to infer how they are feeling. A teacher might even follow this discussion with a variation of a shared reading. The teacher might first read each page aloud alone, while pointing to the words, and then students might chime in together as the teacher and the class reread the page together.

Teachers might discuss the repeated pattern of some of the sentences with a single word change. They might remind students that they could use the illustrations and the letter sounds in a new word to unlock the word. The cow, for example, is jumping in the picture; the pig is rolling. The letters "j" and "r," together with the pictures, help in the decoding. Teachers may want to coach the reader to reread when encountering difficulty in decoding, to cross-check the pictures for help, and to self-correct when necessary. The teacher can also encourage readers to get into the habit of monitoring for meaning.

Teachers might want to discuss features of punctuation and what the various marks signal. Commas, for example, signal a pause in reading. Quotation marks signal words said aloud. The larger print used for the word "LOOK" signals this word was said louder. A hyphen joining two words signals that these two words are read as one word.

Teachers might use this story to discuss the past-tense verb ending *-ed* in the words *jumped*, *rolled*, and *screamed*. *Paddled* might also be used as an example, although the teacher can explain that since the "e" is already there, we don't need to add another one. The words *said* and *went*, while past tense as well, are irregular and should not be included in that discussion.

There are a number of activities teachers may use to review this book. They may ask students to retell the story and discuss why they enjoyed it. Teachers might then want to contrast the book with an informational book on farm animals, discussing actions in this book that ordinarily do not happen in real life. For example, in real life, animals do not get washed in a tub. Students should realize that nonsense stories like this one are written to amuse and entertain, rather than to inform.

A Field Guide to the Classroom Library, Lucy Calkins and the Teachers College Reading and Writing Project, Heinemann, ©2002 Teachers College, Columbia University; http://www.heinemann.com/fieldguides

Book Connections

If students enjoy this book, they will find Joy Cowley's *Splishy-Sploshy* equally amusing. They may also enjoy another wonderful washing story, *Tiny's Bath* by Cari Meisler (Puffin, 1988).

Genre

Emergent Literacy Book

Teaching Uses

Read Aloud; Partnerships; Small Group Strategy Instruction; Language Conventions; Independent Reading; Interpretation

My Cats

Eileen Robinson

Book Summary

This book is about a girl and her cats. The cats follow the girl wherever she goes. On each page the girl says where her cats are. The text follows the pattern "My cats are on the. . . ." For example, page 1 begins by saying, "My cats are on the chair." This pattern continues for six pages. The last page breaks the pattern by having the girl say that the cats are on her.

Basic Book Information

This picture book has a simple structure and inviting illustrations.

Noteworthy Features

By presenting a consistent pattern and beginning each page with the easy sight word "My," the author helps to anchor many Library A readers to the text. The story is partially supported by the illustrations. Children may have trouble with some of the pictures, such as the table and the stairs, which are not very clear.

Teaching Ideas

If a teacher chooses to introduce this book, he might begin by saying, "The title of this book is *My Cats*. In this book a girl tells where her cats are. Let's see where her cats are on this page. . . . Yes, it says, 'My cats are on the rug.' Now let's go to page 6. Where are her cats? (Children will probably say, 'on the table.') Let's point at the word 'table.' Let's go back to the title page. Put your finger under the words. (They will read that part together.) Now read the book independently." Some teachers may choose to direct children to more challenging words such as "washer" on page 4, and some teachers may want to support readers by introducing the last page that breaks the pattern.

This simple "list" book will support emergent readers who are exhibiting behaviors such as using picture clues, matching spoken words with printed words and self-correcting when these do not "come out even" and locating a few sight words on a page.

Reading partners might be inspired to make "text-to-life" connections and to discuss the pets that they have, or wish to have. Children may talk about their pets and where they are allowed in the house. Are they allowed on tables? On the bed?

This book may also be used to support a list book unit of study in the writing workshop. The teacher can read this along with other list books. Children could then be challenged to find more list books in the class library. After they put all the list books they find in a basket they could spend a week reading them and discussing the characteristics of list books.

Illustrator
Diane Palmisciano

Publisher
Scholastic, 2000

ISBN
0439064635

TC Level
1

A Field Guide to the Classroom Library, Lucy Calkins and the Teachers College Reading and Writing Project, Heinemann, ©2002 Teachers College, Columbia University; http://www.heinemann.com/fieldguides

During writing workshop they can be encouraged to write lists about important things in their lives (e.g., the things I like to do with my brother) and develop these lists into list books just like the ones they have been reading.

Genre
Emergent Literacy Book

Teaching Uses
Partnerships; Language Conventions; Small Group Strategy Instruction; Independent Reading; Interpretation; Teaching Writing

A Field Guide to the Classroom Library, Lucy Calkins and the Teachers College Reading and Writing Project, Heinemann, ©2002 Teachers College, Columbia University; http://www.heinemann.com/fieldguides

Nests, Nests, Nests

Susan Canizares; Mary Reid

Book Summary

The heart of *Nests, Nests, Nests* is in the second sentence "A nest can be in a tree." The book continues, listing six places a nest can be. Two photographs on opposite pages illustrate each item on the list. The book ends with the repeated word "nests."

Basic Book Information

This is part of the Scholastic Science series. As with other books in the series, the book contains fascinating color photographs that are sure to ignite conversations among readers.

The book ends with two pages written for adults. These pages are keyed to the earlier pages, with a few sentences amplifying each photograph. These photographs are filled with intriguing bits of information. For example, one bird is called a lily-walker because its feet are so big, it can walk on lily pads. The information is given with the assumption that young children may be curious enough that they'll want to know these very detailed, specific facts about the birds in this book. Given their difficulty, they also assume that the reader has an adult or partner reader who can read or talk about these pages with them.

An index of page numbers and names of birds featured in photographs is included.

Noteworthy Features

The text is repetitive, and uses a large number of high frequency words. The words, "A nest can be in a _____." form the pattern, but this varies somewhat and readers who don't keep an eye on the print may miss this.

Most of the color photographs show mother birds on their nests, and the nests are diverse. Only toward the end of the book do the pictures contain bird eggs, and one shows a baby ostrich sitting among other eggs.

Teaching Ideas

Nests, Nests, Nests can be used to bring readers' attention to high frequency words, or to nudge readers to practice a variety of strategies for figuring out new or unknown words. Readers who are using emergent skills such as one-to-one matching, directionality, checking the picture against the text or "getting their mouth ready" for an unfamiliar word, will find that this book supports these behaviors.

Teachers may want to focus on how readers pay special attention to important or interesting information in nonfiction texts. The teacher might say in a mini-lesson, "I try to first read books like these and pay attention to

A Field Guide to the Classroom Library, Lucy Calkins and the Teachers College Reading and Writing Project, Heinemann, ©2002 Teachers College, Columbia University; http://www.heinemann.com/fieldguides

Publisher
Scholastic Science
Emergent Readers, 1998

ISBN
0590761838

TC Level
1

the big things I'm learning." The teacher might then model this by using Post-Its. Then the class might spend a few minutes trying this out with partners on the rug using another book, putting Post-Its on the important information in the text. This gives the teacher an opportunity to listen in, making sure that children are on the right track and coaching as needed. Children could then disperse to the independent reading part of the workshop where they'd do the same sort of reading work with books from their personal bins or book baggies.

Readers who choose this book will have fun talking about it. As they thumb through the book, the pictures can lead to great discussions between partners. The cover photograph, for example, shows three baby birds, each with a sound bubble holding the word nests. This is odd! Why would baby birds say, "nests?" Children who are given opportunities to have book conversations in partnerships will have even more success when they tackle the print.

Teachers will need to decide how to organize instruction to help children see books such as these as endlessly fascinating for rereading. One option is for a teacher to suggest to the class that they dedicate two weeks of the reading workshop exclusively to nonfiction books, or to "reading like a scientist" or to "reading to learn about the world." During the allotted stretch of time children would still be reading mostly books that were roughly of an appropriate level, but the teacher would have put forward the books in the library that fit the umbrella topic-in this case, nonfiction. "This week, choose your books from the ones in these bins," the teacher could say. Perhaps during this time, the teacher might also encourage children to choose a "study book" for their bins-that is, a book that's much too difficult but which has pictures and charts that merit close study.

Under this plan children might each select books, or, might work in a group of children reading at a similar level. A child or a group of children might choose from baskets of books on a topic, each of a similar reading level. That is, one group might select a basket of three Level 1 or 2 books on nests. Another group might select a basket of say, three Level 3 books on bears. During a read aloud on the rug, the whole class might work with a basket of books on the solar system, baby animals, or plants.

Over time the class could learn that when studying nonfiction, readers can see connections between one page and another and between one book and another; ask questions and reread to see if they can invent tentative answers; categorize what they are learning (i.e., some nests are above ground, some are on the ground); ask, "Does this fit with what I already know from my life experience?" and think about text to self-connections; focus on tiny details across lots of instances (e.g., a reader could focus on the variety of materials with which nests in this book are made).

Book Connections

A book like this will profit from being read alongside other books about birds, nests, or animal homes. Ideally, readers will not only do the work necessary to get through these words, they'll also revisit the book, comparing it to others on related topics, coming to see it as a source of information, questions, theories, and investigations.

A Field Guide to the Classroom Library, Lucy Calkins and the Teachers College Reading and Writing Project, Heinemann, ©2002 Teachers College, Columbia University; http://www.heinemann.com/fieldguides

Genre
Emergent Literacy Book; Nonfiction

Teaching Uses
Partnerships; Small Group Strategy Instruction; Language Conventions; Independent Reading; Content Area Study; Interpretation; Reading and Writing Nonfiction

A Field Guide to the Classroom Library, Lucy Calkins and the Teachers College Reading and Writing Project, Heinemann, ©2002 Teachers College, Columbia University; http://www.heinemann.com/fieldguides

Out in the Weather

Jenny Giles

Book Summary

The book shows the same two children, roughly second graders doing various things together in all sorts of weather. The text pattern is "It is a _____ (e.g., rainy) day./ Look at us."

Basic Book Information

The PM Storybooks, developed in New Zealand and published by Rigby, are written as stories and structured around the traditional story elements of character, plot, setting, change, and movement through time. Even texts that at first appear to be lists are usually stories with characters, a problem, and a resolution. The only exceptions are their earliest books. The PM Readers are known for including a large number of high frequency words, and for controlling vocabulary so that in books of a comparable level of difficulty, the same high frequency words reoccur. The PM Readers use complete sentences: I see a bird./ I see a frog./ to reinforce repetition of high frequency words and simple sentence syntax. However, the fact that PM Readers include so many high frequency words means that sometimes the resulting sentences seem stilted and unnatural.

Noteworthy Features

The text in this 16-page book is consistently placed on the left-hand side of the page. The font is large and easy to read, with black type on a white background.

This book is part of the PM Starters Two Collection, and has more words, and especially more high frequency words, than many other books on this level.

The pictures do not support the phrase, "Look at us." Children must rely on their knowledge of high frequency or sight words to read this, or receive support by way of an introduction. Some of the vocabulary may be tricky (e.g., *windy, frosty, stormy*) especially for English language learners. Some additional support for these weather words is provided through focused mini-illustrations set in a small bubble on the left-hand side beneath the text itself. The "sunny day" bubble, for example, zooms in on an orange sun.

Teaching Ideas

If a teacher wants to set children up for a smooth and successful experience with this text, a book introduction would help. The teacher could say, "*Out in the Weather* is a book about different types of weather. The pictures show us what children can do in each type of weather. For example, on the first page, it is a rainy day and the children want us to 'look at' them. They say

Publisher
Rigby PM, 1996

ISBN
0763541567

TC Level
1

'Look at us.' Keep reading to find out about other activities children can do in different types of weather."

There are two lines of print on each page of this book, making it most appropriate for readers who are a bit more experienced. By the time children read this book, they should already be used to pointing to words while they read and self-correcting if their pointing doesn't match. For example, the child may be more inclined to read, "It is raining," rather than "It is a rainy day," particularly if one-to-one correspondence has not yet been mastered. This isn't a disaster, but anticipating that children might encounter this difficulty can make teachers ready to take advantage of the teaching opportunities it provides.

Readers of this text should also know a handful of sight words, and expect there to be a close match between the picture and print in the books they read. Such a child could, especially while working with a partner, be able to do some good independent reading work in this book. The hardest part may be the title, but these readers could get someone to get them off to a good start by reading it aloud.

Children may also have some work to do discussing the day that is described as a cloudy one. The pictures suggest a bright blue sky with billowing clouds, and some readers might not think of the overall scene on this page as showing a cloudy day. There are other places, too, where the pictures alone won't be enough to help children produce the needed word. This is just as well because children will then need to look at the print and think, "What sound does that letter make?" Children reading at this level are just beginning to use initial letters in combination with pictures to solve unfamiliar words.

When children reread this book, they can be encouraged to focus their talk on the characters and develop theories about them. They seem to be siblings, to be very devoted to each other, to have buoyantly good attitudes, and often choose to wear matching clothes. Are they twins?

Book Connections

This book would work nicely in a reading center about weather, along with books like *Weather Words* by Gail Gibbons.

Genre
Emergent Literacy Book

Teaching Uses
Independent Reading; Partnerships; Interpretation; Language Conventions; Small Group Strategy Instruction

Packing My Bag

Annette Smith

Book Summary

The book goes, "I put my sandwich into my bag" and continues until an apple, a drink, a hat, a book, and a picture are in the bag. Then the narrator puts his spider(!) into the bag and the book ends with the phrase, "for my teacher."

Basic Book Information

The PM Storybooks, developed in New Zealand and published by Rigby, are written as stories and structured around the traditional story elements. Even texts that at first appear to be lists are usually stories with characters, a problem, and a resolution. The only exceptions are their very earliest books. The PM Readers are known for including a large number of high frequency words, and for controlling vocabulary so that in books of a comparable level of difficulty, the same high frequency words reoccur. Instead of relying upon an intensive use of sentence repetition, PM Readers are apt to support very beginning readers by using many high frequency words. They also tend to have longer rather than shorter sentences. Instead of a book going like this: I see/ a bird/ a frog/ and so on, the PM Readers tend to use complete sentences: I see a bird./ I see a frog./. Because PM Readers include many high frequency words, the resulting sentences may seem stilted and unnatural to an adult.

Noteworthy Features

This book is one favorite of the Level 2 books because its story line is a bit mischievous and will often elicit a personal response from young readers. The clear font, black print on a white background, generous spacing between words and lines, simple reoccurring pattern and strong picture support for words that aren't the same on every page, all provide the kind of support beginning readers need. This book goes an extra step by putting a small close-up picture of new vocabulary (i.e., *hat, drink, spider*) beside the printed word that names it. The language feels like the spoken word and there are enough sight words on each page to allow a child to use these words to anchor himself to the text while he reads across the lines. The sentences are divided into two lines to reflect natural speaking patterns and support fluency.

Children who are at the instructional level of Library A may substitute "he" and "his" for "I" and "my" or, "The boy puts . . ." or, "The _____ is in the bag" or some other variation on the actual sentence in the text.

Publisher
Rigby PM, 1996

ISBN
0763541591

TC Level
1

Teaching Ideas

This Library A book supports early emergent readers as they practice a variety of reading behaviors. This text will support children at this reading level as they learn to carry the pattern in a predictable and repetitive text. They will also have opportunities to make use of picture clues. Teachers can model pointing crisply under each word, matching the spoken and written word. When children do this pointing while they read, they begin to notice when the match does not "come out even" and they begin to self-correct. In this book, children will be able to locate one or two sight words on each page. These words will help to anchor them to the text. The teacher can model all these reading behaviors, characteristic of Level 1 readers, during Shared Reading, in mini-lessons and through small-group strategy lessons.

Some teachers choose to give a book introduction that lets children in on the gist of the story. One teacher introduced this book by saying, "*Packing My Bag* is a book about all the different things a boy puts in his bag for school. For example, on the first page the boy puts his sandwich into his bag (the child can supply the word "sandwich"). Read on to find out what else the boy has put in this bag. You may be surprised with the ending!"

The most difficult part of this book is the title and yet, because of the many high frequency words in the text, it's possible for a child to read and comprehend this book without being able to read the title.

Genre
Emergent Literacy Book

Teaching Uses
Independent Reading; Partnerships; Small Group Strategy Instruction; Language Conventions

A Field Guide to the Classroom Library, Lucy Calkins and the Teachers College Reading and Writing Project, Heinemann, ©2002 Teachers College, Columbia University; http://www.heinemann.com/fieldguides

Paint the Sky

Ruth Corrin

Book Summary

Paint the Sky contains two words on each page, beginning with "Red paint" and continuing through all the colors in the rainbow. It ends with, "The rainbow."

Basic Book Information

This book is a part of the Kindergarten Sunshine Series. The Kindergarten Sunshine Series levels the books from AA to D to differentiate the varied needs of kindergarten children. This book is a part of their Guided Reading collection. Big Books in this series also have small book versions that children can use in a listening center or to revisit the book.

Noteworthy Features

This Level 1 book helps children build upon information they already know-in this case, the colors of the rainbow. The pictures in the book direct the reader to the upper left corner of the page each time a new color is painted. It's a great text for beginning readers who need assistance with using picture cues to predict words. The pictures are simple and straightforward and strongly support students who are just learning to use the cues they provide to make reasoned attempts at the text.

Teaching Ideas

A book introduction may be necessary for the reader to understand what the story is about. The teacher might say, "What do you think the girl is doing? What do you think the girl is going to paint?" One might want to call attention to the word "the" on the cover. After discussing the paint colors on the cover, the reader will know to look at the color of the paint on other pages to aid in reading the words.

If the child is an early emergent reader, a teacher might want to picture-walk through the entire book noting the paint colors in the upper left corner on each page. In doing so the teacher will want to be sure to use the word "paint" and encourage the reader to name the color. By then repeating the color named by the child and saying the word "paint" afterward, the teacher provides the child with an opportunity to hear and see the pattern. With this level book, a teacher may instead decide to do a picture walk and simply say the exact sentence.

While reading, the child can practice using his finger to guide one-to-one correspondence on each page. The teacher might prompt him by saying: "I see you are doing some smart reading work. Your finger stopped at the word you aren't sure about. Sometimes when I am unsure of a word I look

Illustrator
Kelvin Hawley

Publisher
Wright Group, 1996

ISBN
0780236971

TC Level
1

A Field Guide to the Classroom Library, Lucy Calkins and the Teachers College Reading and Writing Project, Heinemann, ©2002 Teachers College, Columbia University; http://www.heinemann.com/fieldguides

at the first letter to see what sound it makes. That sound might help me figure out what word it might be." If the reader is not at this stage, the teacher might say, "Sometimes when I do not know what the word is, I look back at the cover to remind me of what the story is about." The image of the paint cans may trigger the word. Or, the teacher might say, "Could it be 'paint'?"

Genre
Emergent Literacy Book

Teaching Uses
Partnerships; Independent Reading; Small Group Strategy Instruction; Language Conventions

A Field Guide to the Classroom Library, Lucy Calkins and the Teachers College Reading and Writing Project, Heinemann, ©2002 Teachers College, Columbia University; http://www.heinemann.com/fieldguides

"Pardon?" said the Giraffe

Colin West

Book Summary

The little frog in this story is trying hard to ask the giraffe, "What's it like up there?" The giraffe is so tall he cannot hear the frog. Therefore the giraffe keeps asking "Pardon?" as the frog hops up on bigger and bigger animals to reach the giraffe. The frog finally hops onto the giraffe's nose. This tickles the giraffe and he sneezes, sending the frog down to the ground. The giraffe ends the story by asking the frog, "What's it like down there?"

Basic Book Information

This is a trade book by a well-known children's author. It is not part of a series as many other early readers are. The book contains 123 words over 17 pages. There is a repetitive pattern in the conversation between the frog and the giraffe that will provide some support to the reader.

Noteworthy Features

The title does not help a reader know what will happen in the book. The repetitive pattern will help the reader once the reader recognizes it. The pattern also lends itself to the teaching of fluency and phrasing.

Teaching Ideas

If a teacher chooses to provide an introduction to this book for a reader or partnership, she might say, "In this book the frog is trying to ask the giraffe 'What's it like up there?' but the giraffe cannot hear him so he says, 'Pardon?' Do you know what pardon means?" Once the readers know it's another way to say excuse me, the teacher can suggest they read to find out what happens as the frog hops higher and higher.

When the frog finally reaches the giraffe's nose the pattern changes and this page may be a challenge for the reader. In a conference, the teacher might prompt the child to search the picture for the meaning while also searching the print to see if there are words, or word-chunks, the child knows. This orchestration of meaning and visual cues will need to be modeled, prompted and/or practiced many times before it becomes automatic for the early reader.

Genre
Picture Book

Publisher
Harper and Row, 1986

ISBN
0397321732

TC Level
4

A Field Guide to the Classroom Library, Lucy Calkins and the Teachers College Reading and Writing Project, Heinemann, ©2002 Teachers College, Columbia University; http://www.heinemann.com/fieldguides

Teaching Uses
Independent Reading

A Field Guide to the Classroom Library, Lucy Calkins and the Teachers College Reading and Writing Project, Heinemann, ©2002 Teachers College, Columbia University; http://www.heinemann.com/fieldguides

Peter's Chair

Ezra Jack Keats

Book Summary

Peter has a new baby sister, and things have changed. He has to play more quietly, and his parents are using all of his old things for her. His high chair is getting painted pink, like the crib and the cradle. He finds his old chair and decides to run away with it. When he tries to sit in it, though, he realizes it is too small. By the time mother calls him inside for a special lunch and a hiding game, Peter feels differently. As he sits in the adult chair around the table, he asks his father if they can paint the little chair pink for his sister Suzie.

Basic Book Information

Caldecott award-winning author and illustrator Ezra Jack Keats offers this picture book, illustrated in his usual collage format, set in a city with the character of young Peter and his small dog Willie, both of whom are featured in many of his other stories. This picture book has about thirty pages. On each double-page spread, there are from one to five lines of print, always on only one of the pages. There is some dialogue, all of which is referenced with a "speaker tag." The book is not based on patterns or repetition, but is instead a story told in chronological order of one afternoon in Peter's life.

Noteworthy Features

As in many of Keats' books, in order to understand the full story, the reader will need to examine the pictures closely. Sometimes the text refers to events described in the illustrations, as when Peter's mother thinks she has found Peter, but it is only his shoes he has placed at the foot of the curtains.

This story begins in the middle of the action. While some readers find this type of opening to be a great hook because it draws them into the book, others find it disconcerting because they begin reading without knowing who, what, where, why, and when.

Teaching Ideas

The primary instructional purpose of *Peter's Chair* in Library A, is as a read aloud. This instruction is based on the research of Elizabeth Sulzby, whose work with kindergarten children informed her of the importance of recreating parent-child interactions around books in the kindergarten classroom. At home, children often ask parents to "read it again" when they hear a favorite story. In school, the teacher's multiple readings of emergent literacy books helps children become familiar with rich narrative, hear the inflection and pacing of storybook language and learn to use detailed

Illustrator
Ezra Jack Keats

Publisher
Penguin, Puffin, 1967

ISBN
0140564411

TC Level
6

A Field Guide to the Classroom Library, Lucy Calkins and the Teachers College Reading and Writing Project, Heinemann, ©2002 Teachers College, Columbia University; http://www.heinemann.com/fieldguides

illustrations to assist them in remembering storyline.

After the story has been read to children at least four times, multiple copies of the book should be added to a basket of "Stories We Love." Children will have opportunities to return to these books at independent reading time. They will refer to the pictures and use their memory of the teacher's reading to recreate the story on their own. Given the opportunity to do this, children pass through a series of predictable reading stages from simply "labeling" pictures on the page, to telling the story off the pictures, to using progressively more dialogue and storybook language, and then moving toward a more "conventional" reading where they use the print. To go on this journey, it is important for children to hear the story read aloud many times, have a lot of opportunities to reread it to a partner and have a supportive teacher nearby who thoughtfully coaches into their reading.

To support this process, teachers can select books that contain more text than emergent readers could decode on their own, that can not be easily memorized, that have elements of drama and suspense, and that have characters that many young children can relate to.

After children have heard *Peter's Chair* and *The Snowy Day*, teachers might want to create an Ezra Jack Keats reading basket. This would be a good time to also introduce *Whistle for Willie*, another book with Peter as the main character. A few of the books together would make excellent material for a character study of Peter. In each of the books, including this one, Peter has some unvoiced, and unexplained, emotions and conflicts that he works through by the end of each book. Readers sometimes like to put these events together to show how Peter has grown. Readers also sometimes like to put the books in chronological order as best they can, based on the kinds of things Peter is doing in his life in each book. In which books does he have his dog Willie? In which books doesn't he? Clues of this sort add to the puzzle of the correct order for the stories.

In classrooms with older children, this book can serve other purposes. Because there are so many similarities between Keats' books-recurring characters and settings, style of illustration and their interdependence with the text and the story structure-he makes a great author to study and this book makes a good addition to such a study. Through read aloud, partner and independent reading, or even in a reading center, readers can build collective knowledge about Keats and his style. What tends to be similar about his books? How is each unique? What can we say about his writing style? His choice of language and setting?

A few of his books together would also make an excellent character study of Peter. In each of the books, including this one, Peter has unvoiced, unexplained emotions and conflicts he works through by the end of the book. Readers sometimes like to put these events together to show how Peter has grown. Readers sometimes put the books in a chronological order as best they can, based on the kinds of things Peter is doing in each book. In which books does he have his dog Willy? In which books doesn't he? Clues of this sort add to the puzzle of the correct order for the stories.

Since the books never explicitly state how Peter is feeling or why, readers need to infer these emotions based on Peter's behavior and their own personal experience. This book is good to read aloud, even in the upper grades. It helps students build their ability to infer and to understand books based on their own experience. Since nearly everyone has experienced a

A Field Guide to the Classroom Library, Lucy Calkins and the Teachers College Reading and Writing Project, Heinemann, ©2002 Teachers College, Columbia University; http://www.heinemann.com/fieldguides

reluctance to share or a discomfort with change, many readers in a class should be able to bring their personal experiences to this story.

It's helpful for readers to look for places in a story when a character really changes. Why does the character change? In this case, why does Peter suddenly feel okay about letting his baby sister have the chair? At first, many readers say it is because the chair no longer fits him, but with further discussion, they come to a deeper understanding of Peter's changing feelings about himself and his role in his family. This type of discussion, both with the whole class and between partners, can teach children to ask these questions when they read on their own.

Book Connections

Ezra Jack Keats has written many great books for children, including *The Snowy Day*, *A Letter to Amy*, and *Whistle for Willie*.

Genre
Picture Book

Teaching Uses
Author Study; Character Study; Read Aloud; Independent Reading; Partnerships; Small Group Strategy Instruction; Language Conventions; Interpretation

Raindrops

Sandy Gay

Book Summary

This book is a first person narrative in which a little girl wakes up, notices that it is raining, goes out to walk her dog in the rain, and watches while the dog rolls in flowers. The book ends with the girl, her father and the dog, indoors while outside it rains. The first sentence on each page follows the pattern, "Rain is falling on my _____." The second sentence of each page is always "Drip, drip, drop." The pattern continues including the final page.

Basic Book Information

This is a Scholastic Beginning Literacy book.

Noteworthy Features

The first page reads, "Drip, drip, drop," which becomes sort of a chorus. The next page, "Rain is falling on my house," is also the text for the last page of the book, but by then the picture has changed so that the girl is no longer in bed but instead, is up and dressed, and cozy in her bunny slippers inside and dry, having already walked the dog.

The text is only moderately supported by the illustrations. Readers will not be able to rely on the pictures alone to discern where the rain is falling; they'll also need to check the print.

Teaching Ideas

Teachers might choose to introduce this book by saying, "The title of this book is *Raindrops*. This book is about a little girl who tells us all the places the rain is falling. She also tells us what the rain sounds like. Let's go to the first page to see what the rain sounds like. It says 'drip, drip, drop.' Let's go to the next page. Here she says 'Rain is falling on my house.' Let's flip through the book to see where else the rain is falling (the window, on her hat, flowers, on her dog and on her dad). Now let's read independently."

This book is particularly appropriate for readers learning to "read with their fingers" or match one spoken word to one written word. Teachers will also find the opportunity to teach other reading behaviors such as encouraging the child to check the picture for information, cross-checking that information with the letters on the page, to "get her mouth ready" for the first sound in a word, and prompting the child to reread when stuck. Teachers will also want to ask readers "Does that make sense?" prompting children to monitor for meaning.

Illustrator
Dorothy Stott

Publisher
Scholastic, 1994

ISBN
0590273701

TC Level
2

Genre
Emergent Literacy Book

Teaching Uses
Partnerships; Small Group Strategy Instruction; Independent Reading; Language Conventions

Ramona the Pest

Beverly Cleary

Book Summary

Ramona Quimby is a thoughtful and imaginative five-year-old who is starting kindergarten. During her interactions with her new classmates, her teacher and her family, Ramona always tries, often unsuccessfully, to do what is right. Her misadventures provide humor and insight into the challenges and rewards of everyday life.

Basic Book Information

Ramona the Pest is an eight-chapter book. The chapter titles and illustrations throughout the book provide some support for the text.

Ramona the Pest is the first in a series of books that tells about Ramona and her family. Read in order, the books give a year-by-year account of Ramona's life from kindergarten through fourth grade. Each book, however, stands quite well on its own.

Noteworthy Features

The text is clear, lively, and well written, and the characters are multi-dimensional. The author's vivid writing and sense of humor portray how everyday events-the first day of kindergarten, new boots, a teacher's criticism-become a pleasure to read about.

The vocabulary is varied and mostly simple. More complicated words can usually be understood in context. Beverly Cleary sometimes uses Ramona's character to define new words or to illustrate potential misunderstandings about certain kinds of language usage. In the opening chapter, for example, Ramona misunderstands her teacher's request that she sit down, "for the present," expecting to receive a gift.

Paragraphs tend to be longer than is currently the norm for this reading level, but the writing is not overly dense. Chapters, too, are fairly long. They have plots without a lot of action, and often don't have an obvious main point. "Ramona's Engagement Ring," for example, covers the purchase of new boots and a mishap on the way to school. Each chapter reads like a short story and can stand on its own.

Teaching Ideas

This book is a fine example of how writing about ordinary life can be made interesting by attention to detail, language, dialogue, and characterization. Listeners are probably much the same age as Ramona. They can empathize with her problems and understand the humor in the story. Teachers who carefully preplan their reading of this book can give children opportunities for thoughtful and reflective discussions.

Illustrator
Louis Darling

Publisher
Scott Foresman, 1968

ISBN
0380709546

TC Level
9

A Field Guide to the Classroom Library, Lucy Calkins and the Teachers College Reading and Writing Project, Heinemann, ©2002 Teachers College, Columbia University; http://www.heinemann.com/fieldguides

Teachers might consider assigning read aloud talk partners. Doing so helps children develop relationships that can support meaningful, text-based conversations. When a chapter is being read, children can sit next to their read aloud partner on the rug. At significant points in the reading, the teacher might ask children to "turn to your partner" and "say something." That "something" might be a prediction, or a connection between the reading and their own lives or another text. Sometimes, to help children stay focused on the text, teachers have children keep a sketchpad or a dry erase board with them on the rug. At strategically planned points in the text, the teacher might stop and ask children to sketch a prediction or a response to the reading. In addition to helping young children stay anchored to the text, it also gives them concrete information for beginning discussions.

Since this is a book that will be read over a period of time, children will get to know the character traits of Ramona and this knowledge will help them in their understanding of the book. To help children organize their thoughts and as a model for future charting of a character's attributes, the teacher and class might consider creating a character web for Ramona. The web can become an ongoing activity, with children adding to it as they learn more about Ramona. This can help children build theories about characters, and lead to class discussions about when a character is acting in character or out of character and how we can tell.

Book Connections

Betsy and Tacy by Maud Hart Lovelace is another chapter book about a kindergarten girl and her exploits during this important year. Betsy and Ramona have traits in common as well as some that are quite unique. If the class also creates a character web for Betsy, the teacher might want to combine the information from both in a Venn diagram that shows where traits overlap and diverge. It might also be interesting to have children include a circle for their own character traits!

Since Betsy and Ramona are both strong-willed children, the class might want to begin a collection of books about strong-willed, spirited children such as *Where the Wild Things Are* and *Amazing Grace*.

Genre
Chapter Book

Teaching Uses
Read Aloud; Character Study; Partnerships

Red Leaf, Yellow Leaf

Lois Ehlert

Book Summary

This is an enchanting nonfiction story of a sugar-maple tree, the young child who planted it, and their relationship. Through exquisite illustrations in vibrant colors and language that evokes strong images, readers are immediately brought into the story. They are provided with a sense of the child and the tree growing up together, while at the same time they follow the journey of a little seedling as it grows into a tree. Readers are left to imagine the process beginning all over again. Though it is written in narrative form, from the point of view of the child telling the story of his tree, many facts are embedded within the context of the story. The story of the maple tree comes to an end, with the little child inviting the reader to become an active participant in the text with the question, "That's my favorite time. Can you guess why?"

Basic Book Information

In this 32-page picture book, illustrations span two pages and the text is written in large black print. The black font set against the brightly colored background supports the reader in attending closely to the print.

Noteworthy Features

As in many of her books, Ehlert's illustrations have a playful feel to them. On the first and last pages, a cut out shape of a maple leaf allows the reader to visualize the leaf with an added dimension. Many pages contain labels and captions that give the reader additional information (e.g., black-capped chickadee, a sugar-maple description, maple seeds). The last four pages form an appendix that gives the reader additional information about this topic. The first part provides a detailed description of the parts of the tree (leaves, buds, roots and sap, seeds, bark, tree flowers) and the last part provides an in-depth description of how to go about planting a tree. The size of the print is significantly smaller on these last four pages.

Teaching Ideas

This text provides an excellent introduction to more complex nonfiction. The print is fairly large and well spaced, but the more complex vocabulary will provide some challenges. The first part of the book is a fairly straightforward story, but as the story deepens, some familiar words are used in ways that will be somewhat tricky (e.g., crown of leaves, winged seeds). The young reader, who for the most part no longer needs to point to words as he reads, may need to in some of the trickier places. As a result, teachers may find themselves coaching children to read and reread to

Illustrator
Lois Ehlert

Publisher
Harcourt Brace, 1991

ISBN
0152661972

TC Level
5

increase fluency.

If a teacher chooses to provide a book introduction, he might begin by saying, "This is the story of a sugar maple tree and the girl who planted it. The girl is going to tell us how the seed started on the ground and then all the different things that happened to it that allowed it to grow into a big wonderful tree. Let's read this and find out how this seed became a maple tree." As the teacher flips through the pages, he would want to call the child's attention to the places that might be somewhat tricky.

This book can also be useful when teaching about the features of nonfiction texts, including how and when to read them. The book includes labels, captions, a glossary of terms (leaves, buds, roots, sap, seeds, bark, and tree flowers), and a how-to page (i.e., how to plant a tree). This is also an example of nonfiction writing in which information is embedded in the context of a story. Children who are familiar with nonfiction features will probably be aware that reading the glossary and the how-to pages will provide them with additional information and a deeper understanding of the concept. They may also know that they can decide to read them either before or after the rest of the text. Unlike those special nonfiction features, however, the story part of this nonfiction book will need to be read from the first page to the last.

Teachers can also take advantage of this text as an opportunity to demonstrate another purpose for rereading. Not only do readers reread to see if something makes sense, but also to gain more information that they might not have caught the first time. Ehlert has embedded a great deal of information in her illustrations that go beyond what's in the text. This leaves the book, and the topic, open to deeper conversations. The labels alone can open meaningful doors. Readers might wonder for example: How do people decide what information to put in the labels and what information to put in the body of the text? Who is meant to be reading these labels? What are the different buds and what type of traits do they have? Teachers should make sure that children immersed in a study of nonfiction texts see a wide variety, including some that are not in a narrative form, and others that contain nonfiction features that aren't found in this book (e.g., a table of contents).

A class engaged in a study of Lois Ehlert would find her books to have a number of similarities. In many of her other books, she offers the reader a gift even before the story begins (i.e., "I've been saving this little leaf from my sugar maple tree so I could show it to you."). Many of Ehlert's books are nonfiction, and most of them contain similar features (e.g., labels, a glossary, or index of words). Her illustrations are imbued with information that goes far beyond what's included in the body of the text.

One teacher used this book in a writing workshop to show students one example of the various ways authors invite readers into the story. In this book, Ehlert ends her story by directly asking the reader a question: Can you guess why? Writers may also want to try that technique in their own writing.

Genre
Nonfiction; Picture Book

Teaching Uses

Author Study; Partnerships; Independent Reading; Small Group Strategy Instruction; Language Conventions; Content Area Study; Reading and Writing Nonfiction; Teaching Writing

A Field Guide to the Classroom Library, Lucy Calkins and the Teachers College Reading and Writing Project, Heinemann, ©2002 Teachers College, Columbia University; http://www.heinemann.com/fieldguides

Rosie's Walk

Pat Hutchins

Book Summary

As Rosie the hen goes for a walk, a fox follows behind her. Seemingly by accident, the hen manages to get the fox caught up in obstacle after obstacle as he pursues her. She arrives home for dinner without incident, with the traumatized fox nowhere in sight.

Basic Book Information

This book has detailed pictures and a short prepositional phrase in the midst of some white space on each page. The font is larger than most books at this level and has no serifs.

Noteworthy Features

The story in this book is played out not only in the words but also in the pictures. The pattern of the story is the hen that walks obliviously around the farmyard with the fox trailing behind her, encountering hazard after hazard. First the text explains where Rosie walked, using a prepositional phrase that is fully illustrated in the picture. Then, the illustrations on the wordless pages that follow, show the trouble the fox gets into as he tries to follow her.

Teaching Ideas

Many teachers like to have this book on hand when they are working with children on making predictions based on clues in the text and pictures. The kinds of things that happen to the fox are based on a predictable pattern; one page shows clues of what could happen to the fox and the next page shows what actually does happen. To figure out what will happen to him, students have to think about the physical evidence presented in the picture, and put that together with what they know has happened to the fox in the past.

Just as this book is good for helping students work on prediction, it is also good for helping students make meaning out of a text in ways that go beyond the words. If a student merely reads the text and does not pay attention to the pictures, the story is boring and pointless-in fact it doesn't make much sense at all. As teachers confer with students about their reading of this book, they may want to be sure that they are monitoring their own comprehension closely enough that they'll pick up on the connection. In most cases, if two students are reading the book together, at least one will notice something is happening in the pictures and soon they will both be involved in the fuller story.

This book can also help those students who are just learning English with

Illustrator
Pat Hutchins

Publisher
Simon & Schuster, 1968

ISBN
0020437501

TC Level
4

A Field Guide to the Classroom Library, Lucy Calkins and the Teachers College Reading and Writing Project, Heinemann, ©2002 Teachers College, Columbia University; http://www.heinemann.com/fieldguides

prepositions. In the pictures, it is very clear what Rosie is doing, and once students can read the words, the graphic illustration of where Rosie is may stick in their minds better than abstract concepts of "through" and "over."

Book Connections

Other books by Pat Hutchins include *Goodnight Owl, Titch, You'll Soon Grow Into Them, Titch,* and *The Doorbell Rang.*

Genre
Picture Book

Teaching Uses
Author Study; Teaching Writing; Partnerships

A Field Guide to the Classroom Library, Lucy Calkins and the Teachers College Reading and Writing Project, Heinemann, ©2002 Teachers College, Columbia University; http://www.heinemann.com/fieldguides

Run! Run!

JoAnn Vandine

Book Summary

The narrator commands the characters from folk tales (i.e., the Three Pigs from *The Three Pigs*, Jack from *Jack and the Beanstalk*, and Red from *Little Red Riding Hood*) to run away to keep the villain from eating them. At the end, the narrator commands Cinderella to stop running away because the prince wants to kiss her.

Basic Book Information

This eight-page picture book follows a consistent pattern up until the very last page. On the bottom of each left-hand page, there are two lines where the narrator names a character from a folk tale and says for example, "Jack ran away from the giant." On the right-hand page, there are two lines where the narrator calls to the character to, "Run, run, the _____ wants to eat you!" On the very last page, the last two lines change to tell the character, Cinderella, to "Stop!" so the prince can kiss her.

Noteworthy Features

Once the reader has realized that each double-page spread will feature a character from a common folk tale, the pictures will support the text more easily. Of course, readers who aren't familiar with *The Three Pigs*, *Little Red Riding Hood*, *Jack and the Beanstalk*, and *Cinderella*, won't really understand the book very well, and certainly won't get much reading support from the pictures.

Teaching Ideas

Because the pattern is so strong in this text, and because so many students know the stories referred to, lots of teachers consider this a good solid book to use at this level for independent and partner reading.

One way to enter the book is to use the cover to predict what the book might be about. A teacher might say, "This book is called *Run! Run!* What do you see on the cover?" The teacher might ask the reader if she already knows these characters. The teacher may also flip to the picture and blurb on the back cover. If this is the first time the reader is encountering a blurb, the teacher might say, "These words tell us about the book. Listen, while I read them to you." In this case the blurb reads, "The Three Pigs, Red Riding Hood and other favorite story characters are all off and running. Can you guess why?" Engaged readers will then read on to check their predictions about the story.

Some teachers use this book not only for helping kids work with print, but also as a reader's introduction to intertextuality. These teachers explain

Illustrator
Kevin O'Malley

Publisher
Mondo Publishers, 1995

ISBN
1572550422

TC Level
2

 A Field Guide to the Classroom Library, Lucy Calkins and the Teachers College Reading and Writing Project, Heinemann, ©2002 Teachers College, Columbia University; http://www.heinemann.com/fieldguides

to readers that sometimes, books and stories are connected to each other, and that sometimes, you can find authors talking about one story "inside" another one. That way you can get all the interesting parts of one story going on in your mind at the same time you have the other story there, and sometimes the mixed up stories make great new ideas. Kids can talk about the new thoughts they have from the mix of stories in *Run! Run!*

Some kids also enjoy discussing the ending of this book, in which Cinderella gets the opposite command to "Stop!" instead of "Run!" Maybe the author just wanted a twist at the ending of the book, and wanted the reader to see that not all fairy tales have characters running away from bad things. The readers will have to decide for themselves what they think the author meant by writing the book the way she did.

Book Connections

Other titles in the *Book Shop* series, from Mondo Publishing include: *Fun with Hats* by Lucy Malka, *Honk!* by Sue Smith, *My Circus Family* by Mary Dixon Lake, and *Will You Play with Us?* by Margaret Yat Sevitch Phinney. JoAnn Vandine also wrote *I Eat Leaves.*

Genre
Emergent Literacy Book; Fairy and Folk Tale; Picture Book

Teaching Uses
Independent Reading; Interpretation; Critique; Partnerships; Language Conventions; Read Aloud

Sally's New Shoes
Annette Smith

Book Summary

In *Sally's New Shoes*, the character, a little girl named Sally, tells us all the things she's going to do in her new shoes. For example on the first page, Sally says, "I'm going to walk in my new shoes." Teachers may elicit the sentence from a child (providing support), thus establishing the pattern. The teacher may then ask the child to read the rest of the book to find out the other things Sally will do in her new shoes.

Basic Book Information

The book has 58 words over 16 pages, with five to eight words and two lines of text per page. The sentence on each page is divided into two lines, reflecting the phrasing of natural speech. The placement of text is consistent throughout, with words on the left page and pictures on the opposite page. Punctuation includes ellipses (...) and an exclamation mark (!).

Noteworthy Features

The text has large, generously spaced print. There is moderately high picture support for action words. For example, the illustration for, "I'm going to dance in my new shoes." shows Sally doing just that before a mirror in a dance studio. Sentences are divided into two lines that support the development of fluency. There is a pattern that remains constant throughout the text with one change at the end, when Sally says, "But I'm not going to . . . swim in my new shoes!"

Text and pictures appear on opposite pages to reinforce the idea that the print carries the meaning. High frequency words: *I'm going, to, in,* and *my,* appear on each page to anchor readers in the text. The pictures appear in thought bubbles where Sally imagines wearing her new shoes in a variety of contexts.

Teaching Ideas

One way to enter the book is to use the cover to predict what the book might be about. The teacher may say, "This book is called *Sally's New Shoes*. The cover can help us know about the book. What do you see on the cover?" Students will notice a little girl, Sally, trying on a pair of shoes. There's a shoebox nearby. Thumbing through the book before reading, will help children get a feel for how the book goes, making reading easier.

Teachers may use this book to support the early reading behaviors of one-to-one matching, directionality, checking information in the picture against the text, or encouraging readers to check the first letter and get their mouths ready for an unfamiliar word.

Publisher
Rigby, 1996

ISBN
076354163X

TC Level
2

A Field Guide to the Classroom Library, Lucy Calkins and the Teachers College Reading and Writing Project, Heinemann, ©2002 Teachers College, Columbia University; http://www.heinemann.com/fieldguides

If students are unfamiliar with "thought" or "speech" bubbles, the teacher may want to have a conversation about why these were used, possibly encouraging students to use them in their own writing.

Book Connections

Other books in this PM Rigby series include: *Sally's Beans, Sally and the Daisy, Sally's Red Bucket,* and *Sally and the Sparrows.*

Genre
Emergent Literacy Book

Teaching Uses
Independent Reading; Language Conventions; Partnerships; Read Aloud

A Field Guide to the Classroom Library, Lucy Calkins and the Teachers College Reading and Writing Project, Heinemann, ©2002 Teachers College, Columbia University; http://www.heinemann.com/fieldguides

Super Hero

John Carr

Book Summary

This book is about a superhero kid who takes off his clothes, one item at a time. Under his clothes he has his "super hero" clothes. The text follows the pattern, "I take off my _____ (e.g., hat)." The pattern continues for six pages with the child taking off different pieces of clothing. The last page reads only, "I take off." Even though these are the same words of the pattern, "take off" in this context has a different meaning.

Basic Book Information

Written by Joy Cowley, the famous New Zealand author of *Mrs. Wishy-Washy*, this fictional book is part of the Sunshine Collection of books published by Wright Group. The book is tiny, and has been written and designed to support very early readers.

Noteworthy Features

The pattern and the fact that each page starts with the easy sight word *I* helps anchor many readers to the text. Other high frequency words include: *my, hat,* and *take*.

The text is highly supported by the illustrations. Once the child has grasped the pattern, he can read the book easily by cross-checking the pictures with visual cues from the text.

Teaching Ideas

A teacher might want to introduce this book to a reader or a reading partnership by saying, "In this book a super hero kid takes off his clothes, one piece at a time. Every page starts by saying, 'I take off...' Let's read the first page, 'I take off my hat.' Look at page 3, it says 'I take off my scarf.' Can you put your finger under the word 'scarf'? Great. Now finishing reading on your own."

Even though the title of the book is *Super Hero*, this word is not mentioned in the text itself. However, on pages 7 and 8, after the child takes off his shirt, the reader will notice the "SH" printed on the shirt. In a conference, the teacher may ask a reader what she thinks the *S* and *H* stand for. The reader may recall the book's title, otherwise the teacher can call attention to it.

A student reading this book independently should be able to point to the words as he is reading. Pulling alongside a child reading this text, the teacher may want to coach the child by prompting him to reread when he encounters difficulty, and to encourage him to check the picture for clues, as well as to get his mouth ready for the first sound of the word. The teacher

Illustrator
Kelvin Hawley

Publisher
Wright Group, 1996

ISBN
0780237226

TC Level
1

can also encourage the child to get into the habit of monitoring for meaning by asking, "Does that make sense?" What is interesting about this book and other books like it is that often, the pictures give more information than the text itself. That is, without the pictures, the text alone will not be as meaningful. The pictures are there not only to embellish the book but to help tell the story. This is not unlike those times in the writing workshop when teachers say to children, "You need to tell part of your story with your pictures and part of the story with words." As they thumb through this book, children will enjoy noticing and talking about these details.

Genre
Emergent Literacy Book; Picture Book

Teaching Uses
Independent Reading; Partnerships; Small Group Strategy Instruction

A Field Guide to the Classroom Library, Lucy Calkins and the Teachers College Reading and Writing Project, Heinemann, ©2002 Teachers College, Columbia University; http://www.heinemann.com/fieldguides

Swimmy

Leo Lionni

Book Summary

In this Caldecott Honor book, a small black fish named Swimmy loses all his little red brothers and sisters to a hungry tuna. He encounters many wondrous things as he swims alone scared and very sad. When he comes across another school of little red fish, he encourages them to stop hiding, and "SEE things!" and he thinks of a way to keep them all safe. The school swims in the shape of "the biggest fish in the sea," and Swimmy makes the eye. While swimming together in this formation, they chase the big fish away.

Basic Book Information

This is a very popular, classic work by well respected children's author Leo Lionni.

Noteworthy Features

Text averages from one to five lines per page, though one sentence continues across six double-page spreads. The lines of print seem to "swim" in the ocean-like page spreads and the small typeface may be somewhat obscured in the lush artwork, presenting a possible challenge for beginning readers.

Teaching Ideas

Before reading this book teachers may want to preview a few of the challenging vocabulary words related to the sea: *mussel, medusa, lobster, sea anemone,* and *school* (as it refers to a large group of fish). Students may also have difficulty with some other words like: *swift, fierce,* and *hungry.*

There are many similes and metaphors in the story, but if children miss them, they probably will not miss the main storyline, though they may get sidetracked in their thinking.

A few children have been known to focus in on the similes and metaphors in the text to the extent that it confuses them. Swimmy describes a lobster, "Who walked about like a water-moving machine." They wondered how could Swimmy be saying that the lobster reminds him of a machine? He doesn't know any machines, does he? And a child might ask why do the sea anemones look like "pink palm trees swaying in the wind"?

In a class discussion about the big idea or meaning of *Swimmy*, a teacher may want to start with questions that nudge children toward interpretation, such as: What is really important about this story? What does this story say about the world? What does this story say about my life? What is the point of this story for me?

Illustrator
Leo Lionni

Publisher
Scholastic, 1992

ISBN
0590430491

TC Level
7

A Field Guide to the Classroom Library, Lucy Calkins and the Teachers College Reading and Writing Project, Heinemann, ©2002 Teachers College, Columbia University; http://www.heinemann.com/fieldguides

Most readers decide that there is a message here: that people who are powerless can work together to vanquish the common enemy-if they have a good leader. Readers find other messages too. Some children think the book's message is that if you lose your family, you have to think of a better way to protect your next family. Some children decide the message is that if you are bullied yourself, you will end up trying to bully other people, too. As in any text, the learning comes not in just taking in another person's interpretation, but instead in deciding if that interpretation fits, or in building a different one, always with supporting evidence from the text. If the class has been studying this theme of community, a teacher might want to challenge the class by asking, "If the little fish, Swimmy, helped *people*, what problems would he see, and how would he help them? How would you?"

Book Connections

Many of Leo Lionni's books including *Frederick*, *The Alphabet Tree*, *Tillie and the Wall* and *Mathew's Dream,* are also parable-like animal fables with powerful messages for study either through the read aloud, in a reading center or as part of an author study.

Genre
Picture Book; Emergent Literacy Book

Teaching Uses
Read Aloud; Interpretation; Content Area Study; Critique; Author Study; Language Conventions

A Field Guide to the Classroom Library, Lucy Calkins and the Teachers College Reading and Writing Project, Heinemann, ©2002 Teachers College, Columbia University; http://www.heinemann.com/fieldguides

Teeny Tiny Tina

Andrea Butler

Book Summary

This simple story lists toys that live in a teeny tiny house. They include a wind-up mouse, a wooden rat, a patchwork cat, a stuffed frog, and a wooden dog. They all live with a straw doll named Teeny, Tiny Tina.

Basic Book Information

This is a seven-page rhyming list book that tells the reader who lives in the teeny tiny house. The text is one long sentence made up of phrases connected by the word "and." The illustrations include easily recognized drawings of a dollhouse and different toys, all done on a broad white background. The main text is printed in large, boldface type and is placed consistently at the bottom of each page, one line per page. In the center of each line are the words "teeny tiny" in smaller, red print.

Noteworthy Features

The repeated words "teeny tiny" are colored red and are in a smaller font. The emphasis on these words steers children to read with inflection and to emphasize the repeating lines. This makes the book sound like a song.

This is an older book, and the pictures are less rich and inviting than those in many newer books. The illustrations suggest that all the "creatures" in the teeny tiny house are toys, and that this is a book about a dollhouse.

The text doesn't have the same highly patterned structure of many other books. It relies on many high frequency words that should not pose a lot of difficulties to readers of books at this level. The text essentially says that a whole lot of creatures-a mouse, a cat, a rat, and so on all live in a house.

Teaching Ideas

Many Level 2 books would sound staccato if read aloud, and this book is a wonderful exception. It is written to support children reading with intonation, pitch, and phrasing, and it deserves to be read and reread with the goal of a smooth read.

Genre

Emergent Literacy Book

Illustrator
Katrina Van Gendt

Publisher
Rigby, 1989

ISBN
0947328106

TC Level
2

A Field Guide to the Classroom Library, Lucy Calkins and the Teachers College Reading and Writing Project, Heinemann, ©2002 Teachers College, Columbia University; http://www.heinemann.com/fieldguides

Teaching Uses

Independent Reading; Read Aloud

The Baby Owls
Beverley Randell

Book Summary

Down on the farm the cows, pigs, and dogs are asleep, but the owl family is awake up in the tree. The baby owls are hungry and Mother Owl goes out hunting for moths. She brings back a moth for her babies. The book ends with the farm animals still sleeping and the baby owls now contented and asleep.

Basic Book Information

The PM Storybooks, developed in New Zealand and published by Rigby, are written as stories, which are structured around traditional story elements. Even texts that at first appear to be lists are usually stories with characters, a problem, and a resolution. The only exceptions are their very earliest books. The PM Readers are known for including a large number of high frequency words, and for controlling vocabulary so that in books of a comparable level of difficulty, the same high frequency words reoccur. Instead of relying upon an intensive use of sentence repetition, hoping children will be given a book introduction and remember what the teacher has told them, the PM Readers are apt to support very beginning readers by using many high frequency words in longer, more complete sentences: I see a bird./ I see a frog./.

Noteworthy Features

The emergent reader who has recently moved on from Level 1 books will find, on the first page of this book, a repetitive pattern that will get him off to a strong start: "The cows are asleep, the pigs are asleep. . . ." The print is large and well-spaced. The engaging illustrations are supportive, but cannot be totally relied upon for figuring out the text. The illustrations use a dark background to indicate a nighttime setting. Black print appears on white pages and white print appears on pages that have a dark background. The word "not" on page 5 is the only word in the text that is written in bold print. This word is vital to an understanding of the text. Children need to understand that all the other animals are asleep, but the owls are awake in the night. The young reader will probably delight in the speech bubble coming out of the owl's mouth, on page 5, saying, "Hoot, Hoot."

Teaching Ideas

Readers who are new to books in this group will likely need some support in their effort to point as they match their spoken words with written words. A teacher might want to gather a group of readers at this level and teach a strategy lesson on the use of sight words as anchors when reading new text.

Illustrator
Elizabeth Russell-Arnot

Publisher
Rigby, PM, 1997

ISBN
076351506X

TC Level
2

For example, in the sentence, "Mother owl sees a big moth," there are several high frequency anchor words. These will probably already be on the word wall. "You know 'see,'" the teacher can say. "Here it says 'sees.' Whenever you see this, it says 'sees.' Look at 'sees.' What do you notice?"

Some readers who encounter this book may have been relying upon using repetition and memorization to figure out words and make meaning. For these children, this book will pose new challenges. For example, a teacher might want to teach such a child that, although the illustration can help with the overall meaning when new words are encountered, it is also important to look at the first letter for help with reading the word.

If this book is a bit of a stretch for a child teachers may want to give a brief book introduction. With the student looking at the cover page, the teacher might ask, "What is mother owl doing?" Then the teacher could confirm, "Yes, she is feeding her babies, and it is nighttime." The teacher will probably let readers figure out on their own that while all the other farm animals are asleep the owls stay up at night, and they are hungry. During the introduction, the teacher may want to help children anticipate that the owl is looking for food for the baby. "Let's see what mother owl got for her baby," the teacher could say.

As children begin reading the whole text to themselves with soft voices, the teacher listens in, moving between them and pulling beside readers, one at a time. She may want to coach one child by prompting him to reread when he encounters difficulty and encourage another to look at the picture and get his mouth ready for the first sound. After a child reads a page, the teacher will ask, "Does that make sense?" encouraging children to get in the habit of monitoring for meaning.

When the child finishes reading, the teacher might draw him back to particular pages to make a point. For example the teacher may return to the words: *pigs, dogs, cows, owls,* and *moths* and call attention to the "s" endings asking, "What's the same about all these words?" Children should be able to see that all these words end with an "s." If the child seems able to do this, she could generate other plural words to show how to use this information to solve other words. The same opportunity is possible for the *-ing* ending on the word "looking" on page 7.

This book can also be a fine addition to a reading center on baby animals and their parents. If the book is set alongside *Baby Lamb's First Drink*, another PM reader, young readers may discuss the different ways that parents take care of their babies or the different ways that babies are fed.

In a writing workshop, young children might benefit from trying to write like the authors of books they read. This book, for example, might be used to inspire young writers to use speech bubbles. In a mini-lesson, the teacher can point out how the author uses speech bubbles to show the sound the animal is making, and invite children to try it out in their own writing. The teacher will want to extend this point so children learn that anytime you want to make a character in your writing talk, one possible way of doing this is through a speech bubble.

Genre
Emergent Literacy Book

A Field Guide to the Classroom Library, Lucy Calkins and the Teachers College Reading and Writing Project, Heinemann, ©2002 Teachers College, Columbia University; http://www.heinemann.com/fieldguides

Teaching Uses
Teaching Writing; Independent Reading; Small Group Strategy Instruction;
Partnerships; Whole Group Instruction

The Big Hill

Joy Cowley

Book Summary

The Big Hill contains a two or three word sentence on each page that explains the actions of children as they play on the slope of a hill. The text begins with "We climb up." Using this same sentence structure, the text describes the children running, falling, rolling, laughing and finally, climbing up the slope once more.

Basic Book Information

This is one of the popular Wright Group Story Box books, and is written by the author of *Mrs. Wishy-Washy* and countless other books for early readers. Some readers enjoy knowing that Joy Cowley lives on a farm in New Zealand, and has her groceries flown in by helicopter.

Noteworthy Features

The expressions on people's faces in the book's illustrations are very funny, and the body postures give a lot of insight into the characters.

The print is large and well spaced and follows a consistent pattern. The high frequency sight word, "we" serves as a useful anchor to the text. Many of the books in Level 1 have very simple pictures but the illustrations in this book are more dynamic and noteworthy than is standard at this level. This helps to make the book both more challenging and more rewarding than many other Level 1 books.

Teaching Ideas

A teacher might want to help readers get started on this book by doing a book introduction. Reading only the title will not support the child's work with the first page. A teacher might say, "The family in this book is telling the story of what they did on the big hill. What do you suppose they are doing here?" The children may say, "They are climbing up the hill," but since this isn't the wording used in the book, the teacher will need to introduce the vocabulary by saying, "Yes, it does say, 'We climb up.'"

It would be worthwhile to call attention to the familiar sight word "we" because it will help the reader to get going on every page of the book. After reading aloud the first page, "We climb up," the teacher may want to say, "You know the word 'we.' It's on our word wall, isn't it? Can you point to 'we' on this page? Read it." Then the teacher may want to put "we" into the context of the sentence by saying, "Let's read the page."

At that point, the children should have enough support to do some good work with the remaining text. The page, "We roll" may present problems because children may not have often talked or thought about this way of

Illustrator
Rita Parkinson

Publisher
Wright Group, 1998

ISBN
0780274180

TC Level
2

moving down a hill. The important thing will be for teachers to let children use the pattern and the pictures and perhaps their knowledge of first-letter sounds to have a go at this text without the teacher doing the first read for the child. When they reach the more challenging parts, this will allow an observant teacher to see the strategies the readers use when encountering difficulties. It is important to give children some time to solve their own problems. If the children are not rereading, checking the picture, and checking the first letter of the word, the teacher can remind them to use these strategies. These observations also will help to plan the direction of future reading mini-lessons and small-group strategy lessons.

Readers of this level of text may not be ready to chunk sounds in words or to divide words into components. If a child has been resourceful and active and is still encountering difficulties, give them the word, perhaps by saying, "Could it be roll?" or, , "Could it be roll or somersault, which one? How do you know?"

It is very important for early readers to become accustomed to reading books with fluency, phrasing, and expression. As children reread the book, they'll work on accurately pointing to words for one-to-one matching and on "making it smooth." This story also lends itself to talking about plot and characters.

Genre
Emergent Literacy Book

Teaching Uses
Independent Reading; Small Group Strategy Instruction

The Big Kick
Beverley Randell

Book Summary

Dad kicks a ball over the fence. Dad and Tom look and look until Tom finds the ball up in a tree. Tom climbs the tree and throws the ball down to Dad.

Basic Book Information

This book contains 67 words over 16 pages. The print, of appropriate size and spacing, is consistently placed on the left-hand side of the page, separated from the illustrations. The illustrations are clear, memorable, and supportive, enabling the reader to make predictions. The author uses quotation marks, bold-faced print, and exclamation points. Many high frequency words are used and repeated.

Noteworthy Features

The book's clear illustrations support the print, and the story follows a simple sequence of events. If the language used in this text is close to the natural oral language of the reader and the experience of losing a ball is a familiar experience for the reader, these features will also assist the reader in making predictions about how the text will go and about what the next words will be.

Teaching Ideas

A possible book introduction could be: "In this book Dad kicked the ball over the fence. Dad and Tom looked and looked for the ball. Read to find out who finds the ball and where the ball is found." Doing a "picture walk" provides an opportunity for teachers to introduce some of the language needed to read this book. In addition, having the reader locate known words will enable the reader to use these as anchors when the text on the page becomes more difficult.

The supportive illustrations offer many chances to model and practice predicting the text and anticipating the dialogue between Dad and Tom. The many high frequency words could then be used to monitor and/or confirm these predictions. For example if the word "said" is substituted for the word "shouted" then children could be encouraged to cross-check the pictures for their anchor words.

Depending on the needs and readiness of the reader, the teacher may take advantage of the opportunities this book provides to model or elicit discussions about the reading of bold-faced print, exclamation points, dialogue, and use of quotation marks.

If the event in the book is familiar to the students from their own experiences, this could lead to a discussion of similar experiences by the

Illustrator
Ernest Papps

Publisher
Rigby PM, 1996

ISBN
0435049100

TC Level
2

reader. These experiences might also stimulate a discussion about how the ball got in the tree, why they did not see the ball at first and who, in the story, was the best finder.

Genre
Emergent Literacy Book

Teaching Uses
Independent Reading; Small Group Strategy Instruction; Partnerships; Interpretation

A Field Guide to the Classroom Library, Lucy Calkins and the Teachers College Reading and Writing Project, Heinemann, ©2002 Teachers College, Columbia University; http://www.heinemann.com/fieldguides

The Birthday Cake

Joy Cowley

Book Summary

The royal bakers plan a birthday for the queen. After the bakers assemble the cake, they sing "Happy Birthday" to the queen. The text begins "A red cake" and continues along with this same basic pattern but with different colors of cake. The text breaks out of pattern at the end with a Happy Birthday shout for the queen.

Basic Book Information

This is one of the popular Wright Group Story Box books, and is written by the beloved Joy Cowley, author of *Mrs. Wishy-Washy* and countless books for early readers. As a Story Box book, this book looks like it belongs in a kit of identical little books but in this library it is interspersed with a lovely variety of shapes and sizes of books. The Wright Company provides professional development as well as books for teachers, and has been a major force in supporting the move toward more literature-based classrooms. The company uses knowledge of readers to publish texts that are supportive of early readers.

Noteworthy Features

This book is a simple list of the different colored cakes that are used to make a bigger cake. The text on its own is not engaging, but the illustrations of the bakers struggling to assemble the towering cake are funny. The illustrations are highly supportive for predicting the text. Both the repetitive pattern and the use of the high frequency word "a" will help an inexperienced reader. The clear distinction between the words and the illustrations also help the reader to find and focus on the print, building their awareness that the print is carrying the message.

The text will support early reading behaviors such as one-to-one matching and directionality. The illustrations provide high reader support by introducing a new color cake on each page. This color corresponds with the new word on that page. The same pattern is repeated on each page, except for the last page. The final page's illustration somewhat supports the text because the chefs are singing the familiar tune, "Happy birthday to you."

Teaching Ideas

This book is about as simple and supportive of early readers as a book could be. It is possible that brand new kindergartners might look as if they were "reading" this book when, in fact, they might not yet not yet have the reading skills necessary for understanding the relationship between the

Illustrator
Jenni Webb

Publisher
Wright Group, 1987

ISBN
0780274873

TC Level
1

written and spoken words. Teachers should not rush all children toward "reading" little books without doing the necessary prerequisite work so they are ready to do one-to-one matching as they read these books.

If a child is ready to do some good work with Level 1 books such as this one, it will do the child no harm and quite a lot of good to have a go at books like this without a teacher first pre-reading the book. On her own, a child who is ready to read Level 1 books can probably deduce the title of this book-by now the child will have met "the" often in shared reading and in her own writing, and the pictures should help. The child will probably be able to discern that the cakes vary by color and may well think the book says *red*, *yellow*, and so on. A teacher will probably want to give a child the opportunity to try to unlock a book like this on her own or with a partner before conferring with the child.

When teachers do confer be restrained as to how much support is provided because it would be easy to do all the work required by this book *for* the child. If a child were reading the book as if it went like this: "Red. Yellow." a teacher might simply say, "Would you point under the words, please." Teaching is more effective if teachers give an instruction like this, rather than doing the work for the child. By keeping intervention to instruction regarding the reading process, teachers allow the children to remain active and in control of the actual reading. If need be, position the child's hand in position to point.

It will soon be clear that the child's oral text doesn't match the written one. A teacher might be tempted to get the child to look across the letters in order to "sound out" *The Birthday Cake*, but this is not usually advisable for a reader reading Level 1 books. This reader should, however, be ready to see that the single word "red" doesn't match with the print, "A red cake." A Level 1 reader should already have done enough shared reading and independent writing to know a handful of sight words, but if the child doesn't "just know" the word "a" it will be important to take advantage of this opportunity to teach that word. After the teacher has read pages aloud, he could draw the child's attention back to the word "a." "So can you find the word 'a'?" (The child points.) "Good noticing. And what do you notice about the word?" The teacher might go so far as to say, "So if you wanted to write 'I want a dog,' how would you write 'a dog'?" "Let's see if we can find that word 'a' somewhere else in the book." (The child turns, searches, points to another "a.") If a child "reads" "A red _____." and is unsure of the final word, there are several options. One might go like this:

Teacher: Let's check the picture. That's what I do.

Child: Cake?

Teacher: Does it look like a cake? Would that fit-"A red cake?" Okay, so cake it is.

Alternatively we could have a conversation like this:

Teacher: Could it be cake? Cake or pie, which? How do you know?

Child: Because (points to the word *cake*).

Teacher: Yes, it looks like a cake. And *pie*, *pie* would start with what letter?

Child: P?

Teacher: Is that a P?

Child: No

Teacher: So cake it is.

A Field Guide to the Classroom Library, Lucy Calkins and the Teachers College Reading and Writing Project, Heinemann, ©2002 Teachers College, Columbia University; http://www.heinemann.com/fieldguides

Or, we could simply say:

Teacher: It says cake. Can you point to the word? Yes, that's cake. Let's reread it. "A-red-cake."

The child should be able to carry on, and if a child reads "orange" instead of "yellow," this shouldn't be of big concern for a reader at this earliest of levels. The goal will be for a child to see that by bringing together what she thinks (from looking at the picture) and the black marks on the page, the child can create a text that matches.

During independent reading with readers at this level, teachers' conferring will probably focus mostly on one-to-one pointing (described elsewhere) and on encouraging children to be active and constructive, doing something themselves if they encounter difficulties. As readers grow, teachers can help them acquire a repertoire of strategies that they can draw on in problem-solving situations. Teachers can use their knowledge of texts and reading process to coach children in using those that are *most* appropriate for their stage of development rather than overwhelming them with a dazzling array from the very beginning.

The child may want to read this book many times. When she meets with a partner, encourage them to reread and retell the book together. It is interesting to realize that later, when children read long rich texts, a retelling is less than the reading; it will be a synopsis of the story. That is, retelling will eventually involve subtracting unnecessary words and details. But at this early level, a good retelling adds to the text. A good retelling of this story, for example might be, "The bakers at the castle are making a birthday cake for the queen. They are going to make a huge cake for her birthday. They get smaller cakes-a red one, a yellow one, and a lot of other ones-and they put them together to make a big cake. Then they sing Happy Birthday."

Genre

Emergent Literacy Book

Teaching Uses

Language Conventions; Independent Reading; Partnerships; Whole Group Instruction; Small Group Strategy Instruction

A Field Guide to the Classroom Library, Lucy Calkins and the Teachers College Reading and Writing Project, Heinemann, ©2002 Teachers College, Columbia University; http://www.heinemann.com/fieldguides

The Carrot Seed

Ruth Krauss

Book Summary

This beloved classic has been around for years because it is simply written and holds the important theme of keeping hope alive. It is the story of a little boy who plants a carrot seed. Everyone in his family tells him that it won't grow. The little boy continues to believe that the seed will grow, despite the discouraging behavior of his family and the seed's lack of progress. He tends to the plant, and eventually the carrot seed sprouts and grows, "just as the little boy had known it would."

Basic Book Information

Many people credit Ruth Krauss, the author of this book, and Margaret Wise Brown with being the two people to break open the field of picture book writing. Ruth Krauss has also written *The Happy Day*, which is a Caldecott Honor Award winner, and *A Hole is to Dig*. *The Carrot Seed*, like these other books, is considered a classic.

Noteworthy Features

The book is illustrated in single lined drawings with shades of brown and white. When the carrot comes up, green is introduced. Then on the final page, there is an orange carrot. The old fashioned feeling of the book doesn't take away from the brilliance of Crockett Johnson's art. The expressions on characters' faces are especially worth noticing.

Some teachers think this book is easier than it is. There aren't a lot of words on the page but the illustrations won't do a lot to help the readers figure out words. Readers also need to be alert to changing patterns. The book is filled with literary language, which can pose some challenges for readers who are more used to the syntax of oral language. For example, the phrase, "Everyone kept saying it wouldn't come up," isn't the sort of phrase people would normally say.

Teaching Ideas

In the A library, the primary instructional purpose of this book is as an emergent literacy read aloud. Through the teacher's multiple readings of this text, children become familiar with the story. After the teacher has read the story at least four times, copies of the book could join a basket of "favorite story books." When they are given the book to read during independent reading time, readers can then use the pictures and their memory of the teacher's readings to recreate the story. When they have had the opportunity to do this, their reading progresses from simply "labeling" pictures on the page, to telling the story off the pictures using progressively

Illustrator
Crockett Johnson

Publisher
HarperCollins, 1945

ISBN
0064432106

TC Level
4

A Field Guide to the Classroom Library, Lucy Calkins and the Teachers College Reading and Writing Project, Heinemann, ©2002 Teachers College, Columbia University; http://www.heinemann.com/fieldguides

more dialogue and storybook language, to more "conventional" reading using the print. It is important for children to hear the stories read aloud many times, and to have a lot of opportunities to reread it with a partner while a teacher is near by to thoughtfully coach the reading.

The Carrot Seed is a classic story written around the familiar motif of the youngest child who prevails in the end. This is not unlike the story of Cinderella, the youngest of the daughters who in the end marries the prince or of Titch who has only the littlest things, but whose seed grows into the mighty plant.

The characters' facial expressions provide an opportunity to demonstrate the importance of reading the pictures and how they can be used to help in making inferences. When the mother and father say, "I'm afraid it won't come up," there is a picture of the mother and father leaning into the picture with wide eyes and concern on their faces. When the big brother leans into the picture, he has a smile on his face and he pronounces, "It won't come up." Teachers can point out the facial expressions of the characters and demonstrate, using their own voice inflection, how they imagine the characters might sound when they speak.

One teacher, during a guided reading book introduction, discussed how the illustrated facial expressions help us to understand the story. She said, "The mother looks worried here in the picture. How do you think she would say the words, 'I'm afraid it won't come up.'" One young reader replied, "Oh, she doesn't want to disappoint the boy, so she says it softly, carefully. She doesn't want him to be hurt."

When young readers are working in partnerships, they may alternate the pages, taking on the parts of different characters while reading this book to each other. Readers can practice the different ways the lines could be said. This can develop a reader's sense of fluency and phrasing.

Although this is a Level 4 book, it can be used with more advanced readers in upper grades who are ready to understand that stories often have themes. Some teachers talk about the theme as the "under story," or as the story beneath the surface. In *The Carrot Seed*, the boy's undying belief in his seed illustrates the value of keeping faith in each other and in ourselves.

This is one theme in *The Carrot Seed*, but of course each reader needs to construct her own sense of a book's theme. One first grader noticed that this book is about the way some people and things grow-slowly at first, and then in bursts. This child pointed out that the carrot was rather like Leo from *Leo, the Late Bloomer*. Other readers will think that this book carries the message that if someone believes enough, their belief will come true. This interpretation doesn't always match our life experiences, and readers who know that things don't always turn out well may question *The Carrot Seed*.

All this can make for some great book talk. Teachers may remind children that if they suggest a theme is present in a book, they must demonstrate accountability by returning to the text for supporting evidence.

Book Connections

This book might be added to a reading basket of "Books about people who believe in themselves or others," along with *Leo the Late Bloomer* (Windmill, 1971) and other more recent books by Robert Krauss.

A Field Guide to the Classroom Library, Lucy Calkins and the Teachers College Reading and Writing Project, Heinemann, ©2002 Teachers College, Columbia University; http://www.heinemann.com/fieldguides

Genre
Picture Book

Teaching Uses
Independent Reading; Partnerships; Critique; Interpretation; Read Aloud;
Language Conventions

A Field Guide to the Classroom Library, Lucy Calkins and the Teachers College Reading and Writing Project, Heinemann, ©2002 Teachers
College, Columbia University; http://www.heinemann.com/fieldguides

The Cat on the Mat

Brian Wildsmith

Book Summary

A dog, a goat, a cow, and an elephant join the cat on the mat. The cat becomes more and more angry with the addition of each new animal. In frustration he arches his back and spits at the other animals. This frightens off all the animals and leaves the cat alone on the mat wearing a satisfied grin. The text ends as it begins with, "The cat is on the mat."

Basic Book Information

Brian Wildsmith is prolific and has written and beautifully illustrated numerous books that range from retold fairy tales and fables (*The Hare and the Tortoise: A Classic Oxford Fable*), to biblical stories (*Exodus, The Christmas Story*), to some terrific ABC concept books (*Brian Wildsmith's ABC*), to informational nonfiction (*Squirrels*). This book has a traditional plot where more and more is added until, finally there is too much. This is similar in theme to the story line of *Stone Soup*, where vegetables keep getting added to the cooking pot, and *The Napping House*, where more and more people come into the bed.

Noteworthy Features

This book is bigger and bolder in color than many Level 1 books, and has a sophisticated feel to it despite the repetitive and simple prose. The lively illustrations support the needs of the emergent reader while adding to the subplot and drama of the story.

A single sentence repeats itself. The only variation is the changing of the animal's name, depending on which animal is joining the group on the rug. On page 9 and 10, the animal's name-the elephant-is long enough that the sentence can't fit in its usual spot on the upper left hand corner and so in this one page it is centered on the page.

A few very useful high frequency words are important in this book.

Teaching Ideas

This book is at an appropriate level for children at the early stages of reading print. It supports the practice of beginning reading strategies such as: directionality (understanding that print goes from left to right), one-to-one (matching word to print by pointing to each word as it is read), checking for picture clues, and using initial letters to self-check. The goal for a reader at this level is not that she will be able to word-solve unfamiliar words. Instead, the goal is that the child will understand that print holds meaning. The reader won't be able to sound out unfamiliar words or use word families and patterns to decode just yet. For now, if the child can attend to letters

Illustrator
Brian Wildsmith

Publisher
Oxford University Press, 2001

ISBN
0192721232

TC Level
1

and match letters to sounds he is ready to begin looking at the first letter in a word to help figure it out, and to notice some of the high frequency sight words on a page.

For the reader of this book, the biggest job may be to point under each word as she voices it, and to check that the spoken word matches the printed one. Some readers may notice when there is a mismatch between the sounds the reader says and letters on the page, as when the reader points to "Cat" on the title, reads "The" and realizes this couldn't be right because the number of words doesn't match up (i.e., Child's version: The cat on the mat; Text: Cat on the mat).

The child will find that he is continuing to say words after all the print "has been used up." The teacher will want to let the child receive this feedback from the print so that ideally it's the print not the nearby teacher that rings the alarm bell.

A teacher may want to give a reader a quick introduction to this book. A possible book introduction could be: "In this book you are going to meet a cat who sat on a mat. Other animals sat on the mat with him, but they make it too crowded."

The teacher will decide whether it's necessary to go farther and do a picture walk with the reader so as to elicit the names of the animals. This will probably be most worthwhile for helping youngsters produce word-perfect reproductions of the text. For example, without previewing the animals, it's likely that some readers will mistake the goat for a sheep. If it were important to a teacher, a visit to that page would be in order. At that point, the child could be encouraged to check the first letter of the word before rereading.

Book Connections

This book could be introduced for independent reading after the children have heard *The Napping House* and *Stone Soup* as read alouds. Given this opportunity, they might take the initiative of creating a basket of storybooks about "Too many things!"

Genre
Picture Book

Teaching Uses
Independent Reading; Partnerships; Language Conventions; Small Group Strategy Instruction

The Chick and the Duckling

Mirra Ginsburg

Book Summary

The Chick and the Duckling is a story of a duckling exploring his world as a chick follows close behind and mimics each of the duckling's actions. Every time the duckling tries something new he says what he is doing, "I am taking a walk." "Me too," said the chick. Finally, when the chick almost drowns while trying to swim like the duckling, he is saved by the duckling and decides to stop mimicking him.

Basic Book Information

This book has been translated from the Russian story of V. Suteyev. It has 110 words over 29 pages with an average of five to eight words per page. The placement of text changes from top to middle to bottom and some pages have no text. There is one sentence on each page.

Noteworthy Features

The text is highly supported by colorful illustration and will support early reading behaviors such as one-to-one matching and directionality. The same two sentences are alternatively repeated on each page with the only difference being the verb. A small change occurs at the end of the book when the verb changes from *said* to *cried*. The last sentence breaks the pattern that runs through the book. Quotation marks are used in each sentence.

Teaching Ideas

If a teacher wants to support a reader by giving a book introduction, she might tell a student, "This book shows a newborn chick learning from a newborn duckling by copying everything the duckling does. On the first page, it says 'A duckling came out of his shell.' Then a pattern begins when he says, 'I am out!' At the end of the story, there is a surprise for the chick."

This book includes many high frequency words including *I*, *am*, *said*, *the*, *me*, and *too*. For readers who haven't yet mastered one-to-one correspondence, who don't always check the picture against the first letter or who are ready to expand their sight word vocabulary, this book offers many learning and teaching opportunities. The book offers the opportunity for teaching about quotation marks. Although the text is a simple one, there are topics and issues to be discussed within the text. Children can talk in partnerships about "things that birds do." They can also discuss why they believe the chick is copying everything the duckling does and relate this to their own lives. Children may find humor (or grief) in the story when the chick falls in the water and is saved by the duckling. Finally, a good topic of

Illustrators
Jose Aruego; Ariane Dewey

Publisher
Simon & Schuster, 1972

ISBN
068971226X

TC Level
3

discussion could be how and what the chick learns at the end of the story.

Genre
Picture Book

Teaching Uses
Independent Reading; Partnerships

The Go-Carts

Beverley Randell

Book Summary

The text of the book begins "Here comes a red go-cart." The same sentence is repeated with orange, yellow, green, blue, purple, and white go-carts. At the end the pattern changes to announce the winning go-cart.

Basic Book Information

The PM Storybooks, developed in New Zealand and published by Rigby, are written as stories and structured around traditional story elements. Even texts that at first appear to be lists are usually stories with characters, a problem, and a resolution. The only exceptions are their very earliest books. The PM Readers are known for including a large number of high frequency words, and for controlling vocabulary so that in books of a comparable level of difficulty, the same high frequency words reoccur. That is, instead of relying upon an intensive use of sentence repetition, hoping children will be given a book introduction and remember what the teacher has told them, the PM Readers are apt to support very beginning readers by using many high frequency words. They also tend to have longer rather than shorter sentences. Instead of a book going like this: I see/ a bird/ a frog/ and so on, the PM Readers use complete sentences: I see a bird./I see a frog.

The fact that PM Readers include many high frequency words means that sometimes the resulting sentences seem stilted and unnatural to an adult, especially. The most common other way to support very beginning readers, however, also has its limitations. Is it better to give young readers an endless stream of books that have repetitive captions on every page and a twist at the book's end, or to give them books like these, with somewhat stilted language? Probably the best diet includes both.

Noteworthy Features

There are six words on each page, except the last page, which has four words. This book introduces and reinforces high frequency words: *here, comes, a, the, go*. This text follows a simple pattern and the one word that changes-the color-is strongly supported by the illustration. The book will support early reading behaviors such as directionality, one-to-one matching, and monitoring to a known word.

Teaching Ideas

This book is ideal for children who are just beginning to read the words (rather than do an emergent reading based on the pictures) in very supportive books. These readers will already know some letters-and-sounds and will use these to do invented spellings. They'll also know a few sight

Illustrator
Roger Harvey

Publisher
Rigby PM Starters One, 1994

ISBN
0763541494

TC Level
1

words and will profit from seeing these words in the context of a story. Because these readers are just starting to read the print, it's very helpful to give them an introduction to the text. The introduction will mean the text they say can align with the words on the page. As students are looking at the cover page, a possible book introduction could be: "This book is called *The Go-Carts*. Have you ever seen a go-cart? There are seven go-carts on the cover and each one of them is a different color. They're in a race. What colors do you see? (The student or students might predict who will be the winner.) Let's look over the book and see who will be the winner." As the teacher and student(s) look at the first page, the teacher will want to say "Here comes the. . . . " This will establish the language pattern.

This book is appropriate for readers learning to match one spoken word to one written one. The teacher can cue the reader to find the know sight word *the*, which will serve as an anchor for a one-to-one match. References can be made to the word wall, or other print posted in the classroom if any of the sight words are on it.

Teachers might also ask a child to find an unknown word by using the picture and the initial letter. For example, "Can you find the word *red* on page 2? What letter would you expect *red* to start with?" It helps to point out that there are two ways to check themselves-the picture and the letter.

This book also provides teachers an opportunity to teach other early reading behaviors such as prompting children to reread when stuck, drawing children to look closely at the picture, and encouraging the child to get his mouth ready for the first sound in a word. Teachers will want to ask, "Does that make sense?" on a regular basis, reminding children that reading is all about making meaning.

Book Connections

This book will support children's study of the numbers one through seven. It could be added to a basket of counting books along with other library A books such as *Count!* and *The Cheerios Counting Book*.

Genre
Emergent Literacy Book

Teaching Uses
Independent Reading; Small Group Strategy Instruction; Language Conventions; Partnerships

A Field Guide to the Classroom Library, Lucy Calkins and the Teachers College Reading and Writing Project, Heinemann, ©2002 Teachers College, Columbia University; http://www.heinemann.com/fieldguides

The Good Bad Cat
Nancy Antle

Book Summary

The Good Bad Cat is a 31-page book about a cat that gets into trouble, but manages to redeem himself by chasing away a mouse. Interestingly, the setting appears to be in a home for elderly men or some sort of gathering place for elderly men who play chess and read. The cat is called a "Bad Cat!" after running over a chess game, then almost knocking over a man sitting in a chair, and finally jumping on the table. In the middle of the story, the cat sees a mouse and so do the men. The cat chases the mouse out of the room and is deemed a "Good Cat!" for doing so.

Basic Book Information

The Good Bad Cat is a 31-page story. It is a favorite for many readers for lots of reasons. For one, it's an oversized book with illustrations that are more artistic and literary-seeming than those children will generally encounter in the very supportive books.

Noteworthy Features

The characters and setting in this book are both unusual. The four old men in the story seem to be in a nursing home. Each appears to be quite a character, and one can imagine whole life-stories to accompany these people. Some children will identify with the scoundrel cat in the story.

The first half of the text will be much easier for a child to read than the second half. Beginning readers will find that by page 18, there are three lines of text and only minimal picture support. This is when the reader must use graphophonic knowledge across the whole word to work through the prepositions *under*, *over*, and *across*, along with checking the picture for meaning.

Teaching Ideas

Children who are reading Level 3 books will probably not encounter a lot of trouble with the beginning of this book. It helps that many of the sentences begin with a concrete reference, "The cat ran . . . " that repeats itself often in the book. Readers can then focus attention on the rest of the sentence, "The cat ran over the game." The picture will help with the nouns at the ends of sentences such as *game* and in another instance, *table*.

The reader must figure out prepositions including *under*, *over*, and *on*. The reader might look at the picture and speculate that the cat jumped on the game but a quick effort to match this word with the print would tell the reader that no, it's a longer word. If a teacher can coach this reader, the teacher might help the reader to look all the way across the word, while

Illustrator
John Sanford

Publisher
A School Zone Start to Read Book, 1996

ISBN
088743410X

TC Level
3

remembering the cat's journey over the game board. A teacher might want to warn the reader that soon the sentences will get long!

A teacher might want to coach readers toward phrasing. This book is written in phrases that need to be "put together," such as the prepositional phrases. Readers may also need help with the phrase "everyone else" on page 17. "Can you put your words together?" a teacher might say. "Can you read it smoothly?"

The interesting setting for this book lends itself to discussion about where the readers think the cat is and what his place is in this particular community. Partners may want to talk about how the cat gets in trouble just for doing what cats do, for example, chasing after balls, jumping on things, and running under things.

Genre
Emergent Literacy Book

Teaching Uses
Partnerships; Language Conventions; Independent Reading; Critique; Interpretation

A Field Guide to the Classroom Library, Lucy Calkins and the Teachers College Reading and Writing Project, Heinemann, ©2002 Teachers College, Columbia University; http://www.heinemann.com/fieldguides

The Lazy Pig

Beverley Randell

Book Summary

When the sun rises, the rooster tells the animals on the farm to wake up. They do, one by one. "I am up," said the cow. "Moo-moo. Moo-moo. I am up." The sheep is up and says so in a similar way. The pig says that it is still asleep. Only when the farmer comes with food for the pig does the pig say it is awake. It runs over to the food proclaiming its hunger.

Basic Book Information

PM Readers are an important resource for teachers because there are so many of them at the early reading levels, and PM Readers are designed to meet the needs of early readers. PM Readers are especially good at providing an easy text composed of many high frequency words. They also contain text in complete sentences such as: "I see the cow. / I see the pig." Also, a great many of even the earliest PM Readers are stories. Other books at this level tend to be label-books, organized in a repetitive list structure. The PM Readers give beginning readers the opportunity to read stories that have problems, resolutions, and characters, many of which they can follow across a series of stories. Just as more sophisticated books may feature the Boxcar Children across a series of tales, PM Readers often feature Ben, Sally, or other familiar characters, across a series of books.

Noteworthy Features

Each of the animal's words is in quotations, referenced with a "speaker tag." In the case of the rooster, his entire speech is in a speech balloon. Because the balloon takes up much of the page, children may have difficulty noticing that this is a speech bubble.

The farmer in this story is a woman. This is an uncommon sight for many children and it sometimes provokes an interesting discussion.

Teaching Ideas

Readers who are new to books at this level will likely need some support in their effort to point as they match their spoken words to written words. A teacher might want to gather a group of readers at this level and teach a strategy lesson on the use of sight words as anchors when reading new text. For example, in the sentence "I see the cow," there are several high frequency anchor words. These will probably be on the word wall. "You know *see*," the teacher can say, to help the child work across the print.

If the book is a bit of a stretch for a child, the teacher may want to give a book introduction and encourage the child to make predictions based on the cover illustration. The teacher may also coach a child by prompting him

Illustrator
Trish Hill

Publisher
Rigby PM Story Book Collection, 1994

ISBN
043504902X

TC Level
2

to reread when he encounters difficulty. Another child might need encouragement to "Look at the first letter of the word and get your mouth ready to read." Children should also be encouraged to get in the habit of monitoring for meaning by asking while reading, "Does this make sense?"

Opportunities for discussion may come up as children begin to think about the book, and begin trying to truly comprehend it. With the goal of gaining deeper comprehension, it's often useful for readers to ask themselves why the characters have acted the way they have. In this case, why do all the animals except the pig wake up? Is this the rooster's job, or is he just bossy? Are they frightened of the rooster? What motivates them? At first, many readers think the pig is lazy and therefore bad. After discussing this they might wonder what makes him lazy and what work should he have been doing? What were the other animals doing up so early? Were they up early in order to eat? Wasn't it perfectly reasonable that the pig would sleep until there was something better to do, like eat? Sometimes, after a discussion, children might change their original opinions. Some end up thinking that the pig wasn't lazy, but instead wise.

In a writing workshop, young children benefit from trying to write like the authors of books they read. This book can inspire young writers to use speech bubbles. In a mini-lesson the teacher can demonstrate how speech bubbles show the sound the animal is making. The teacher will want to extend this point so children learn that anytime you want to make a character in your writing talk, one possible way of doing this is through a speech bubble.

Genre
Emergent Literacy Book

Teaching Uses
Teaching Writing; Small Group Strategy Instruction; Interpretation; Independent Reading; Partnerships

The Letter
Nancy Gjoding

Book Summary

The book traces the journey of a letter as it is put in an envelope, stamped, arrives at the post office until the letter reaches a boy and the text says, "A letter for me!"

Basic Book Information

Developed and published by Wright Group (now, Wright Group/McGraw-Hill), Twig Books were developed as a nonfiction series for emergent readers. Supported by stunning photographs and a variety of illustrative styles, young readers will be inspired by these books about the natural world and everyday life. These titles are most appropriate for small-group instruction and are leveled to support the early reader from the early emergent to upper emergent levels.

Twig books offer level-appropriate text exploring a wide range of topics from creatures and community to history and helpers. Twig Books are easily integrated across the curriculum-especially in math, science, and social studies.

Noteworthy Features

This is an eight-page list book with a twist at the end. It is interesting to note that this is not only a list book, but also a book that follows a sequence or "story line."

The pattern, the sequence, and the word "The" that starts each page can all combine to help anchor the reader to the text. However, the book has many words that are not high frequency words, and the sequence of the letter's journey from writer to reader is a little confusing. The woman on page 2 slips a letter into an envelope, and addresses it to Matt in Washington. She puts it in the mailbox on the street, and a postal worker collects it. The next page may be a little confusing. It shows a few different people working at the counter in a post office. The implication is that behind the scenes, the letter is being sorted, but we lose track of the letter on this page. On the last page, the letter is delivered to Matt.

The text is large and black on a white background, and consistently placed at the bottom of the page. This consistency helps the child to focus on the text more easily than in books where the placement or font varies.

The illustrations provide only moderate support for the text. Children may have trouble reading the word "envelope" if they rely on the picture to

Illustrator
Molly Hashimoto

Publisher
Wright Group, 1998

ISBN
0780288696

TC Level
1

generate this word, and the same with "post office." In this book and other books like it, the pictures tend to give more information than the text itself. That is, the text alone would not be as meaningful without the pictures. The pictures not only embellish the story, but instead tell key parts of it.

The book also provides a back page for the teacher with "Things to Know" and "Things to Do." They provide additional information about the U.S. postal service and mail delivery.

Teaching Ideas

The text of this book isn't as easy as it might at first seem. First, the "sentences" are shorter than those we use in normal speech, and there is a high density of new words. The text would be easier to read if it said, for example; "I see the envelope." instead of just "The envelope." Then, too, the new words aren't as supported by the illustration as they could be. The picture supporting the phrase "the stamp" for example shows an envelope with a stamp and an address. The text, "The mail truck" is accompanied by an illustration that shows a postal worker crouching beside the mailbox with the truck in the background. For this book, then, a teacher will probably want to do a book introduction and a picture walk. A teacher might say, "The title of this book is *The Letter*. Let's look at the cover. Someone is writing a letter. Let's go to page 4. The lady is putting the letter in the mailbox. Let's find the word "mailbox." Let's go to page 7, that girl is the mail carrier; she is delivering the letter that the lady wrote. Now let's read independently."

One way to bring the literate life into our classrooms is to search for and cherish books in which characters read and write, and this is one such book. Children may want to be on the lookout for books like this one and to keep these books in special places. In writing workshops children may be inspired to write, and send, a letter they've written to a family member, friend, or favorite author.

Book Connections

In a study of letter writing or books about letters, teachers may also want to use *The Jolly Postman: Or Other People's Letters* by Janet and Allan Ahlberg and *A Letter to Amy* by Ezra Jack Keats. Many K-1 teachers study the post office as part of a social studies curriculum focused on community. This book would be a helpful addition to such a study. Other books to add might include *The Post Office Book: Mail and How it Moves* by Gail Gibbons and *Good-Bye, Curtis* by Kevin Henkes. *The Gardener*, a Caldecott Honor book by Sarah Stewart illustrated by David Small, tells the story through letters of how a young girl named Lydia makes a big impact.

Genre
Emergent Literacy Book; Nonfiction

A Field Guide to the Classroom Library, Lucy Calkins and the Teachers College Reading and Writing Project, Heinemann, ©2002 Teachers College, Columbia University; http://www.heinemann.com/fieldguides

Teaching Uses

Content Area Study; Small Group Strategy Instruction; Independent Reading; Partnerships

A Field Guide to the Classroom Library, Lucy Calkins and the Teachers College Reading and Writing Project, Heinemann, ©2002 Teachers College, Columbia University; http://www.heinemann.com/fieldguides

The Lion and the Little Red Bird

Elisa Kleven

Book Summary

A little red bird sees a lion with a tail that is strangely green in color. The bird tries to ask the lion why its tail is green, but receives no reply. Instead the lion just smiles because he does not understand the bird's language. The little red bird decides to follow the lion as he plays among the flowers and butterflies. Then the bird follows the lion to his cave, where the lion sleeps while the bird builds a nest outside. The next morning the lion's tail is orange and again the bird asks about this strange tail that has now changed color. Again, the lion only smiles. They go to play in the blue lake, under the blue sky and again the bird follows the lion home, sleeping outside his cave. Again, the bird follows the lion as he goes on his way.

That night they again return to the cave and the bird sleeps outside in her nest. When a storm hits, the lion comes out to rescue the bird and brings her into his cave. The bird discovers that the cave has a beautiful wall mural that shows all the lovely places they have visited. As the bird watches, the lion dips his tail in the red berry juice and paints a picture of the bird on the mural. The bird sings with delight at the beauty of the painting. Now the bird knows why the lion's tail changes color.

Basic Book Information

This 32-page book contains colorful collage pictures, which usually span a two-page spread. The pictures are detailed and encourage close examination by the reader. Many pages have seven or eight lines of text, but the line breaks are not always traditional, nor is the text consistently located in any one particular place. Some words are even printed in slopes and curves so that they become part of the picture. Many sentences start on one page and are completed on the next.

Noteworthy Features

There is a strong picture-word correlation in this book, though the pictures provide details that go beyond the text. For example, other animals and sometimes people are portrayed in the pictures, even though they are not mentioned in the text. There is some dialogue in the book and a few lines are repeated (though not with exactly the same words) throughout the story. The text contains some interesting punctuation including dashes, and unusual line breaks, with sentences occasionally extending from one page to the next. These characteristics would present challenges to an independent reader. As this book is intended primarily as a read aloud in Library A, the teacher may want to point out some of these characteristics in a rereading, once children are familiar with the story.

Illustrator
Elisa Kleven

Publisher
Puffin Unicorn, Penguin Books, 1992

ISBN
0140558098

 A Field Guide to the Classroom Library, Lucy Calkins and the Teachers College Reading and Writing Project, Heinemann, ©2002 Teachers College, Columbia University; http://www.heinemann.com/fieldguides

Teaching Ideas

In Library A, the primary instructional purpose of this book is as an "accountable talk" read aloud. We want to encourage children to have rich book talks and some texts lend themselves especially well to the modeling of strategies for thinking and talking about texts. When teachers use the read aloud to model how to talk about books, they are giving children the opportunity to practice the kinds of thinking and talking about books they want them to do when the children read independently. Teachers can prepare for an accountable talk read aloud by choosing and marking in advance those sections of the text they plan to refer to. Over time, teachers can help children generate a list of comments that can help readers to stay grounded in the text. These might include things like: Show me what you mean. What makes you say that? I'm not sure I agree, because remember what happened on the last page. . . .

Many teachers assign long- or short-term talk partners for read aloud. When the teacher is ready to begin a read aloud, these partners get next to each other on the rug. At pre-selected moments in the reading, the teacher might ask these partners to turn to each other and "say something." Having long-term partnerships allows children to become more proficient in their interactions. At first, the "say something" might be just a thought or reaction to the text, but over time teachers can challenge children to think even more carefully about what they've heard and respond in more specific ways.

There is so much in this book to discuss. Students who are studying the story elements of character, plot, setting, change, and movement through time will find this book a good one for getting started. The character and setting are easy to identify. The passage of time is noted with phrases like "one afternoon" and "in the morning," as well as through more subtle phrases like "with the sun setting" and "the warm starry night." There are enough changes in the book for children to start with the most concrete-the changing color of the lion's tail-to the more abstract-the ability of the two animals to form a friendship without a common language.

As a text for helping children to see the greater meaning or "big idea," behind a story, this book again works well. The big idea of friendship reaching beyond differences is one with which children are likely to identify. Further, they will be able to hold on to the whole story, given its simplicity, as they use the pictures and text to support their ideas about the text. The subject matter also makes it a book that lends itself easily to comparison with other books with which the children are familiar.

This is an excellent book to read aloud a number of times with emergent readers. The strong story line allows emergent readers to hold on to the story and to start making sense of the natural rhythms of storybooks. The book has strong characters and a clear setting that young children can easily identify which will help them to make sense of the story. As this book is read to the children repeatedly, the children will come to be able to "read" the book through the pictures on their own. In other words, they will use the pictures and their recollection of the book to retell the story.

The dialogue and repeated lines allow children to retell the story with expression and give them a real feel for how stories should sound as they are read. By reading this book many times to a group of emergent readers, we

A Field Guide to the Classroom Library, Lucy Calkins and the Teachers College Reading and Writing Project, Heinemann, ©2002 Teachers College, Columbia University; http://www.heinemann.com/fieldguides

help them to hear and imitate the "story voice." Over time they will become more and more adept at retelling the book with the language and expression with which it has been read to them. This kind of "reading" helps children to internalize how fluency, expression and language help us to make sense of reading.

This text would be also an appropriate one to share in a writing workshop mini-lesson. For children at the beginning of kindergarten, their illustrations usually hold the story. When we can find a book, like this one, where the author also does the illustrations, we can have deep conversations with children about the decisions the author/illustrator makes regarding what will be said in words and what will be said in pictures. The seemingly simple idea that the words and pictures should match, or go together, is an important concept for our youngest readers to grasp.

While young writers will scarcely be able to read this text, and therefore be unable to use it as writing mentor, the message of the text is well suited to the writing workshop. In the story, the lion uses his life experiences to express himself artistically, just as the children do in their writing. Though the lion is unable to tell the bird what he is doing in words, the writing he creates does that job for him. His expression of love for his world is right there for the bird to experience.

Genre
Picture Book

Teaching Uses
Partnerships; Small Group Strategy Instruction; Critique; Language Conventions; Interpretation; Read Aloud; Teaching Writing

The Merry-Go-Round

Beverley Randell

Book Summary

The book begins with the discovery of the merry-go-round and then moves to the first pattern: "Look at James. James is up on a pig." After this basic pattern is repeated, there is a new pattern where Dad suggests a car or a plane as a merry-go-round ride for Nick to ride on, but Nick refuses each one. Finally, Nick happily gets up on the horse. Then, after a few non-patterned lines, the final pattern appears. "James is up on a pig," and so forth until the last line, "Nick is up on a horse."

Basic Book Information

The New PM Story Books are part of the Rigby PM Collection, published by Rigby. Story Books tend to come in kits in which every book looks exactly like every other book. Some teachers think this is less than ideal because at every level, a library should be full of books, each with its own individuality. On the other hand, these Story Books are an important resource for teachers for two reasons. First, because there are so many of them at the early reading levels and secondly, they recognize and provide the supports early readers need. Teachers feel the PM Story Books are especially good at providing a lot of easy text, full of high frequency words. The PM Story Books use complete sentences: I see the cow. /I see the pig.

The PM Readers are also special because a great many of even the earliest books are stories. Other early books tend to be label-books, organized in a repetitive list structure, and it's nice to be able to also give beginning readers the opportunity to read stories that not only have problems and resolutions, but also characters they can follow across a series.

Noteworthy Features

The print is large and well spaced. Although there are many lines of text in this little book, early readers will find support in the repeated use of many words and phrases. The text is also highly supported by colorful illustrations. Familiarity with the characters from other books in the series is also likely to boost their confidence.

Teaching Ideas

Teachers may want to give a book introduction. Pointing out the cover, the teacher might begin by saying, "This is a book called *The Merry-Go-Round*," and ask the child if he has ever visited a merry-go-round. As the teacher and child thumb through the pages, they'll notice that Nick is having difficulty choosing a ride. "Let's see what Nick decides," the teacher may say as the child begins reading himself, and she listens in.

Illustrator
Elsbeth Lacey

Publisher
Ribgy Story Book PM Collection, 1996

ISBN
0435049046

TC Level
2

Readers who have been practicing emergent reading skills such as one-to-one matching, directionality, checking the picture against the text or "getting your mouth ready" for an unfamiliar word, will find that this book provides support for those behaviors.

In addition to the word-level uses of this text for the teaching of reading, this book will also be useful for teachers who want to help children read emotions into stories, or read between the lines by inferring emotions and motives. When partners meet to talk about the book, they may well begin by talking about why Nick didn't want to ride the car or the airplane. Sometimes the conversations revolve around the supposition that Nick wants only an animal to ride. Sometimes readers just think he is angry that James and Kate got to choose what they wanted first and they think that Nick just needed some time to get over his anger, and that's why he finally climbs on the horse. The teacher may want to point to the bold type and exclamation point emphasizing Nick's "NO!" Also, the last line of text emphasizes Nick's choice of a "horse." In any case, this discussion can help readers learn to infer and read deeper meaning into texts when such a reading is called for.

Book Connections

Some readers like to take this book together with the others in the series that are about this same family and see what they can determine about Nick's character.

Genre
Emergent Literacy Book

Teaching Uses
Partnerships; Critique; Small Group Strategy Instruction; Independent Reading; Language Conventions; Interpretation

The Napping House

Audrey Wood

Book Summary

In this cumulative, rhythmic verse, the inhabitants of the napping house each begin to sleep piled up atop a napping granny. One by one they climb on top of one another until the wakeful flea at the top of the pile bites the mouse who scares the cat, who claws the dog and so on, until no one in the house is left napping.

Basic Book Information

This cumulative tale is rich in literary language. It tells of a cozy bed with a snoring granny, a dreaming child, and a dozing dog. Donald Wood's full-page illustrations are lush and intriguing. The author/illustrator team also created *King Bidgood's in the Bathtub*, a Caldecott Honor Book that is similar to this book.

Noteworthy Features

The cumulative pattern and repetition makes this a delightful book to use as a read aloud where excited listeners will join in as the refrain "in a napping house,/ where everyone is sleeping" repeats itself.

Teaching Ideas

The enticing pictures, engaging rhyme, simple cumulative structure, and lush language make this a favorite in early elementary classrooms everywhere. After it has been read to children a time or two, once they get the hang of the pattern and the repetition in the book, it usually becomes easy for children to read along, despite the challenging literary language.

Teachers who work with young readers become accustomed to looking at a book in order to ascertain the supports and challenges it will provide for them. The simple cumulative structure of this book and the repetition that's built into the structure will support young readers and give them the security and confidence necessary to solve the unusual words like *slumbering, dozing,* and *wakeful.* Meanwhile, children's work with this book is sure to pay off because the end result is a story-like reading, and because the illustrations are endlessly fascinating.

This is a great book to use to help children feel rewarded and satisfied by close reading and close observation of the pictures because there is much to find in them. After several readings, children tend to notice that each of the

Illustrator
Don Wood

Publisher
Harcourt Brace, 1984

ISBN
0152567089

TC Level
5

creatures-the granny, the child, the dog, the cat, the mouse, and the flea, can be found in every single picture, even the illustrations in which the character hasn't yet been mentioned. Finding these characters can be fun for groups poring over the pictures.

Next, children tend to notice the color changes in the book as the story progresses. "Why does everything turn yellow?" With a little detective work, children can usually discover on their own that the rain at the beginning of the naptime makes the day dark, and that as the sun comes out, the day gets brighter and cheerier, just as the folks are waking up from their naps.

Very observant or very persistent readers will probably notice the change in perspective that is evident over the course of the book. As each creature joins the pile, the perspective of the viewer changes, until the point where the flea bites the mouse. Thus we move from a perfect side view to a nearly perfect top or overhead view. Then, as everyone wakes up, the perspective slowly, picture-by-picture, moves back down to a side view. These readers may well notice that the book opens and closes with a front view of the napping house, one in rain and one in sunshine, one with everyone asleep and one with everyone awake.

Readers who notice this may also notice that the house in the author photo on the back cover of the book looks suspiciously like the napping house itself. This usually provokes great excitement for young readers.

Sometimes discussion centers around odd questions like, "Why is everyone piling on the granny?" or "Why do they let the flea be in the house?" but even these seemingly irrelevant questions can lead to central issues in the book, like the tone of love and comfort and coziness and snuggling.

Some readers will already know the Woods from their popular book *Quick as a Cricket*. That book has similar illustrations and children might be interested to compare the appearance of the two characters in the books.

Book Connections

Of course, there are many, many books that have this building, repetitious pattern. *Drummer Hoff* by Ed and Barbara Emberly is one well known one, as is *King Bidgood's in the Bath Tub*, also by the Woods. Readers will enjoy comparing *The Napping House* to *Just Like Daddy, Who Took the Farmer's Hat,* and *Hattie and the Fox*. This is an "all fall down" story and can be compared to Brian Wildsmith's much simpler book of that title. Books that feature the poem *The House that Jack Built* or the song, *I Know an Old Lady Who Swallowed a Fly* also largely follow this pattern and are great choices for a read aloud and choral reading.

The Woods have also collaborated on *Heckedy Peg, Elbert's Bad Word,* and *Piggies*. Teachers may want to collect these books for children to study either in a reading center or as part of an author study/illustrator study.

Genre
Emergent Literacy Book; Picture Book

A Field Guide to the Classroom Library, Lucy Calkins and the Teachers College Reading and Writing Project, Heinemann, ©2002 Teachers College, Columbia University; http://www.heinemann.com/fieldguides

Teaching Uses

Author Study; Whole Group Instruction; Interpretation; Read Aloud

The Snowy Day
Ezra Jacks Keats

Book Summary

One morning when Peter wakes up he sees that snow has fallen during the night; the snow covered everything "as far as he could see." Peter puts on his snowsuit and goes outside to play. He makes all kinds of tracks, finds a stick and smacks a snow-covered tree. He makes a snowman and snow angels. Before he goes into his warm house, he puts a snowball in his pocket to save for the next day. When he checks his pocket for the snowball, he discovers that it's no longer there. That night Peter dreams that the sun had melted all the snow away. But when he woke, he saw that snow was still everywhere and new snow was falling. The story ends as Peter calls to his friend across the hall and "they went out into the deep, deep snow."

Basic Book Information

The Snowy Day is the recipient of a Caldecott Medal. It is widely regarded as a classic. The book has clear and colorful illustrations made from collage.

Noteworthy Features

This book can be a great example of making a wonderful story out of everyday events. The simple acts of playing in the snow, written carefully and truthfully, make a great story. Children can feel the fun in whacking a snowy tree with a stick, or in makng funny footprints in the snow. Reading aloud stories like this one can help young writers learn to make a story out of their everyday lives.

Teaching Ideas

The Snowy Day is an appealing children's classic. It is a perfect choice for emergent reading. After children have heard the story read over and over, they can construct the story by "reading" the pictures. From hearing the story over and over, children will begin to learn how stories work and understand the structure of language. They will learn to anticipate and connect events. Children will begin to "talk like a book" , as Marie Clay says, and will be rehearsing fluent and expressive reading. Some children will point to the pictures and use them to recreate the story. Others will begin to sweep at the print while "reading." Eventually, some children will begin to notice some words in the text. All of these behaviors are important stages in emergent reading.

The Snowy Day is an engaging read aloud. Children can easily "say something" and make personal connections, sharing these thoughts with a read aloud partner.

The Snowy Day provides an excellent opportunity to teach the strategy of

Illustrator
Ezra Jacks Keats

Publisher
Penguin Books, 1962

ISBN
0140501827

TC Level
6

prediction. An ideal stopping point might be page 24 when Peter puts the snowball in his pocket and goes into his warm house. Readers can use prior knowledge of their own experiences to predict what will happen to the snowball. This provides a clear and simple way for children to begin making inferences.

Book Connections

After children have heard and reread many emergent literacy books, teachers might want to segue into a reading center cycle. Since Ezra Jack Keats has written a series of "Peter" books, such as *Peter's Chair* and *Whistle for Willie*, children might enjoy reading a basket of these books. This provides them with a rich opportunity to discuss the character Peter and how he changes through time.

Genre
Picture Book; Emergent Literacy Book

Teaching Uses
Teaching Writing; Read Aloud; Partnerships; Whole Group Instruction; Interpretation; Author Study

A Field Guide to the Classroom Library, Lucy Calkins and the Teachers College Reading and Writing Project, Heinemann, ©2002 Teachers College, Columbia University; http://www.heinemann.com/fieldguides

The Three Billy Goats Gruff

Paul Galdone

FIELD GUIDE

Book Summary

This version presents the traditional folk tale about the three Billy Goats Gruff who want to cross the bridge and go to greener pastures to graze. In their way is a mean troll who lives under the bridge. When the first little goat crosses the bridge and the troll threatens to eat him, he convinces the troll to let him pass because a bigger goat is on his way. This is repeated with the middle goat who convinces the troll to wait for the biggest billy goat. Finally, the big goat comes along and proves too big for the troll to handle. The biggest billy goat gruff butts the troll into the river and joins his brothers on the hill to feast on grass and grow fat.

Basic Book Information

In this 28-page book, the text always appears on one side of the full-page illustrations. The detailed drawings catch the reader's attention and draw him in for a closer look. Generally the pages contain no more than four or five lines of text, though one has nine lines.

Noteworthy Features

This particular version of this folk tale is straightforward. It is short and traditional, adding no new details of its own. Descriptions are simple, such as "mean as he is ugly" for the troll. However, the detailed illustrations allow children to bring a deeper level of visualization to the text.

Teaching Ideas

In Library A, *The Three Billy Goats Gruff* is included as a read aloud. This instruction is based on the research of Elizabeth Sulzby, whose work with kindergarten children informed her of the importance of recreating parent-child interactions around books in the kindergarten classroom. At home, children often ask parents to "read it again" when they hear a favorite story. In school, the teacher's multiple readings of emergent literacy books helps children become familiar with rich narrative, hear the inflection and pacing of storybook language and learn to use detailed illustrations to assist them in remembering the storyline.

After the story has been read aloud at least four times over the course of two weeks, multiple copies of the book should be added to a basket labeled "Stories We Love" (or something similar). Children will return to these books at independent reading time. They will refer to the pictures and use their memory of the teacher's reading to recreate the story in their own rereading. Children who tell you that they "can't read yet" should be encouraged to read it "the best way that they can." Given the opportunity to

A Field Guide to the Classroom Library, Lucy Calkins and the Teachers College Reading and Writing Project, Heinemann, ©2002 Teachers College, Columbia University; http://www.heinemann.com/fieldguides

do this, children pass through different reading stages from simply "labeling" pictures on the page, to telling the story off the pictures, to using progressively more dialogue and storybook language, and then moving toward a more "conventional" reading where they use the print. To go on this reading journey, it is important for children to hear the story read aloud many times, to have a lot of opportunities to reread it to a partner and to have a supportive teacher nearby who thoughtfully coaches into the reading.

Researchers such as Elizabeth Sulzby and Marie Clay, in their studies of emergent readers, have found that when children are given opportunities to do this type of "pretend reading" (referred to as "reading" or "rereading") they go through these predictable stages of reading development. To support this process, teachers should select books with more text than readers could decode independently, books which can not be easily memorized, which have elements of drama and suspense, and characters that young children can relate to.

Young children enjoy repeating the "Trip trap, trip trap" and "Who's that tramping over my bridge" refrains, joining in with the teacher as the story is read aloud. They also naturally begin to dramatize the plot. Teachers might consider supporting this behavior by adding copies of the book to the block area and dramatic play center.

Although this text may be too sophisticated to become a writing mentor for emergent writers, it does serve to build an awareness of story conventions such as repetition, sound words, dialogue in quotes, and a traditional storybook beginning ("Once upon a time...") and ending ("This tale's told out.").

This is also a great book for older readers. Discussions of exactly what the troll looks like, in this story and in other versions can be fascinating for children, and a good exercise in visualization. This can be an even stronger exercise in envisioning if children are willing to let go of the image of the troll in the pictures and create their own from the words alone.

Within the plot alone there are many opportunities for discussion. Was the bridge the troll's to begin with? Did he have a right to block people from using it? Or was it everyone's bridge, and the troll just terrorized people who tried to use it? Did he have a reason for being protective of it? Why didn't the goats try to protect each other, instead of turning each other in as they crossed? Or was it all a big plan to get the troll to fight the biggest goat? If that was the plan, why didn't the biggest goat just go first so that his smaller brothers wouldn't have to risk anything? Why didn't the goats all work together to fight the troll? And why didn't they try to think of a plan that involved outsmarting the troll instead of violence?

Some of the language in the book may be strange to some readers. In the first lines, the book says the name of all three billy goats was "Gruff." Some readers think it's their first name. They find it odd that all three goats would have the same name. Later in the book, the troll calls out "Who's that tripping over my bridge?" and some readers picture the goats actually tripping and falling. This may throw children off track as they try to make sense of the story unless they are familiar with the story or already know what these expressions mean.

Some children even discuss the morality of the story. Did the big billy goat really need to toss the troll into the river to drown? Couldn't he have just threatened or hurt him enough so he would leave the goats alone? Some

A Field Guide to the Classroom Library, Lucy Calkins and the Teachers College Reading and Writing Project, Heinemann, ©2002 Teachers College, Columbia University; http://www.heinemann.com/fieldguides

kids decide the biggest goat is a bully. And why exactly did the troll let the first two goats go anyway? Was he nicer than he looked? Was he just ugly and everyone assumed he was mean? Were the goats appealing to his sense of fair play when they said wait for my bigger brother, or were they appealing to his appetite? And if it was his appetite, couldn't he have eaten them all since the first two were pretty small?

Reading different versions of a familiar fairy tale like this one lends itself to comparison across texts, something we want our young readers to be able to do. As they read each version, they build a set of expectations and knowledge about the story, the characters and the style of each, as well as repeated experience with a familiar vocabulary providing them with opportunities to increase their fluency and comprehension.

Because most everyone does know this story, it's a good one to encourage children to talk to their parents and at-home relatives about. They can bring the fruits of the classroom discussion home to talk over and bring back to the room.

Book Connections

Paul Galdone has written many versions of these old folk tales. Each is fairly simple and fairly traditionally told. His books include *The Three Little Pigs, The Three Bears* and other stories that are well known and well loved.

Genre
Picture Book; Emergent Literacy Book

Teaching Uses
Read Aloud; Language Conventions; Partnerships; Independent Reading

A Field Guide to the Classroom Library, Lucy Calkins and the Teachers College Reading and Writing Project, Heinemann, ©2002 Teachers College, Columbia University; http://www.heinemann.com/fieldguides

The Tiny Seed
Eric Carle

FIELD GUIDE

Ⓐ Ⓒ

Book Summary

This book tells the story of the life cycle of a tiny seed. The story is told in narrative form, with the tiny seed as the main character. To emphasize the unending continuity of the theme, the author has used a circular structure for the narrative. Beginning in autumn and ending the following autumn, the story goes full circle and full cycle. The process of natural selection (where seeds survive or not, depending on location, circumstances, etc.) weaves its way through the story. Teachers, however, should be aware that all of the information presented is not necessarily scientifically correct. The tiny seed, the smallest seed of all, grows into a plant that is larger and taller than houses. In reality, small seeds usually grow into small plants. Teachers might want to discuss the concept of "poetic license" to avoid children drawing erroneous conclusions.

Basic Book Information

There are 15 double-page spreads, with text consistently starting at the top of a page. Each page is illustrated by Eric Carle in his trademark tissue paper collage style and printed in full color. The text is in bold print and contrasts strongly with the white background of the page. The print size is medium with medium spacing between words and lines. Pages are not numbered.

Noteworthy Features

As a nonfiction book about the life cycle of a seed, the text does not use any sophisticated or technical terms. It is a botany lesson without any botanical language. Instead, the information is conveyed by way of a fiction story told in accessible, everyday language. Although the scenes change often, these scenery changes are clear and direct. The names of the seasons are highlighted by capitalization of the first letter. For example, "It is Autumn," "Now it is Winter," "Now it is Spring," "It is Summer," "Now it is Autumn again." It would be difficult to overlook these markers that indicate the passage of time and a change of scene.

The sentence structure is short and simple, with no clauses and very few complex or compound sentences. Most sentences contain the subject, verb, and object, elaborated with adjectives and adverbs.

Although Eric Carle creates impressionistic illustrations, these pictures are well supported by the text. Each spread contains an illustration of the main idea from the accompanying text.

Teaching Ideas

In Library A, the primary instructional purpose of this text is to support an

Illustrator
Eric Carle

Publisher
Scholastic, 1987

ISBN
0590425668

TC Level
5

Eric Carle author study. After listening to many of his books read aloud and having opportunities to reread them on their own, children are likely to notice that many of them are about scientific concepts, and each teaches us something new. These include *The Very Hungry Caterpillar*, *Today is Monday*, *The Very Busy Spider*, and *Have You Seen My Cat?* Children might observe that, although they appear to be nonfiction, they all contain exaggerated truths and even some misinformation.

Eric Carle is a very accessible author for young children to study. Children easily recognize his strong, consistent style of illustrations. The books often contain biographical information, sometimes accompanied by a photograph of the author. Many of his texts contain repetitive patterns and children enjoy joining in on the refrain as the teacher reads aloud to the class.

Eric Carle's books lend themselves to partner reading. After the children have heard the book read to them many times, they will have internalized the story. Using the illustrations to support their retelling, they can then recreate the story as they read to each other in their partnerships.

If the class is doing an inquiry study of plants, this book could be added to a basket of books on the topic. If there were two baskets of books on the topic, fiction and nonfiction, an interesting discussion might ensue around deciding where this book belongs. Children could be encouraged to support their opinions by returning to the text for evidence.

Book Connections

The A Library also contains the book, *The Carrot Seed*. These two books would make an interesting pairing for partner reading or reading centers.

Genre
Picture Book; Nonfiction

Teaching Uses
Author Study; Content Area Study; Partnerships; Read Aloud; Interpretation; Reading and Writing Nonfiction

A Field Guide to the Classroom Library, Lucy Calkins and the Teachers College Reading and Writing Project, Heinemann, ©2002 Teachers College, Columbia University; http://www.heinemann.com/fieldguides

The Very Hungry Caterpillar

Eric Carle

Book Summary

This book portrays the metamorphosis of a caterpillar into a colorful butterfly. The caterpillar starts out as an egg, transforms into a "very hungry caterpillar" and then becomes a beautiful full-grown butterfly. Over the course of the week, the caterpillar eats through many foods: apples, pears, plums, strawberries, and oranges. On the sixth day, he is still hungry and eats an array of junk food and ends up with a terrible stomachache. On the seventh day, after only eating through one leaf, he makes the final transformation into a gorgeous butterfly.

Basic Book Information

This picture book includes 13 die-cut pages. The number of sentences on a page as well as the length of the sentences varies throughout the book. There are many short, repetitive, simple sentences (e.g., "But he was still hungry, on _____, he ate through _____.") But there are also lengthier and more complex sentences and groups of sentences on a page (e.g., "He built a small house, called a cocoon, around himself. He stayed inside for weeks. Then he nibbled a hole in the cocoon, pushed his way out.").

Noteworthy Features

The pages are beautifully illustrated in Carle's trademark collage style. Often the illustrations are dramatically spread across two pages, with text written on only one side. On other pages, the text is set alongside a single page illustration. On many pages, the illustrations are marked with a hole in the middle. This suggests to the reader, none too subtly, that the hungry caterpillar has been nibbling the illustrations, enhancing their understanding of the concept.

Eric Carle successfully takes the sophisticated topic of metamorphosis and simplifies it for the young reader. He begins the book by presenting the image of the egg lying on the leaf at night, and then moves into the daylight. After the first few pages, the text shifts into a repetitive pattern: "On Monday he ate through one apple, but he was still hungry." Each succeeding page is highly predictable. Many young children are cognizant of the days of the week and are able to accumulate the food that is being eaten each day by both the visual representation as well as the expectation of what will follow. On the sixth page, the pattern begins to break down. Many children find some tricky words on this page, since the pictorial representations are more abstract and not as familiar. The book is so engaging that young readers are usually able to comprehend the text even though there are some specific words that might be tricky.

Illustrator
Eric Carle

Publisher
Philomel Books, 1987

ISBN
0399213015

TC Level
6

Teaching Ideas

This book is an excellent one to include in an author study on Eric Carle. It is similar to Carle's other books about insects-*The Very Busy Spider* and *The Very Quiet Cricket*. After reading many of his books, children will notice that a number of them are about insects, and that though they appear to be nonfiction, they all contain exaggerated truths. Children will notice the repetitive patterns in many of his books and will want to join in on the refrains (e.g., "But he was still hungry.").

Eric Carle books also provide attainable writing models for children. In their own writing, children will want to try out some of Carle's literary techniques such as combing nonfiction and fiction, using repetition and strong, repetitive patterns, and using the paper creatively.

Eric Carle's books lend themselves to partner reading. Often when children are reading this book in a partnership, sitting close together with one book between the two of them, they make a deliberate decision on how to read the repetitive parts. Partners may decide to each read a different page, and then in unison read, "But he was still hungry." Another partnership might decide to each read the entire repetitive part before switching back and forth.

This book might lead to an inquiry study of change. This investigation might last over a period of several weeks, with one part of the study focusing on the process of change from a caterpillar into a butterfly. If the discussion of change involved the eating habits of the caterpillar this might develop into a conversation about whether or not the foods listed in the book were typical foods for a caterpillar. The concept of "exaggeration" might be discussed. This could also lead to a reading center on books about metamorphosis, where children might ponder this question as they look across books, coming to their own conclusions about truth or poetic license.

Book Connections

Other Carle texts include *The Very Busy Spider, The Very Quiet Cricket*, and *The Grouchy Ladybug*.

Genre
Picture Book; Emergent Literacy Book

Teaching Uses
Author Study; Read Aloud; Independent Reading; Partnerships; Interpretation; Teaching Writing

There's a Mouse in the House

Alan Trussell-Cullen

Book Summary

The first page of this book says, "There's a mouse in the house." Then on each of the succeeding pages another animal is substituted, so that there is a cat in the house, a dog in the house, and so forth. By adding the pictures to the words, readers can construct the harrowing tale of a mouse that is chased by a cat, then by a parade of other animals. The book ends with all the animals collapsed, exhausted, on a carpet.

Basic Book Information

Mondo Publishing, a company with roots in Australia, produces this book. Mondo combines its knowledge of the characteristics of emergent readers with a commitment to publishing books that hold real appeal for inexperienced readers.

Noteworthy Features

This book is special because of its large size and literary appearance. The illustrations give details that support the reader. There is ample spacing between words and a font that reads like an alphabet chart.

Teaching Ideas

This text provides support for the emergent reader who needs to practice behaviors such as: carrying the pattern in a predictable text, referring to pictures for information, and using left to right directionality when reading one or two lines of print. With this text, a child will also have an opportunity to practice matching spoken words with printed words and self-correcting when these don't "come out even," paying attention to spaces between words to signify the end of one word and the beginning of another and locating one or two known words on a page to anchor their reading. Teachers may use their reading conferences to coach students in these behaviors.

Children may benefit from an introduction to the book before reading independently. For many readers reading Level 1 books, a slightly stronger-reading classmate could do the job of reading the title and children only need to be encouraged to ask a friend for help. In this book, emergent readers might find the word "there's" to be a struggle without the benefit of an introduction or some scaffolding by the teacher or a peer.

The illustrations on each page give readers a clue for predicting what is coming next. For example, on the first page where the printed words read, "There's a mouse in the house," the picture shows a mouse in the foreground, and in the background the reader can glimpse a cat's tail. On

Illustrator
Winifred
Barnum-Newman

Publisher
Mondo Publishing, 1998

ISBN
1572555262

TC Level
1

the next page, the cat is pouncing on the mouse, and the text reads, "There's a cat in the house." Again, if the reader looks carefully, she can see a dog's nose poking out from behind a door in the background.

With a partner, readers may want to use Post-iIts to mark these clues and notice the pattern throughout. They may also want to talk about why the author chose to put the animals in the order that they appear in the book. The teacher might follow this discussion by asking the children if their knowledge about animals helped them with their predictions and if these predictions made their reading easier.

Genre
Emergent Literacy Book

Teaching Uses
Whole Group Instruction; Independent Reading; Partnerships; Language Conventions; Small Group Strategy Instruction

This Quiet Lady
Charlotte Zolotow

Book Summary

A young girl who is trying to understand the relationship between her life and her mother's life narrates this picture book. In it the little girl looks through photo albums and framed pictures of her mother's life from baby through childhood, schoolgirl through bride. Until the last two-page spread with both mother and daughter where the text reads, "And here is where I begin." The final single page is of the little girl herself as a baby that's labeled simply, "The Beginning."

Basic Book Information

Charlotte Zolotow is the acclaimed author of many beloved children's book such as *My Grandson Lew* and *William's Doll*. This is a beautifully illustrated 19-page picture book. The text, which consists of one complete sentence broken into three to four lines of type, is consistently placed on the left side of a double-page spread. The text is clearly written in a large black font on a white background.

Noteworthy Features

The book is set up like a photo album with the young narrator shown on the left hand side in a smaller illustration of black, white, and gray, studying a full-page color "picture" of her mother in a chronological sequence of life stages on each page to the right. It's as if the reader as well as the narrator, is examining and learning about the mother's life page by page.

Each double-page spread has one single sentence beneath the narrator's picture. Each sentence repeats, "This..." and ends with, "...is my mother." This sentence structure may support some early readers in getting through the words of this book.

Teaching Ideas

This is a good book to read aloud and discuss with children. Children might notice the cycle of life in this story and think about how this cycle of life happens to parents and children. This book might also bring out family stories of their own. Many children will be eager to share the stories they have heard about the members of their own families. They might also want to bring in photographs from home to share with other students.

Students will also enjoy time to revisit this book independently. They might read the pictures and the words. Children might also create stories that go with the picture illustrations on both pages, which are always rich in detail. The repeated sentence structure of, "This . . . is my mother" and picture clues offer support to young readers

Illustrator
Anita Lobel

Publisher
Harper Trophy, 1992

ISBN
0688175279

A Field Guide to the Classroom Library, Lucy Calkins and the Teachers College Reading and Writing Project, Heinemann, ©2002 Teachers College, Columbia University; http://www.heinemann.com/fieldguides

This book is also appropriate for use as a model in the writing workshop. In a mini-lesson a teacher might say, "Let's notice the kinds of things that Charlotte Zolotow did as a writer so we can try some of those things ourselves." Children will notice for example, the author's use of descriptive language (e.g., "This baby smiling in her bassinet under the crocheted throw is my mother." or "This bride like a white flower is my mother.").

Teachers may also point out the ending that reveals the circular theme of the story, "And here is where I begin." Here we see the narrator with her dolly in her lap holding a picture of her mother holding her, a newborn baby girl. As readers turn the page, they see the baby and read, "The Beginning." Once children notice these things they might want to try some or all of these techniques in their own writing.

This book might be a good starting point for story reflections on children's younger years, possibly to begin a memoir study.

Book Connections

When I Was Five by Arthur Howard and *When I Was Little: A Four-Year-Old's Memoir of Her Youth* by Jamie Lee Curtis are also books where the narrators reflect back on an earlier life through memoir writing.

Genre

Emergent Literacy Book; Picture Book

Teaching Uses

Critique; Interpretation; Teaching Writing; Read Aloud; Independent Reading

Tiger, Tiger

Beverley Randell

Book Summary

This story is set in a jungle. All of the animals are asleep-tiger, mother monkey, and baby monkey. When the baby monkey gets hungry, he strays from his tree branch to feast on some berries below. Unfortunately, the tiger wakes up hungry, too. He goes after baby monkey. Luckily, mother monkey wakes up just in the nick of time and yells below, "Baby monkey! Come up here! Come up here!" Baby monkey scampers up the tree to safety, barely escaping the tiger.

Basic Book Information

This book contains 43 words across 16 numbered pages. The large and generously spaced text does not appear in a uniform location on each page, but is always set against a white background. John Boucher provides colorful illustrations that emphasize the ferociousness of the tiger and the vulnerability of the cute baby monkey. The expressions on the animals' faces throughout the book effectively convey the emotions of the story.

The PM Readers is a series published by Rigby. The PM Readers tend to come in kits where every book looks exactly like every other book. Some teachers think this is less than ideal because at every level, a library should be full of books where each has its own individuality. On the other hand, the PM Readers are an important resource for teachers for two reasons. First, there are many of these at the early reading levels and second, the PM Readers recognize the supports that early readers need and offer these. Also, the PM Readers use complete sentences: I see the cow./ I see the pig./ to reinforce the repetition of high frequency words and simple sentence syntax.

Finally, the PM Readers are special because a great many of even the earliest books are stories with characters, a problem, and a resolution. Just as more sophisticated books may feature characters like the Boxcar Children across a series of books, the PM Readers contain many books about Ben and Sally, or other characters, also across a series of books.

Noteworthy Features

Tiger, Tiger contains a lot of repetition as evidenced even by its title. Though the sentences do not always begin in the same way, they do almost always begin with high frequency words. On several pages, there are multiple sentences, some of which "wrap around" to a second or third line.

The text is fairly straightforward, but there is one instance where the author uses boldface type for emphasis. The last line of the book reads, "Baby Monkey is **safe**." Young readers may not be familiar with an author's use of boldface type for emphasis. Others may have only seen boldface type in dialogue, indicating someone speaking in a raised voice, shouting, or

Illustrator
John Boucher

Publisher
Rigby PM Collection, 1994

ISBN
0435049003

TC Level
2

yelling.

The story may be somewhat intense for some young readers. And not all children will infer that when the tiger is hungry, he may want to feed on the baby monkey. Teachers should be mindful of the fact that some children might be upset by the storyline.

The pictures convey a strong sense of the story. John Boucher truly captures the peacefulness of sleep, as well as the panic of the moment Mother Monkey discovers her baby is in danger; however, the pictures are not always directly supportive of the corresponding text.

Teaching Ideas

Tiger, Tiger contains illustrations that are not directly supportive of the text. Children who rely heavily on the pictures to gain meaning may need to be reminded to cross-check the picture with the initial consonant sound of the word. It is important that children who are reading on this level are able to use multiple cueing systems to process text.

The text provides students with an opportunity to predict how they think the story might go. In the beginning of *Tiger, Tiger,* the story reads, "Tiger is asleep. Mother Monkey is asleep. Baby Monkey is asleep." The story is set-up with the vicious tiger and a baby monkey asleep in close proximity. Some children may already predict trouble to come. Making predictions is an early reading behavior that should be fostered in young readers because it provides a framework for understanding the story, and helps keep the reader engaged with the text.

Tiger, Tiger is a wonderful book for helping students develop fluency and phrasing. In coaching and read aloud sessions, it's important for teachers to model the way books should sound when read. This book, for example, provides opportunities to model how different punctuation should be read. On page 15, the text reads, "Here comes tiger!" This page could be used in a reading mini-lesson for children who need to work on how sentences with exclamation marks should sound. Another reading mini-lesson might focus on how to read bold print. On page 16, the text reads, "Baby Monkey is **safe**." Teachers can put extra emphasis on the word "safe" while reading aloud and point out that bold print indicates that this word should stand out from the regular reading of the text. Learning how to read a variety of punctuation enhances children's fluency and improves their comprehension. Emphasizing certain sentences and words can also provide additional emotional layers to the reading of a story.

Tiger, Tiger will surely fascinate children who are interested in animals. This book might be grouped with other animal books in a classroom library. Book discussions may revolve around questions like "Why would a tiger want to eat a monkey?" or, "Why would monkeys sleep so close to a dangerous tiger?" The book also deals with issues of feeling safe and being in danger. These are emotions with which young children will surely identify. By discussing such themes with children as they come up, teachers can help students begin to see that books can be related to their own experiences.

Genre
Emergent Literacy Book

A Field Guide to the Classroom Library, Lucy Calkins and the Teachers College Reading and Writing Project, Heinemann, ©2002 Teachers College, Columbia University; http://www.heinemann.com/fieldguides

Teaching Uses
Independent Reading; Read Aloud; Small Group Strategy Instruction; Whole Group Instruction; Partnerships; Language Conventions; Interpretation

A Field Guide to the Classroom Library, Lucy Calkins and the Teachers College Reading and Writing Project, Heinemann, ©2002 Teachers College, Columbia University; http://www.heinemann.com/fieldguides

Titch

Pat Hutchins

Book Summary

Titch is little. He has a sister Mary, who is big, and a brother Peter, who is bigger. Compared to his siblings, everything Titch has is small-until Titch gets a tiny seed. When he plants his seed with Mary's pot and Peter's spade, the seed grows bigger, and bigger, and bigger.

Basic Book Information

Pat Hutchins is a British author of a number of well-known books including *Rosie's Walk* and *Good-Night Owl*. *Titch* is part of a series of books about the same character: *You'll Soon Grow Into Them Titch* and *Tidy Titch*.

Noteworthy Features

It's worthwhile for teachers to understand that a book such as this is written with hopes that a reader will soon "get" how the whole book goes, so the reader already knows that poor Titch will have the smallest item even before it happens.

Teaching Ideas

A teacher may choose to provide an introduction to this book for a particular reader, knowing that by doing so, he might then go on to read other *Titch* books with more independence. One way of introducing this text is by engaging the child in a conversation about what it's like to have a big brother and sister who always seem to have the bigger and better stuff.

A child who is reading books at this level may not need to point to the words anymore; if that is the case, a finger can get in the way, becoming more of a hindrance than help. "Just keep your finger close and bring it out if you get to a hard part," the teacher can say. The hard parts in this book might include the expression, "flew high above" on pages 8 and 9, and, "wooden whistle" on page 15. The word *spade* may also be an unknown word, and if a teacher is close by he or she may want to tell the child that this is a special kind of shovel.

While conferring, teachers might help readers practice putting together all they've learned about the process of using information in the text-searching, checking, and using phonological information-on the run, while reading. For example, on page 2, a student might read, "His sister Mary went a bit bigger," the teacher might prompt the child by saying, "You said 'went a bit bigger,' does that make sense?" Again on the last page, if the child read, "And Titch had the nails," the teacher might prompt the child to check again by saying "You said . . . I'm glad that you made sense, but does that look right?" Alternately, the teacher could simply ask the child to

Series
Titch

Illustrator
Pat Hutchins

Publisher
Macmillan Publishing, 1971

ISBN
0689716885

TC Level
4

A Field Guide to the Classroom Library, Lucy Calkins and the Teachers College Reading and Writing Project, Heinemann, ©2002 Teachers College, Columbia University; http://www.heinemann.com/fieldguides

reread, "There was something wrong on this line. See if you can find what was wrong." The teacher could also watch the child's word-solving strategies. For example it'll be interesting to see what the child does with compound words such as *pinwheel* and *flowerpot*. If the students are having difficulty with the word *hand*, attention can be focused on parts of it that look like familiar words, like *and*.

Book Connections

Titch is part of a series written by Pat Hutchins. Other books include *You'll Soon Grow Into Them Titch* and *Tidy Titch*. Other books in the library at about the same level include *George Shrinks!* by William Joyce.

Genre
Picture Book; Emergent Literacy Book

Teaching Uses
Independent Reading; Small Group Strategy Instruction; Read Aloud

Underground

Rebel Williams

Book Summary

This book poses questions and supplies answers about many underground-dwelling animals.

Basic Book Information

Underground is part of the red level/early emergent Twig book set. Each one of these books includes a "Things to Know" summary on the inside back cover as well as a few suggestions for "Things to Do" after reading the book. These books are also available in Spanish.

This eight-page book has 31 words. The text is patterned with a question on the left side of each double-page spread and the answer on the right side. The pattern changes on the last page.

Noteworthy Features

Underground is an early level nonfiction book. It follows a question and answer format and includes some animals that may not be familiar to many early readers.

Teaching Ideas

Because of the many unfamiliar animals that this text refers to, teachers would probably want to begin this book with an introduction. This will give children the opportunity to identify the various animals as they join the teacher in a "picture walk" through the book.

Teachers might consider introducing this text as part of a genre study of "question and answer" books. This book could then be added to a basket of books with a similar format.

There are many features in this book to support emergent readers such as larger font, good spacing between words, and a highly patterned text. The illustrations provide only minimal support for figuring out unknown text because many children will not know the names of some of the animals pictured (e.g., coyote, anteater, platypus). The question and answer structure may offer challenges to students who have not read many nonfiction texts. As often found in earlier level texts, the switch out of the pattern on the last page may also offer some challenge.

Children who are reading this level text are practicing behaviors such as rereading and self-correcting, reading with some fluency, cross-checking one cue against another, monitoring for meaning by checking to make sure what has been read makes sense and sounds right, and recognizing common chunks of words. The vocabulary in this text will provide opportunities for children to decode new words by using their knowledge of onsets and rimes

Publisher
Wright Group, 1998

ISBN
0780290755

TC Level
3

A Field Guide to the Classroom Library, Lucy Calkins and the Teachers College Reading and Writing Project, Heinemann, ©2002 Teachers College, Columbia University; http://www.heinemann.com/fieldguides

and compound words (e.g., ant/eater, under/ground).

Children who read this book can learn about animals, their habitats, and predators. Children could be encouraged to read other books on the same topic. This will help them understand how we can accumulate knowledge on a topic by reading many related texts.

Genre
Emergent Literacy Book; Nonfiction

Teaching Uses
Reading and Writing Nonfiction; Independent Reading; Content Area Study

Wake Up, Dad

Beverley Randell

FIELD GUIDE

Book Summary

It's morning and Kate, James, and Nick are up. Dad is asleep and won't wake up. Together with their mother, Kate, James, and Nick pile onto their father's bed. Over and over, they tell him to wake up. After pulling on his bed sheets and yelling at him, they finally rouse Dad by knocking him out of the bed. From the floor dad ironically says, " I am up."

Basic Book Information

This is a 16-page book with 67 words. This book is part of the popular PM collection for early readers and it features characters that reoccur in a number of PM Readers. The colorful and realistic illustrations occupy their own page, opposite the page of corresponding text. The only exception to this layout is on the last page of the book, where the text and illustration share the page.

The PM Storybooks, developed in New Zealand and published by Rigby, are written as stories, which are structured around traditional story elements. Even texts that at first appear to be lists are usually stories with characters, a problem, and a resolution. The only exceptions are their very earliest books. The PM Readers are known for including a large number of high frequency words, and for controlling vocabulary so that in books of a comparable level of difficulty, the same high frequency words reoccur. Instead of relying upon an intensive use of sentence repetition, the PM Readers are apt to support very beginning readers by using many high frequency words. They also tend to have longer rather than shorter sentences. Instead of a book going like this: I see/ a bird/ a frog/ and so on, the PM Readers use complete sentences: I see a bird./ I see a frog./.

The fact that PM Readers include many high frequency words means that sometimes the resulting sentences seem stilted and unnatural to an adult, especially. The other common way to support very beginning readers, however, also has its limitations. Is it better to give young readers an endless stream of books that have repetitive captions on every page and a twist at the book's end, or to give them books like these, with somewhat stilted language? Probably the best diet includes both.

Noteworthy Features

It is worth mentioning that this book contains a good deal of dialogue. Most of the dialogue is referenced, however, there are instances where it's not. Page 12 is particularly challenging. It reads, "Look Mom! Look at Dad!" All three children are depicted in the illustration opposite page 12, so it is nearly impossible to figure out who is speaking.

Three wrap-around sentences make for another noteworthy feature of

Illustrator
Elispeth Lacey

Publisher
Rigby PM Collection, 1994

ISBN
0435067303

TC Level
2

A Field Guide to the Classroom Library, Lucy Calkins and the Teachers College Reading and Writing Project, Heinemann, ©2002 Teachers College, Columbia University; http://www.heinemann.com/fieldguides

this text. For early readers, continuing the same idea across two lines may prove challenging and they may need some support.

For children who think very literally this book may seem puzzling. Only on the first page, where Dad is introduced, is he truly asleep. On all of the corresponding pages, where the children are urging him to, "Wake up!" the father is already awake. Readers must infer the sense of play in the story. The family is having fun trying to get Dad out of bed, and Dad is having fun pretending to resist.

Punctuation is another pertinent feature of this book. There are many commas, quotation marks, and exclamation points throughout the text. In addition, on page 14 some of the dialogue is in bold face to indicate emphasis.

Teaching Ideas

This book is repetitive in structure. The phrase, "Wake up, Dad!" is repeated six times throughout the short text. This repetition will allow young readers to gain some confidence as they make their way through the text. This repeated phrase will reinforce children's recognition of the high frequency words *Wake, up,* and *Dad.* After children have mastered them, teachers can post these words on a word wall and do some work during word study time with the rimes -*ad* and -*ake* to expand children's vocabulary. Children may feel empowered when they discover that by knowing the rime -*ake* they can also know the words: *make, take, fake, bake,* and so forth.

Wake Up, Dad is more challenging than other books in the PM series. The sentences do not always start with high frequency words or repetitive phrases. A number of the lines begin with the name of the speaker (i.e., James, Kate, Nick). While these names are monosyllabic and fairly simple, decoding them requires the use of multiple cueing systems. Students will not be able to figure out any of the names by merely looking at the pictures.

The pictures are not fully supportive of the text and this might present a challenge for children who rely heavily on this strategy. Teachers working with children suitably matched with this book may want to focus their reading conferences on using multiple cueing systems. In a reading workshop mini-lesson or conference, teachers may want to advise children that this is an example of a book in which you can not always rely on the pictures to tell you what the story says. This is a good opportunity to teach how and when to use multiple strategies as they read new text. Children should be taught to ask themselves: Does that makes sense? Does that word sound right? Does it look right? Teachers may want to remind children when they are self-correcting to look at the picture, and to look at the word, and to "get your mouth ready" when they give the sentence another try.

Teachers may want to use this book in a strategy lesson on punctuation. Lessons can focus on exclamation points, commas, or bold face type. For instance, *Wake Up, Dad* contains dialogue in bold face on page 14. Teachers can model how such typeface is to be read and instruct young readers that bold font indicates that this part of the book is to be read in a stronger voice. In this case, mom is yelling, **"Wake up, Dad!"**

Since this book contains a lot of dialogue, reading partners may want to take on the roles of the different characters. This type of dramatic reading can help students become more facile at figuring out who the speaker is

A Field Guide to the Classroom Library, Lucy Calkins and the Teachers College Reading and Writing Project, Heinemann, ©2002 Teachers College, Columbia University; http://www.heinemann.com/fieldguides

when dialogue is not referenced. In addition, this type of reading helps to develop children's fluency and phrasing.

There is a sense of playfulness in the story that surely will amuse some readers. Kate, Nick, James, and Mom try everything to get Dad out of bed. They jump onto Dad's bed, pull off his blankets and keep yelling, "Wake up, Dad!" Dad is in on the game, and tries his hardest to stay in bed, despite his family's efforts. In the end, Dad comes tumbling out of his bed and the entire family shares a laugh. Children may strongly identify with this story and want to discuss times their own family shared a happy time like this. It is important for teachers to help children make these text-to-self connections and to understand how they can help them develop a deeper comprehension of the story. Children are learning the rudiments of book discussions in these partnerships, and they are practicing skills that will make them lifelong readers.

Genre
Emergent Literacy Book

Teaching Uses
Independent Reading; Language Conventions; Partnerships; Interpretation; Whole Group Instruction; Small Group Strategy Instruction

A Field Guide to the Classroom Library, Lucy Calkins and the Teachers College Reading and Writing Project, Heinemann, ©2002 Teachers College, Columbia University; http://www.heinemann.com/fieldguides

What Do Insects Do?

Susan Canizares; Pamela Chanko

Book Summary

What Do Insects Do? begins with the title question and then lists 11 things that insects do: "They jump./They fly./They eat. . . ." Magnified photographs illustrate various insects doing what is described in the text.

Basic Book Information

What Do Insects Do? is part of a series of books by Susan Canizares and Pamela Chanko. It has detailed photographs of insects in their natural habitats. Each unnumbered page has one line of print (a full sentence) placed consistently beneath each photograph. The print is large and well spaced.

Noteworthy Features

Photographs do not end at the seam of the book but carry on to the opposite page. This may be both distracting and impressive for early readers. This book is part of Scholastic's Science Series for Emergent Readers. Like others in the series, it contains beautiful color photographs that are sure to prompt questions, pique their curiosity, and get them wondering.

The last two pages, called "What Do Insects Do?" include even more detailed facts and information about the insects depicted in the text. It also identifies and names of each insect, referring the reader back to a page number in the text, which unfortunately is not printed on the page itself. The index is written for the teacher and is accompanied by black and white drawings of the insects shown in the photographs. Overall, this index is not as helpful a reference source as it could be.

Each page contains the word *they*, which should become a sight word pretty quickly and then also contains the action word (*fly, bite, build, hide*) that matches the picture. These action words though, can't be derived simply from the picture, as there are many ways to describe what the picture shows.

Teaching Ideas

A book such as this one will be used in countless ways by a class full of readers and learners. First and foremost, it can be part of a library full of choices for children to draw from during independent reading. Research has shown that many children, and especially boys, prefer nonfiction books to fiction. All children benefit from growing up with a balanced reading life that includes reading that helps them learn about the world (nonfiction).

When a teacher confers with a child who is reading this book during the

A Field Guide to the Classroom Library, Lucy Calkins and the Teachers College Reading and Writing Project, Heinemann, ©2002 Teachers College, Columbia University; http://www.heinemann.com/fieldguides

Publisher
Scholastic Science
Emergent Readers, 1998

ISBN
059039794X

TC Level
2

independent reading part of the workshop, she will want to first just sit nearby and watch as the child continues to read. While watching a child read this book, a teacher will want to notice whether the child points crisply under each word, matching the word she is pointing to with the oral word she says. If a child's matching does not "come out even," the teacher will want to note whether the child seems to catch the error and self-correct.

While observing this reader, the teacher will also want to note if she uses both the print and the pictures to help figure out the words. Are the child's eyes flicking between picture and print? If the text says, "They fly . . ." and the child reads, "They run . . ." does anything about the print give the child feedback that fly can't be spelled r-u-n? If we intervene to say, "Check it" or, "Does that look right?" can the child then see the problem? If so, can she repair it?

Then, too, the teacher would want to note whether the child seems to be merely plowing through print in this book, or is the child actively making meaning? During partnership time when readers talk about the book, we should be able to hear some reactions to the pictures in their talk. Does the child wonder at the drop of water that's been magnified so that it's fist-sized? Does the child notice the funny horns on the short-horned grasshopper? Does the child try to see the stinger on the mosquito? Does the child see that there are two interlocked insects on the, "They fight" page? Teachers may want to nudge children to reread to "grow ideas" and to put Post-Its on things they find intriguing. The teacher might even be more specific and tell readers that it is smart to look between pages and notice things that are similar, or things that go together. Do they see any patterns?

Finally, *What Do Insects Do?* contains a number of sound and letter patterns that make it ideal for launching various word studies, perhaps with readers who normally read more difficult books. This book contains examples of the /i/ sound written in three different ways: *fly, fight,* and *bite*. A teacher might use *What Do Insects Do?* to launch a word study of the /i/ sound.

What Do Insects Do? also contains three different functions of the letter *y* as in *fly, carry,* and *they*. A teacher might use this book to launch a study of the letter *y*.

This book may be used to support the science curriculum. For example, a teacher might want all of her students to study insects. She might organize five small groups of readers, each with appropriate texts and a question to research. One group's question could be, "What are insects' homes like?" Another group's question could be, "What are insects' legs like?" and so on. This book could be filed under the latter question and children would learn a lot if challenged to approach this book with an inquiry question in mind.

This book could also be a mentor text for children who, in the writing workshop, were writing books about topics on which they are experts. They would notice that some books begin with a question that is then answered throughout the text, or that some of these books might be structured like a list.

Genre
Nonfiction; Emergent Literacy Book

A Field Guide to the Classroom Library, Lucy Calkins and the Teachers College Reading and Writing Project, Heinemann, ©2002 Teachers College, Columbia University; http://www.heinemann.com/fieldguides

Teaching Uses
Independent Reading; Content Area Study; Teaching Writing; Small Group
Strategy Instruction

A Field Guide to the Classroom Library, Lucy Calkins and the Teachers College Reading and Writing Project, Heinemann, ©2002 Teachers
College, Columbia University; http://www.heinemann.com/fieldguides

Wheels

Susan Canizares; Susan Moreton; Daniel Moreton

Book Summary

This is a nonfiction book with repetitive text and photographs depicting all kinds of wheels: wheels on bikes, wheels on tractors and trains, as well as a Ferris wheel, and a pottery wheel. The text asks the question "What do wheels do?" Each double-page spread repeats the answer, "Wheels turn." on the left-hand page, with a repeated descriptive word (i.e., "steer, steer, steer" or "Dig, dig, dig:") on the right-hand page. On the last page of the text, the pattern changes with the full sentence, "Wheels turn round and round!"

Publisher
Rigby, 1988

ISBN
0439081238

Basic Book Information

This book has 15 unnumbered pages and is appropriate for beginning readers given its patterned and predictable text. Each page has one line of print, consistently placed beneath a large full-color photograph.

Noteworthy Features

This book is part of the Scholastic Science Series for Emergent Readers. Like others in the series, it contains beautiful color photographs that are sure to prompt questions and generate discussion. The pictures, however, are not entirely supportive of the text and readers must check the print across the entire word.

The last two pages of the book provide the teacher with an informal index and "picture glossary" of terms with reduced-size pictures of the wheels depicted in the text and even more facts and information about these wheels, what they do and how they work.

Teaching Ideas

Teachers may want to do a walk-through of the text, inviting students to identify the various wheels in the photos first, assisting them with prompts when the photo is not recognized.

Teachers may use this text to support the early reading behaviors of directionality, getting your mouth ready for an unfamiliar word, and for cross-checking the picture against the text.

A student reading this book should be able to point to the words as she is reading. While observing a child read this book during independent reading workshop, a teacher can note whether she is catching any errors or self-correcting when the matching does not "come out even."

Teachers might also want to contrast *Wheels* with a fiction book they have read-one that is clearly fiction, such as *Mrs. Wishy-Washy*. Once students have made the distinction between books that give us facts and books that tell stories, the teacher might show students other books-and let

A Field Guide to the Classroom Library, Lucy Calkins and the Teachers College Reading and Writing Project, Heinemann, ©2002 Teachers College, Columbia University; http://www.heinemann.com/fieldguides

them categorize the books as nonfiction or fiction.

This book may also be used to support the science curriculum or placed in a reading center with other nonfiction texts about wheels. Students may compare and contrast the information presented in each text and how it is presented.

Genre
Nonfiction; Emergent Literacy Book

Teaching Uses
Independent Reading; Content Area Study; Whole Group Instruction; Reading and Writing Nonfiction

A Field Guide to the Classroom Library, Lucy Calkins and the Teachers College Reading and Writing Project, Heinemann, ©2002 Teachers College, Columbia University; http://www.heinemann.com/fieldguides

When I Was Five

Arthur Howard

Book Summary

The author of this humorous picture book writes from the point of view of a six-year old child. Arthur Howard sets his text up so that it is a comparison between the boy's life at age five and the boy's life at age six. This book begins by a young child telling us about himself at age five. He lets the readers into his past by telling them about such things as what he wanted to be when he grew up (an astronaut or a cowboy), his favorite car, his favorite dinosaur, his favorite hiding place, and who his best friend was, Mark.

In the middle of the picture book, the boy switches to the present and tells us what his life is like now at age six. Just like in the beginning of the book, the boy tells us about such things as what he wants to be when he grows up, his favorite dinosaur, and his favorite hiding place. However, things have changed. He now wants to be a major league baseball player or a scuba diver. His favorite car is now flashier and his favorite dinosaur is fiercer. He won't even reveal where his secret hiding place is. The only thing that has not changed is his best friend, Mark. The final page shows the narrator of the book with his arm around Mark, with the words, "Some things never change."

Basic Book Information

Because the narrator is supposed to be a six-year old child, everything about this picture book is child-like-from the large print, to the humorous child friendly illustrations. The illustrations are especially inviting because they are enlarged and spread out over two pages and the text is embedded within the illustrations.

Noteworthy Features

The text has some repetition and patterns that may support some of the earlier readers. The pictures are also clear and students will be able to use them to help with the text.

The illustrations are large and detailed, sometimes matching the words on the page and sometimes adding to them. Children can learn how to illustrate in this same way.

Teaching Ideas

Some young children will be drawn to read this book especially because the author writes about things that can matter quite a bit to five- and six-year olds (dinosaurs, best friends, hiding places).

This is a good book to read aloud and discuss with children. Children are eager to see if they liked the same things that the narrator liked. They might

Publisher
Harcourt Brace, 1996

ISBN
0152020993

TC Level
5

A Field Guide to the Classroom Library, Lucy Calkins and the Teachers College Reading and Writing Project, Heinemann, ©2002 Teachers College, Columbia University; http://www.heinemann.com/fieldguides

want to think about what things change and what things remain the same in their own lives.

Although the author of this book takes on the voice of a young child, he also tackles the sophisticated theme of friendship and the importance that is placed on family and friends. As the narrator of this book matures, many of his ideas change, but his best friends don't. Teachers might want to facilitate a discussion where students reflect upon how friends and family impact their own lives.

This book is particularly appropriate to use as a teaching tool in the writing workshop. In a mini-lesson a teacher might say, "Let's take a look at the kinds of things that Arthur Howard did with his words and pictures so that we can try some of the same things out in our words and pictures." The book begins with everything that the boy likes when he is five and ends with everything that he likes when he is six. Children can learn how to structure their own writing in this "now versus then" way. The book also ends with a message-some things will never change. This ending sums up the book and leaves readers understanding why the author compared his life at five and at six. Students can learn how to end their own books with this kind of relative stance.

Book Connections

When I Was Little by Jamie Lee Curtis is another memoir in this library and it, too, is structured like a list that moves between then and now.

When I Was Young in the Mountains by Cynthia Rylant also starts each page with a refrain, "When I was young," and might be a nice structural companion to this book. It might also lead to a rich discussion of the kinds of things that each author chose to write about, and what was important to each.

Genre
Picture Book

Teaching Uses
Interpretation; Critique; Teaching Writing; Read Aloud

A Field Guide to the Classroom Library, Lucy Calkins and the Teachers College Reading and Writing Project, Heinemann, ©2002 Teachers College, Columbia University; http://www.heinemann.com/fieldguides

When I Was Little

Jamie Lee Curtis

Book Summary

A four-year-old makes a series of comparisons between what she can do now and what she could do when she was a baby. Each comparison starts with "When I was little . . ." and presents a small thing that used to happen or that she used to be able to do. "Then" is contrasted with "Now" and a short description of the kind of girl she is today.

Basic Book Information

When I Was Little is a memoir. This is Jamie Lee Curtis' first book. This picture book is 29 pages long and has brightly colored illustrations on each page. The illustrations are similar to those in the Annie Bananie books that were also illustrated by Laura Cornell. Each page begins predictably with, "When I was little. . . ."

Noteworthy Features

The colorful, exuberant watercolors and the small amount of type coupled with the large, hand-lettered font make this an attractive, inviting book for children to read.

Many children won't know what, "I went to Mommy and Me" means. If they inquire, it would help to explain that this is a name for a class mom's can take with their babies. The page that says that she slept in a zoo as a baby may also perplex children.

Teaching Ideas

Many kindergarten and first grade children are eager to share stories about their own lives and about their families. These are both important themes that are studied in these grades. *When I Was Little* lends itself to these studies. This book would be a wonderful addition to a basket of books about "Families."

Before adding this book to a reading center basket, the teacher probably will want to read and discuss the story with the class. In discussion, children may want to compare their lives with the author's life, remembering back to when they were babies and four-year-olds. That discussion is the cornerstone for deeper understanding of the text. We can help children deepen their personal responses to the text by helping them move beyond simplistic, "Me, too!" answers. Teachers may lead the discussion toward more reflective responses that speculate on why there are differences and similarities between the book's character and themselves.

Character studies can be extremely interesting with this book, and can lead to many deep understandings of both the book and of our society

Illustrator
Laura Cornell

Publisher
HarperCollins, 1993

ISBN
0064434230

TC Level
7

A Field Guide to the Classroom Library, Lucy Calkins and the Teachers College Reading and Writing Project, Heinemann, ©2002 Teachers College, Columbia University; http://www.heinemann.com/fieldguides

today. Children may believe that the character is a girly-girl who likes to talk about herself a lot. They may notice how the girl likes to do things with hair and make-up and is talking about swimming with boys as if she cares whether the kids are boys or girls. It might be interesting for readers who have thought about the character of the little girl in this book to know more about the famous actress who has written this book. This may or may not contribute to their character study.

Readers, who study this book carefully, will probably wonder why the main character tends to be so scornful of babies, or of her own past. Why shouldn't babies like goo? And isn't it great when babies make up words? Aren't they supposed to cry a lot? Just because she does different things now, doesn't mean the things she used to do (and that other babies still do) aren't great. Some children speculate that the character has a little sister that she is jealous of and that is why she looks down on babies. Other children may be of the opinion that the girl, not demeaning the accomplishments of babies, is merely proud of herself. Voicing these two opposite opinions can lead children to study the text in deeper and more fruitful ways.

This book is also a good model for writer's workshop if children are writing personal narratives. Each page tells something about when she was a baby and that page is sometimes followed by how she is as a girl now. Once children discover the predictable pattern, reading becomes easier.

This pattern is easy to understand, making it a good book to be used as a model for children who are trying to write a memoir of their own. Some children name this as a then/now pattern or a see/saw pattern, incorporating the structure into their own writing.

Book Connections

Like *When I Was Five*, Margaret Wise Brown's *The Most Important Thing*, also a memoir, reads as if a young child wrote it. Children who are writing personal narratives can use both books as models for incorporating contrasting elements in their writing.

When I Was Young in the Mountains by Cynthia Rylant also starts each page with a refrain "When I was young" and might be a nice structural companion to this book. It also might lead to a rich discussion of the kinds of personally important things authors choose to write about.

When I Was Five by Arthur Howard is another memoir in this library which flip-flops between then and now and is also structured like a list. Again, readers may contrast Arthur Howard's list of important ways that he's changed with Jamie Lee Curtis' list. Arthur Howard believes that he was different but not worse when he was younger. Jamie Lee Curtis, on the other hand, seems to scoff at her younger self.

When I Was Little contrasts in fascinating ways with *Messey Bessey*, another book in this library. Notice the different gender roles the two girls take on, with Jamie Lee playing with make-up and high heels and Bessey, with paint, dinosaurs, planetary charts, and checkers.

Genre
Emergent Literacy Book

A Field Guide to the Classroom Library, Lucy Calkins and the Teachers College Reading and Writing Project, Heinemann, ©2002 Teachers College, Columbia University; http://www.heinemann.com/fieldguides

Teaching Uses
Teaching Writing; Interpretation; Critique; Character Study

A Field Guide to the Classroom Library, Lucy Calkins and the Teachers College Reading and Writing Project, Heinemann, ©2002 Teachers College, Columbia University; http://www.heinemann.com/fieldguides

Where's the Bear

Charlotte Pomerantz

Book Summary

A villager sees a bear and brings her neighbors into the words, with sharp tools, to look for it. They can't find it and keep asking, "Where's the bear?" to which she keeps answering, "There." or, "There's the bear." Finally, the bear is found and the villagers run away in a panic, dropping most of their "weapons." The bear watches them go with a satisfied "Yeah." to end the book.

Basic Book Information

This book has about 30 pages, some of which have no text. Other pages have several sentences, but if there is more than one sentence, it is a repeated sentence. The text is consistently at the top of the page and is never more than one line. The attractive pictures are black outlines filled in with bold basic colors without shading or small detail.

Noteworthy Features

To read this book well, readers need to gather sense not only from the words, but also from what is happening in the pictures. Otherwise, the repetition of the phrases in the story makes no sense at all and is merely monotonous. With the pictures, the repeating phrase can build suspense and questions regarding the whereabouts of the bear. The first page of the book has no words and this format helps get readers into the habit of looking at the pictures to add to their understanding of what is going on in the tale.

Teaching Ideas

This book is in Library A as a leveled text for children to read during independent reading. This book would give children practice in using punctuation as a tool toward understanding how the intonation and meaning of a sentence can change without the actual words of the sentence changing. Students who read without attending to the punctuation, will find they need to go back and reread with attention to these end marks.

For similar reasons, this book is also a good one for practicing reading with expression. For this exercise, in order to assume different voices, children will first have to determine who is speaking. This is not an easy task because, although the speaker changes often, there are no quotation marks and no paragraph changes to indicate a change of speaker. The readers will have to determine what makes sense according to the words and pictures. This is a necessary part of reading the book and will lead children toward reading "with expression."

Illustrator
Byron Barton

Publisher
Mulberry Books, Greenwillow, 1984

ISBN
0688109993

TC Level
2

There is a lot of storytelling that can go between the pages of this book. That makes it a good one for partnership reading or even reading aloud and having a class discussion. The events in the pictures and the expressions and behaviors of the people make this an easy book to talk about. Children might wonder, "Why are they carrying their tools?" or "Why are they looking for the bear?" or "Why are they running?" and "What does the final page mean?"

While children are reading the book, they may notice that "where" and "there" follow the same word pattern, or that they rhyme. This can help them read the second word if they can already read the first. When children don't notice this, teachers can point it out.

Students can use this text to learn about making inferences and predicting what is going to happen. They can also do some rhyming and word pattern work with: *where, there, bear.*

Genre
Emergent Literacy Book

Teaching Uses
Independent Reading; Language Conventions; Interpretation

A Field Guide to the Classroom Library, Lucy Calkins and the Teachers College Reading and Writing Project, Heinemann, ©2002 Teachers College, Columbia University; http://www.heinemann.com/fieldguides

You'll Soon Grow Into Them, Titch

Pat Hutchins

Book Summary

When Titch outgrows his clothes, his big brother Pete and his big sister Mary give him their hand-me-downs. They always say, "You'll soon grow into them." Mother tells Dad to take Titch shopping and buy him some brand new clothes. At the end of the story, Titch decides to give his hand-me-downs to his new baby brother.

Basic Book Information

This book has 191 words written over twenty-six pages. Sentence structure and phrasing are consistent with early reading patterns and will help beginning readers make meaning.

Full-page color illustrations are on each page. Text is placed consistently on the top. The illustrations provide high to moderate support. This book uses many high frequency words.

Noteworthy Features

Pat Hutchins, the well-known British author of many wonderful children's books, wrote this text and others about Titch.

The cover picture of *You'll Soon Grow Into Them, Titch* is exactly like the picture on the first book, *Titch*, with Titch still wearing a blue tunic-top and brown/red trousers. But this Titch looks much older, with a thinner face and baggy clothes. Titch's siblings, Peter and Mary are each older too, and a cat has joined their family. If a reader looks at the cover and notices that Titch is older now, this observation will lead directly into the first page of the book where Titch can't fit into his trousers anymore.

Throughout this story we see the passage of time illustrated by such things as a bird building a nest and then having babies, and flowers just starting to come up and then blooming.

Teaching Ideas

Children who are able to read *You'll Soon Grow Into Them, Titch* and other similarly challenging books will find that though many of these books continue to have a pattern, the patterns are more complex. This was true, for example, of *Titch* or *Cookie's Week*, which are both structured like lists of repeating episodes. This book has a similar structure. Titch can't fit into his clothes and his bigger siblings give him theirs, which are always too large. Titch instead goes shopping. But soon his newborn baby brother arrives home. Titch does to the baby brother what others had done to him. He gives his old clothes to the baby, saying, "He'll grow into them soon." Students may be able to predict the outcome of the story, by paying close attention to

Series
Titch

Illustrator
Pat Hutchins

Publisher
William Morrow, 1983

ISBN
0688115071

TC Level
5

this pattern. Students may want to read with a partner, sharing and revising predictions about how the story will turn out.

A child who rereads this book may spot various things in the story that change, marking the passage of time. The bulbs grow into plants. The mother knits clothes that the baby soon wears. The bird builds a nest and then has babies. Mary and Pete also grow-into and out of *their* clothes just like everyone else. Teachers may want to encourage other readers to look for evidence of change and the passage of time in their own books, using this text as a model in a mini-lesson. Students may also make text-to-self connections about how they experience similar changes in growth and share similar feelings about hand-me-downs and older siblings in general. Partners or Group may also want to discuss these changes.

While conferring, a teacher will want to monitor reading comprehension. One way to do so is to assess any substitutions the child makes while reading, considering which cueing systems he seems to be using effectively and which he might make better use of. If the student reads, ". . . that Titch *shout* have some new clothes" the teacher might prompt the child to monitor and search by saying, "You said '*shout* have some new clothes.' The beginning chunk matches, but does that word make sense there?" Again, on the last page, if the child reads, "And Titch *had* the nails," rather than "And Titch *held* the nails," the teacher might prompt the child to search and check by saying, "You said. . . . That makes sense, but does it look right?" Once attention is drawn to the substitution, the child could probably correct the word *had* to *held*. Alternatively, the teacher might also choose to simply prompt the child to find and correct the error by saying, "There was something wrong on that line. See if you can find what was wrong."

Some children discuss issues of fairness raised in the text. Why doesn't Titch have new clothes all for himself? Why might this be?

Book Connections

You'll Soon Grow Into Them, Titch is part of a series written by Pat Hutchins. Other books include *Titch* and *Tidy Titch*.

Genre
Picture Book

Teaching Uses
Independent Reading; Partnerships; Critique

Index